The Election of 1860 Reconsidered

CIVIL WAR IN THE NORTH

Series Editor, *Lesely J. Gordon, University of Akron*

THE

ELECTION

OF 1860

RECONSIDERED

Edited by A. James Fuller

The Kent State University Press · *Kent, Ohio*

© 2013 by The Kent State University Press, Kent, Ohio 44242
All rights reserved
Library of Congress Catalog Card Number 2012037934
ISBN 978-1-60635-148-2
Manufactured in the United States of America

Library of Congress Cataloging-in-Publication Data
The election of 1860 reconsidered / edited by A. James Fuller.
    p. cm. — (Civil War in the North)
 Includes index.
 ISBN 978-1-60635-148-2 (hardcover) ∞
 1. Presidents—United States—Election—1860. 2. United States—Politics and
government—1857–1861. I. Fuller, A. James.
 E440.E45 2012
 324.973—dc23
                          2012037934

17 16 15 14 13   5 4 3 2 1

For the Civil War Study Group

Contents

List of Illustrations

Acknowledgments

In the months surrounding the 150th anniversary of the election of 1860, scholars around the country gathered for conferences dedicated to analyzing this event. One such meeting was the third annual symposium of the Civil War Study Group on September 17, 2010. Hosted by the Institute for the Study of War and Diplomacy at the University of Indianapolis and funded by an Eli Lilly InQuery Grant, the symposium featured papers by four historians. More than twenty scholars offered their responses in the cordial discussions that followed each reading. Those papers became the foundation for this book. Charged with organizing the symposium and writing one of the papers, I saw the possibilities for something more and began to think about what a book-length reconsideration of the election of 1860 might include. I sought out other scholars who might be able to contribute. The result is a collection of essays, each of which stands on its own as an insightful study of the election.

The authors themselves deserve my thanks. Jack McKivigan participated in the symposium and graciously agreed to include his superb essay on Frederick Douglass, which reinforces his well-deserved reputation as a leading historian of abolitionism. Doug Gardner allowed me to conscript him into service for the meeting and applied his wit, insight, and elegant writing style to the historical literature. He learned the duties of friendship the hard way by agreeing to write on a subject outside the scope of his own immediate interests. Mike Green did an old friend a favor and, as usual, wrote a fine piece of scholarship. His essay here demonstrates that his work on Lincoln, the Republicans, and the politics of the 1850s is authoritative and groundbreaking. Jim Huston came on board and produced an excellent chapter on Stephen Douglas. His timely work and amiable attitude are models of professionalism, as is his essay. Tom Rodgers made such insightful comments at the symposium that I asked him to contribute to the book. He agreed to do so, although it was late in the process. Working under the looming shadow of a rapidly approaching deadline, he wrote a first-rate essay that is a tremendous addition to this volume. Larry Sondhaus was supportive of my ideas about the symposium and the book from the very beginning. When asked to contribute, he wrote about the European view of the election as only an accomplished and prolific scholar can. His exceptional chapter proves his dedication as a friend, a department chair, and a historian.

Joyce Harrison at Kent State University Press saw the value of this project and offered helpful guidance throughout the process. The series editor, Lesley Gordon, supported my idea for this collection; her insightful criticisms made this a better book. The two readers for the press offered excellent suggestions and constructive criticism aimed at improving the volume. Krista Kinslow is always willing to proofread and ask questions that make me write more clearly. I greatly appreciate her help and encouragement while I wrote my essays and during the revision process. My late wife, Brenda, displayed great patience with my work during her losing struggle with ovarian cancer and I regret that she did not live to see this project appear in published form. I also wish to thank my son, Carson, for sometimes managing, somehow, to contain his four-year-old enthusiasm while Daddy was trying to write and edit. I dedicate this book to the little band of scholars who make up the Civil War Study Group, founded in 2008 by Stephen E. Towne. Their friendly encouragement and willing participation have created an intellectual community that inspires each of us to undertake new projects in the field about which we all are so passionate.

A. James Fuller
Indianapolis, Indiana
Fall 2012

Introduction

The Election of 1860 Reconsidered

A. James Fuller

The most important presidential election in American history took place in 1860. The electoral contest marked the culmination of the sectional conflict and led to the secession of the Southern states and the beginning of the Civil War. Over the past century and a half, scholars have offered a number of different interpretations of the election, but surprisingly few works have been dedicated exclusively to the presidential contest itself. Most explanations of the campaign appear in general histories or in biographies of Abraham Lincoln or the other presidential candidates. Although nearly every succeeding generation of historians has managed to produce at least one full-length study, scholarship on the election of 1860 remains relatively rare. The sesquicentennial anniversary of the election offered an opportunity to fill this gap in the literature. Historians have taken up the cause, producing several new books on the subject, including this one.[1]

This volume reconsiders the election and offers fresh insights on the campaigns for the presidency. In his concluding essay, Douglas G. Gardner examines the historiographical tradition regarding the election, noting that scholars across the generations have focused on Abraham Lincoln and Stephen A. Douglas, with scant attention paid to the other candidates or to other related topics. Two of the essays clearly fall into that scholarly tradition—Michael S. Green argues that Lincoln played the role of master politician during the campaign, and James L. Huston explores the significance of Douglas's southern tour. The other chapters move in different directions, and even those chapters dedicated to the Rail Splitter and the Little Giant provide new interpretations of the two most famous presidential

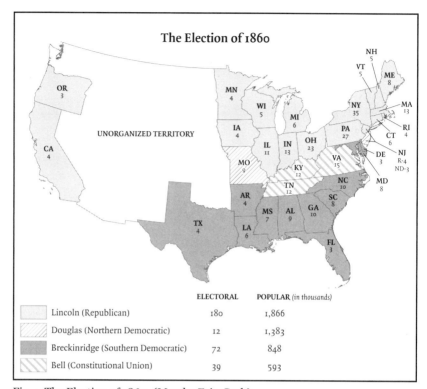

Fig. 1. The Election of 1860. (Map by Erin Greb)

candidates. But this book breaks new ground by seeing the election as more than Lincoln's victory and Douglas's loss. Historiographical innovation appears in interpretations of the other candidates, the view from Europe, abolitionist perspectives, and close examinations of voter turnout and the presidential election at the state level.

Several themes unify the various essays. Perhaps the most important theme of this book is political biography, a genre no longer fashionable among academic historians. In addition to the studies of Lincoln and Douglas by Green and Huston, I offer chapters on the other two major candidates for president, the Southern Democrat John C. Breckinridge and the Constitutional Union candidate John Bell. John R. McKivigan explores the election through a biographical lens focused on Frederick Douglass. These biographical studies look at candidates and the election in the context of a life—that is, they go back several decades or even more to demonstrate why and how later decisions were made. Biographical approaches require biography, even in an essay format. In studying the lives of individuals, the authors demonstrate how the critical presidential contest in 1860 was related to and resulted from the life experiences of their subjects. Thus, in his chapter on Lincoln, Green challenges the traditional interpretation that sees the Republican as a passive candidate who let his operatives do the work in the campaign while he sat on the sidelines. Rather, Honest Abe was a superb politician and candidate. Seemingly passive on the surface, behind the scenes Lincoln pulled the strings and controlled his entire campaign. In the end, his ambition and political skills enabled him to organize for electoral victory. Huston focuses on Stephen A. Douglas, Lincoln's longtime rival and the man widely considered the favorite in the presidential race. He argues that Douglas's tour of the Southern states during the campaign was actually a tool with which the Northern Democrat tutored Southerners on the procedures of democracy. Huston demonstrates that, ultimately, Douglas's campaign reveals why the vast majority of Northern Democrats rejected secession and supported the Union.

Moving beyond the two candidates who have enjoyed the most scholarly attention, in my chapter on Breckinridge I examine the historical literature on this Southern Democrat's run for the presidency in 1860, showing that the scholarship remains deeply divided over the true nature of that campaign. I then offer a novel explanation, arguing that honor is the best lens through which to interpret the actions of Breckinridge and his supporters. In the essay on John Bell, I explore the campaign of the least known of the four major candidates, challenging the traditional view of the Constitutional Union nominee and his party. Although most historians have dismissed the conservative Bell, I argue that he actually was the last true Whig candidate for president, showing that his campaign was really a principled call for compromise rather than a hollow avoidance of the issues. Biography continues to be the focus as John R. McKivigan turns to Frederick Douglass and the abolitionist view of the presidential race. Starting with an examination of the political attitudes and practices of the abolitionists from the 1830s to John Brown's Raid in 1859, McKivigan focuses on Frederick Douglass but also includes other Garrisonian activists and radical abolitionists. He argues that in 1860 the abolitionists were initially ambivalent about Lincoln but then exerted the full force of their well-honed political action organizations and propaganda in his support.

Another important theme that animates these essays is ideology. Ideas mattered and were not just campaign rhetoric spouted by politicians hoping to win the election. James Huston's interpretation of Stephen A. Douglas reveals the ways in which the Northern Democrat wrestled with the idea of democracy, while McKivigan's Frederick Douglass struggles with how to put his abolitionist ideas into political practice. Ideology is the focus of Thomas E. Rodgers's essay as he examines the contested process of computing election turnouts. He suggests that a combination of republicanism and party ideology is the key to understanding the general pattern of presidential elections and argues that, in 1860, republicanism was the essential element that drove turnout. Republicanism also plays a part in my chapters on Breckinridge and Bell, because those two candidates both accepted the tenets of that ideology. For Breckinridge, republican ideas mingled with honor, whereas Bell's views on compromise clearly expressed the republican ideology of the Whig Party. But this is not to say that Rodgers and I agree completely. Despite similarities, we have important disagreements about the role and nature of republicanism as well as the true motives of voters. Such contrasts invite the reader to engage questions about motivation and the significance of ideology.

Related to ideology is a third theme, political culture. In 1860, the values and morality of republicanism mattered to voters and to candidates. The ideology of republicanism included the principle of virtue, which required individuals to put the public good before their own interests to maintain the American system of ordered liberty. At the same time, honor was a foundational principle of Southern political culture; moral and social reform stemming from evangelical Christianity and the ethics of individualism motivated Northerners. Issues such as slavery, immigration, and corruption made sense in the context of 1860 in different ways than they would to later generations. In my chapter on political realignment theory, the political culture of Indiana emerges as an important factor in the election. This state provides a useful case study through which to assess the traditional theory of realignment. Political culture is at the center of Thomas Rodgers's essay on turnout and Huston's piece on Stephen A. Douglas, and it is the framework for my biographical chapters on Bell and Breckinridge. Readers will find some repetition of certain themes within that political culture, such as the tradition of candidates' not campaigning publicly, a fact important to several of the interpretations offered here. Gender and social relations mattered in mid-nineteenth-century America. My biographical chapters include personal and family concerns that will remind readers of the role of women and private matters in antebellum politics.

Beyond these themes, the book offers readers interdisciplinary studies and new angles of approach to the election of 1860. Rodgers's chapter on voter turnout and my essay on realignment theory both move across disciplinary lines to engage the work and interests of political scientists. McKivigan's essay on Frederick Douglass offers a new view of the election by taking an abolitionist perspective. Lawrence Sondhaus's chapter on the European view of the election explores how outsiders interpreted the contest in a transatlantic context. Going beyond the traditional treatment of English and French opinions, he includes the lesser-known views of German and Austrian leaders and opinion makers, finding surprising opinions while concluding that Europeans generally showed little interest in the election and failed to predict its consequences.

But not all of the themes presented here are new. The authors also engage the traditional questions that one might expect to find in a volume of essays on the election. The issue of slavery and its territorial expansion is familiar ground, covered throughout the book. Additionally, the debate between contingency and determinism pervades many of the chapters. Some of the scholars see the election's outcomes as an inevitable result, whereas others insist that the end was uncertain. For example, James Huston takes a strong stand for determinism in his essay on Douglas, but I later employ contingency as a counterpoint to realignment theory. Again, such contrasting views invite the reader to ponder important problems from different sides of the debate, allowing plenty of room for drawing independent conclusions. On these and many other topics, the essays provide a splendid exploration of the historical literature on the election, the candidates, and the politics of the antebellum era. Gardner's closing essay studies the traditional view of the election and traces the literature on this presidential contest over several generations of historical writing. But scholars also will find the notes of the various essays useful and provocative, as the authors engage the various interpretations and guide those interested through the literature and the historiographical issues involved. In a sense, this volume is a primer for anyone interested in pursuing research on the election.

As a collection, then, these essays revolve around main themes such as political biography and ideology and offer some interdisciplinary approaches to this presidential race as well as different ways of seeing that contest. At the same time that they challenge old interpretations and provide innovative explanations, they also breathe new life into the traditional approaches of the long-neglected field of political history. Taken together, they bring fresh perspectives and make a significant contribution to the literature. After 150 years, with such a surprisingly small amount of scholarship that has nearly always taken a remarkably similar view of what remains the most important presidential contest in American history, it is time to reconsider the election of 1860.

1. The most recent titles to be published are: Michael S. Green, *Lincoln and the Election of 1860* (Carbondale: Southern Illinois Univ. Press, 2011); Douglas R. Egerton, *Year of Meteors: Stephen Douglas, Abraham Lincoln, and the Election that Brought on the Civil War* (New York: Bloomsbury Press, 2010); Bruce Chadwick, *Lincoln for President: An Unlikely Candidate, An Audacious Strategy, and the Victory No One Saw Coming* (Naperville, Ill.: Sourcebooks, Inc., 2009); Gary Ecelbarger, *The Great Comeback: How Abraham Lincoln Beat the Odds to Win the 1860 Republican Nomination* (New York: St. Martin's Press, 2008). At the time of this writing, Jonathan Earle is working on a book on the election for the Pivotal Moments in American History Series published by Oxford University Press.

1

The Political Organizer

Abraham Lincoln's 1860 Campaign

Michael S. Green

"Seward will be first on the ballot, Chase next—then Bates or Cameron. . . . My policy has been to keep down my name everywhere as a candidate for the first office. . . . Seward's friends generally prefer me after himself," and "I think without doubt Chase's friends will go for me after himself." This was the optimistic analysis of the 1860 Republican convention that one of the presidential candidates, Cassius Marcellus Clay, a Kentucky abolitionist, shared with Caleb B. Smith, a longtime Indiana Whig who had become a far more conservative Republican than Clay would ever be. Clay was hopeful, as most candidates tend to be, and more so than he had reason to be. Given their desire to carry border slave states and appeal to moderates and conservatives, Republicans would gain little support by nominating a candidate who was radically antislavery. But Clay's strategy for winning the Republican presidential nomination made sense. Indeed, it worked perfectly—for Abraham Lincoln.[1]

Like almost every aspect of his life, how Lincoln won the nomination and then the presidency has been the subject of analysis, myth, and debate. One of the problems with understanding his role in the 1860 election lies in the history of his story. Because he was, as his law partner William Herndon observed, "the most secretive—reticent—shut-mouthed man that ever existed," much about him remains shrouded in mystery: his existing correspondence is limited, and he controlled how much he revealed to those around him. That has freed us to see Lincoln as we wish: as the self-made man, the Great Emancipator, the working man, "Honest Abe," and even as the humorous yet melancholy man who becomes a martyr to a higher cause.[2]

Fig. 2. Hon. Abraham Lincoln: Republican candidate for sixteenth president of the United States. (Library of Congress)

At times, those images diverge from the many examples of Lincoln as the crafty backwoods-turned-urban but never entirely urbane lawyer. Yet many of us prefer not to replace one word that too many associate with evil—lawyer—with another similarly and wrongly abused word involving trickery: politician. If the law became Lincoln's occupation, politics always remained his preoccupation, from organizing Whigs for campaigns every other year to nearly fighting a duel with a Democratic opponent over an exchange in the press. That preoccupation with politics was evident when he sought the presidency. In 1860, many deserved credit for the political organization and plotting that made Lincoln the nominee and likely victor, but none deserved more credit than Lincoln.[3]

The views of two Lincoln biographers, divergent in their approaches and times but deeply connected, are important to understanding why he deserved the credit—and, perhaps, why he has received less of it than he should. One is by William Herndon, who referred to Lincoln's ambition as "a little engine that knew no rest." The other is by David Herbert Donald, who published biographies of Herndon and Lincoln nearly half a century apart.[4] Both of these authors focused on a crucial aspect of Lincoln's life and personality: his friendships, how he dealt with others. "Those who knew him best came to realize that behind the mask of affability, behind the façade of his endless humorous anecdotes, Lincoln maintained an inviolable reserve," Donald wrote. Yet he also echoed Herndon's point, which suffered from what Donald called "only a little exaggeration," that "no man ever had an easier time of it in his early days—in . . . his young struggles than Lincoln had. He always had influential and financial friends to help him; they almost fought each other for the privilege of assisting Lincoln." And so it remained for much of Lincoln's life, at least in Illinois, until he won a job that placed him above all of those old friends. Many seemed to consider themselves his close friends when they were not. At times they seemed divided mainly over which of them loved Lincoln more or could accomplish more for him. How he dealt with these friends, close friends, and acquaintances—the temptation is to say that he handled them, and that word may be more appropriate—proved crucial to his political future.[5]

Donald and Herndon described the same man in ways that are not mutually exclusive but part of the same mosaic. Although historians increasingly have accepted the information that Herndon obtained in the process of trying to write Lincoln's biography, they always have doubted his attempts to interpret Lincoln's mind. But Herndon certainly knew and understood Lincoln well enough to characterize his ambition and the benefits he derived from friends who wanted to help him. As Donald demonstrated, Lincoln had a capacity for or interest in maintaining truly close friendships only with a select few. Although he could work with a diverse group and benefited from their help, he also was and had to be self-contained and self-reliant in many aspects of his life, especially politics.

With all of the help that he received from friends, Lincoln fitted Richard Hofstadter's ironic analysis of him as representative of "the self-made myth." More Lincoln scholars should view Hofstadter's observation, "The first author of the Lincoln legend and the greatest of the Lincoln dramatists was Lincoln himself," in the broadest sense. Early in life, Lincoln harbored hopes of escaping what seemed to be his fate of following in his father Thomas's footsteps as a yeoman farmer. Living in New Salem from 1831 to 1837 and after that in Springfield, Lincoln benefited from community support—thus the importance of his friendships—but he also exhibited a drive to succeed. He tried several professions in New Salem and embarked on a quest for self-improvement that never really stopped, if overcoming his lack of a formal education to become an attorney and the pride he expressed at learning Euclidean geometry while in his forties are any indication.[6]

Clearly, though, Lincoln found another avenue to advancing himself: politics. Not only did he learn, study, and think about candidates and issues but he also involved himself in a political party. Lincoln was not a joiner: the social clubs that attracted many attorneys and the would-be socially mobile appear to have held little charm for him. He enjoyed the camaraderie of his fellow lawyers on the circuit. In terms of belonging to a group, though, his political party mattered a great deal to him, and that required him to think of both his own ambitions and the greater good of his organization. Thus, he was willing to support candidates such as William Henry Harrison and Zachary Taylor against his political hero, Henry Clay, for the presidency and was unwilling to break with the Whig party over slavery during the 1840s. His experience in political parties would prove valuable when he sought the presidential nomination in 1860.

Lincoln famously lacked national office-holding experience—after all, he had spent one undistinguished term in the House of Representatives and lost two Senate races in the five years before the 1860 convention. But he had a distinct advantage over his competitors: none of the three main front-runners for the nomination had the breadth or depth of his experience in organizing campaigns for elective office. One of the Republican Party's leading radical voices, William Henry Seward, served two terms as governor and two terms as a U.S. senator from New York. Although Seward was an excellent backroom operator in the Senate and convivial in his personal relations, no one doubted that he left the details of political management to his close friend and ally, Thurlow Weed. The editor of the *Albany Evening Journal,* Weed served as a Whig and then as a Republican boss. Seward reportedly declared, "Seward is Weed and Weed is Seward. What I do Weed approves. What he says, I endorse. We are one." That was not entirely true: Seward's determined opposition to slavery sometimes vexed Weed politically and ideologically. But the freedom that Seward enjoyed from day-to-day political operations also left him more naïve than his Illinois counterpart about the scutwork of politics and left him open to criticism when Weed's lobbying and investments raised questions about his probity.[7]

Salmon P. Chase and Edward Bates reflected opposite ends of the spectrum. Even more radically antislavery than Seward, Chase ran his own campaigns and found it difficult to confide in anyone, but his deal making and sanctimony won him far more enemies than lasting alliances. Nor did he ever dedicate himself to a political party as Lincoln did first with the Whigs and then with the Republicans. He dedicated himself to the cause, antislavery. He saw whatever he did that he benefited from politically as part of a higher calling. Although his actions enabled him to become Ohio's governor and U.S. senator, they also generated the kind of attitude unlikely to make it easy for him to win over those who doubted his efficacy as a candidate. The barely antislavery Bates avoided the damage that Seward and Chase suffered by refraining from political activity, but that merit also proved to be a demerit: Bates ended up with little political experience of any kind and few significant allies in the Republican rank and file, especially because the Republican Party in Missouri was limited in size and scope. Led by the unusual Republican tandem of Francis Preston Blair, a longtime Democratic operative and Andrew Jackson confidante, and Horace Greeley, the reformist editor of the *New York Tribune* and onetime Whig, Bates's supporters resorted to arguing, "We frankly admit that Judge Bates has not long been distinctively a Republican: how many of us have been? We are a young party, rising gradually from nothing to ascendancy: such parties, when destined to succeed, are always liberal toward accessions and careless of antecedents." That might not have been a problem if Bates had been active enough politically to build a network or a sense of good will, but instead he had little political credit on which to draw.[8]

In contrast to Bates, Lincoln dedicated most of his adult life to politics—not just thinking deeply about what he believed and why but also the important electoral tasks of campaigning and dealing with the day-to-day drudgery of organizing parties and campaigns. Soon after arriving in New Salem in 1832 at the age of twenty-three, Lincoln sought a legislative seat, and although he lost, he won 277 of the 300 votes in his new community—a sign that he had made himself known to local voters, who found him appealing. In 1834, he tried again and won, partly through cunning that involved the slate of candidates from which voters would choose several legislators. First, with New Salem solidly for Henry Clay's "American System" of internal improvements and farmers in the hinterland strongly Jacksonian, Lincoln avoided repeating any of his pro-Clay comments from 1832. Second, he agreed to a Democratic plan to funnel votes to him and thereby siphon votes from the presumed front-runner, his future law partner, John Todd Stuart, who encouraged him to take the deal. The Democratic plan worked far less well than Stuart's and Lincoln's: Lincoln drew enough votes to win, but so did Stuart. This campaign marked Lincoln's first lesson in—and foray into—political deal making and organizing.[9]

As a legislator and Whig, Lincoln worked from the minority, and his success demonstrated his growing political acumen. In addition to his legislative achievements—most notably, perpetuating Whig economic policies and shifting the state capital to Springfield—Lincoln made a name for himself in putting together his party's campaigns and seeking to broaden his party's reach. The Whigs suffered from two image problems that contained considerable truth. First, many thought them moralizers who saw themselves as above petty political activity. Second, they were seen as an elite, especially in comparison with the Democrats, whose name seemed to fit them with both a small "d" and a capital "D." Lincoln looked beyond businessmen and evangelicals, the groups to which Whigs most appealed, toward a larger constituency. He hoped to convince new voters of the benefits of his party's pro-business proclivities (He even suffered in his efforts when he married Mary Todd, who came from a higher social class than he.) He hoped to win the 7th Congressional District—the only Whig district in Illinois—and engaged in protracted negotiating and behind-the-scenes maneuvering with other Whigs to ensure that they supported both his campaign and rotating the job among party members so that he would have his chance. He put his organizational skills to work on local and national campaigns, including in 1840, when he drew up what David Herbert Donald called "a semimilitary plan for getting out the Whig votes" that included local and county party workers who would ensure "that every Whig can be brought to the polls." He made similar efforts in 1844 and resented the antislavery Liberty Party and the staunchly anti-slavery Whigs for declining to support Clay's election that year.[10]

Lincoln entered Congress as a little-known party regular, but though his term was short, he made as much of it as he could. His most famous legislative action was a failed attempt to end slavery in the District of Columbia, and how he went about it demonstrated both his desire to unify his often divided party and his preference for seeking a consensus. He also campaigned in New England and again put party fealty above ideology when he backed the nomination of Zachary Taylor over Clay because he realized that the general had a better chance of winning.

Although the end of Lincoln's congressional term in 1849 prompted a five-year hiatus from his pursuit of elective office, he proved more active in party plotting and organization during this period than he appeared. He advised Whig candidates seeking office through elections and patronage. He delivered eulogies in 1850 for Taylor and in 1852 for Clay—duties that someone less political minded might have ceded to a Whig office seeker. These two eulogies revealed something of Lincoln as a coalition-building politician. His account of Taylor played down the divisions that "Old Rough and Ready"'s presidency had both highlighted and created within the party, especially his opposition to the Compromise of 1850. Having already established a record of disliking slavery, Lincoln certainly could have discussed that issue in some detail but chose not to do so, perhaps because his feelings were mixed on the subject. His eulogy for Clay said less about his American System of internal improvements, which Lincoln had once celebrated and sought to emulate within Illinois, and far more about Clay's opposition to slavery and his defense of liberty and union. In both cases, Lincoln sought to heal or avoid party schisms and discuss issues around which Whigs could unite as he continued to refine his own thinking about party and issues.[11]

However, unity proved to be a pipe dream for the Whigs, and Lincoln's longtime political nemesis, Stephen A. Douglas, provided both the means for a new party to coalesce and a new issue to capture Lincoln's attention. In 1854, the introduction and passage of the Kansas-Nebraska Act, repealing the Missouri Compromise and permitting the extension of slavery into new territories, brought Lincoln out of the political wilderness. Although he quickly won attention for his speeches on slavery, reflecting the considerable thought he had been putting into the issue, Lincoln also dedicated himself to managing two campaigns. He helped guide Richard Yates, a fellow antislavery Whig, to victory in his race for the House of Representatives from Illinois. Lincoln lost his own bid for a U.S. Senate seat at the 1855 legislature, but not for lack of effort—including a great deal of letter writing—or cunning. With the political parties in flux, legislative Democrats opposed to Douglas refused to vote for a longtime Whig such as Lincoln. Instead, after Lincoln released his supporters rather than allow a Douglas acolyte to be elected, the antislavery Democrat Lyman Trumbull overcame Lincoln's large lead to win the seat. In turn, Trumbull and his supporters pledged to back Lincoln in the next Senate election, in 1858, against Douglas.

By the time Lincoln and Douglas faced off, much had changed. Douglas had broken with James Buchanan, the president from his party, over what the Little Giant attacked as the corruption of his policy of popular sovereignty in Kansas, costing himself the national and local party patronage and support that had been so helpful to him in previous campaigns. Lincoln had worked behind the scenes successfully to moderate the new Republican Party's platform in Illinois and unsuccessfully to ease differences between former Democrats and former Whigs as he prepared to run for the U.S. Senate against Douglas. Although the seven Lincoln-Douglas debates did a great deal to define the differences between the candidates and their parties inside and outside of Illinois, Lincoln also immersed himself in the day-to-day workings of politics, from strategy to fund-raising—sometimes directly, sometimes through intermediaries so that he could keep clear of any controversies. His loss had more to do with the gerrymandering of Illinois legislative districts and Douglas's ability to appeal to conservative former Whigs unwilling to associate themselves with what they perceived as the radically antislavery Republicans than with any organizational failings on his part.

By forcing him to voice positions popular in Illinois but not in the South, the debates did a great deal to harm Douglas's chances of winning the Democratic nomination in 1860. They also put Lincoln on the presidential map. Soon after the vote for the legislators who would choose the next U.S. senator from Illinois made clear that Douglas would be reelected, the *Lacon Illinois Gazette* declared, "Abraham Lincoln for President in 1860." Lincoln had nothing to do with that call, or the one the next day at a Republican meeting in Mansfield, Ohio. When his friend Jesse Fell and then other Republicans in Springfield made similar noises, Lincoln pooh-poohed his chances. But he also appears to have made clear that he would like to be president, and that seeming too interested, especially in an era in which the office sought the man, might prove counterproductive. By April 1860, though, he confessed to Trumbull, "I will be entirely frank. The taste *is* in my mouth a little." His statement begs the question of what he did to satisfy that hunger. The best way to look at this election and Lincoln's role in determining his fate is to consider it in three stages: what Lincoln did to lay the groundwork for his presidential candidacy, what he did to prepare for the national convention that nominated him, and what he did during the general election campaign.[12]

Although Republican insiders had known Lincoln because, thanks to the efforts of the Illinois delegation, he received 110 votes as the runner-up for vice president at the 1856 Republican convention, the debates with Douglas in 1858 brought him to national prominence. In keeping with traditional practice, other candidates traveled abroad, as Seward did, or generally stayed home. But Lincoln accepted invitations to speak in several states, including Indiana, a swing state that Republicans needed to carry if they hoped to win in 1860. He also went to Ohio, where his speeches enabled him to present himself as a moderate alternative to the radical senators Salmon P. Chase and Benjamin F. Wade and the conservative Supreme Court justice John McLean. For what became his most famous campaign speech in 1860, he agreed to go to Brooklyn for an appearance, but his hosts relocated it to New York's Cooper Union, where he impressed Republicans seeking an alternative to the front-runner, William Seward. He tailored his speeches to his audiences closer to home and did so even more carefully for his eastern appearance, producing a scholarly treatise on the history of efforts to limit the spread of slavery.[13]

Just as Lincoln built support outside Illinois, he worked hard at unifying the bickering Republican Party within his state. Keeping former Democrats such as the state party chair, Norman Judd, and Whigs such as Judge David Davis united with him even as they fought with one another, he allowed each to complain about the other to him without taking positions on their disputes. It was not that he was free from vexation: "Long" John Wentworth, a newspaper publisher and the mayor of Chicago, despised Judd. Wentworth's taste endeared him to Davis, who constantly overrated how much support Lincoln would receive from the Chicago operative. It was significant that Lincoln also assured almost from the outset that he would be his state's favorite-son candidate at the Chicago convention rather than a possibly more plausible choice, its highest-ranking Republican officeholder, Trumbull. Although the senator seemed uninterested in the presidency, the willingness of his supporters to back Lincoln for the prize certainly said something about Lincoln's planning and cultivation of good relations—especially because Lincoln sought his advice and information. When Trumbull's name came up as a possible vice-presidential nominee for Justice McLean, the senator made clear to Lincoln that "I wish to be distinctly understood as first and foremost for you."[14]

Lincoln's contrast with his main opponents—especially the front-runner—was telling. The "firm" of Seward, Weed, and Greeley had long since dissolved, and the mercurial *New York Tribune* editor had joined forces with such former Democrats-turned-Republicans as the *New York Evening Post* editor, William Cullen Bryant, to pursue an alternative to Seward. Thus, New York's Republican Party normally would have been bifurcated between radicals and conservatives, but these divisions ran much deeper and posed more danger to Seward's candidacy. Ohioans divided over Chase—to Lincoln's advantage, because he and some of Chase's opponents engaged in mutual cultivation. In Missouri, Edward Bates remained indifferent to the fray. In Pennsylvania, Simon Cameron was the pivot on which the Republican Party turned, with his machine as committed to him as ever and his opponents equally convinced of his corruption and mendacity.

Lincoln's efforts paid off, especially with Judd. The former Democrat reminded Trumbull of the need to keep Seward from gaining support wherever possible and, more crucial, to unify the Illinois delegation behind Lincoln. Judd used his connections to the editors of the *Chicago Press & Tribune*—like him, former Democrats—to support Lincoln's candidacy. More important, Lincoln wrote, "I find some of our friends here, attach more consequence in getting the National convention into our State than I did, or do. Some of them made me promise to say so to you." Whether Lincoln felt ambivalent or thought it best to be subtle and diffident, Judd understood the point and voted at the Republican National Committee meeting to locate the nominating convention in Chicago, giving Lincoln what would prove to be a crucial home-field advantage.[15]

First, though, Lincoln shaped the team that would play on his home field. On May 9, 1860, about six hundred Republicans met for the Illinois state convention in Decatur. When the delegates learned that Lincoln was present, they cheered, lifted him onto their shoulders, and carried him to the platform, then gave him three great gifts. One was their unanimous support for the Chicago national convention. The other was a new persona, created when John Hanks, a cousin of Lincoln's mother Nancy, and Isaac Jennings entered the "Wigwam," as the convention hall was known, with two fence rails and a banner proclaiming "ABRAHAM LINCOLN THE RAIL CANDIDATE." That day, Lincoln became the "rail splitter,"

Fig. 3. The Republican Convention in the Wigwam, Chicago, May, 1860. (Library of Congress)

a workingman's candidate, a far more appealing image than the accurate depiction of him as a successful attorney and man of property.[16]

The third present revealed Lincoln at his shrewdest and demonstrated his talents for political strategy and tactics. The convention permitted Lincoln to select four of the twenty-two delegates it would send to the national convention at the larger "Wigwam" in Chicago. Sitting in a nearby grove with Davis, Judd, Leonard Swett, and other Republicans, he made his choices. Picking Gustave Koerner appealed to the Republican Party's strong German contingent and might help him overcome that group's support for Seward, who had opposed the nativist Know-Nothing movement far more vocally than Lincoln had. Judd deserved to go anyway as the state party chair but Lincoln made it certain that he would be there, assuring him of a steadfast supporter and blocking Davis's choice, Wentworth, the loosest cannon in the Illinois Republican Party. Lincoln appeased Davis by naming him a delegate and, by dint of their longtime relationship and Davis's standing as a judge, his manager in all but name at Chicago.

Lincoln's choice as his fourth delegate proved to be a master stroke. Lincoln chose one of his oldest friends, Orville Browning, who had told Lincoln

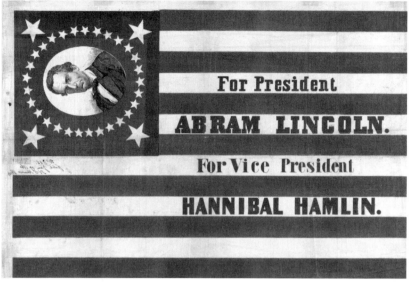

Fig. 4. Lincoln Campaign Banner, 1860. (Library of Congress)

that he preferred Bates to win the nomination. Lincoln handled Browning so well and wisely that the conservative former Whig thought that his friend shared his feelings about the nomination. But Lincoln had known him since his earliest days in Springfield and told the group that Browning "will do more harm on the outside than he could on the inside." Besides, Lincoln was "satisfied that Bates has no show. When Orville sees this he'll undoubtedly come over to me, and do us some good with the Bates men." Events proved the soundness of his judgment. Lincoln took other steps to prepare for the convention. Mark Delahay, an Illinois friend who had moved to Kansas, needed money to attend the convention; Lincoln paid his way and suggested that he lobby the Iowa and Minnesota delegates, his fellow westerners. He instructed the Illinois delegates on his views on the tariff—still Whiggish and thus potentially reassuring to the key swing state of Pennsylvania—but asked them to avoid discussing the matter if possible, thereby avoiding creating problems with old free-trade Democrats.[17]

With the state convention over, Lincoln returned to Springfield with no choice but to wait and hope that his friends could deliver for him. Because he had chosen so carefully and united the delegation behind him, as William Jayne told his brother-in-law Trumbull, the Illinois delegation "worked like Turks for Lincoln's nomination." They also worked the delegations. Because Swett came from Maine, he lobbied that state's representatives, while Judd dealt with Democrats, Browning with the conservatives, and Koerner with the Germans, whose influence proved vital to winning over the Indiana delegation and giving Lincoln a solid bloc of votes on the first ballot. Judd also used his power as state party chair to help Lincoln again by persuading the railroads to reduce fares to Chicago, enabling more Illinoisans to come to town, fill the galleries, and cheer for Lincoln. He also used his position to decide where each delegation would sit in the hall. He put Illinois close to Indiana and Pennsylvania and isolated the known pro-Seward delegations, making it difficult for Weed and his minions to circulate on the convention floor when they most needed to do so.[18]

Fig. 5. Lincoln and Douglas in a Political Foot Race. (Library of Congress)
In this pro-Lincoln cartoon, a very tall Lincoln out-races a very short Stephen Douglas while a black man caught in a rail fence cheers the Republican on to victory.

THE NATIONAL GAME. THREE "OUTS" AND ONE "RUN".
ABRAHAM WINNING THE BALL.

Fig. 6. The National Game. (Library of Congress) In this pro-Lincoln cartoon, the Republican, his foot on "Home Base," advises the other candidate, "Gentlemen, if any of you should ever take a hand in another match at this game, remember that you must have a good bat' and strike a fair ball' to make a clean score' & a home run.'" His "good bat" is a wooden rail inscribed "Equal Rights and Free Territory." Lincoln wears a belt inscribed "Wide Awake Club." The skunk symbolizes how the other candidates have been "skunk'd." Breckinridge holds his nose and complains, "I guess I'd better leave for Kentucky, for I smell something strong around here, and begin to think, that we are completely skunk'd.'" His bat is labeled "Slavery Extension" and his belt "Disunion Club." At far left John Bell of the Constitutional Union party notes that, "It appears to me very singular that we three should strike foul' and be put out' while old Abe made such a good lick.' Bell's bat says "Fusion" and his belt "Union Club," and his bat "Fusion." Stephen Douglas replies, "That's because he had that confounded rail, to strike with, I thought our fusion would be a short stop' to his career." His bat is labeled "Non Intervention."

Across the Republican Party spectrum, Davis proved even more vital than Judd when the time came for on-site wheeling and dealing. How much wheeling and dealing he actually did, though, remains open to question. When Swett supposedly told him that Lincoln had instructed him to "make no contracts that will bind me," Davis shot back, "Lincoln ain't here." Davis met with the Pennsylvania delegation, emerged, and said, "Damned if we haven't got them." How they had gotten them? "By paying their price,"

Fig. 7. Storming the Castle. (Library of Congress) In this pro-Lincoln cartoon, the Republican is dressed as a "Wide-Awake," and carries a wooden rail as he approaches the White House to prevent the other candidates from sneaking in to office. Incumbent James Buchanan struggles to pull Southern Democrat John C. Breckinridge in through a window. The weary President gasps, "I'll do what I can to help you Breck, but my strength is failing and I'm afraid you'll pull me out before I can pull you in." Breckinridge cries, " . . . I'm too weak to get up—and we shall be compelled to dissolve the Union," a reference to his supposed plan to push the South toward secession. Northern Democrat Stephen A. Douglas works to unlock the White House door, while Constitutional Union party candidate John Bell, seeing Lincoln coming, calls, "Hurry up Douglas! and get the door open, so that I can get in, for the watchman is coming." Douglas replies that none of his three keys (inscribed "Regular Nomination," "Non Intervention," and "Nebraska Bill") "will open the door . . . so I'd better be off, for old Abe is after me with a sharp stick."

which was a Cabinet seat. Whether Davis actually went beyond what Lincoln wanted and promised a Cabinet post to Cameron or some other Pennsylvanian remains unclear: Davis told another Republican, "Mr. Lincoln is committed to no one on earth in relation to office. He promised nothing to gain his nomination and has promised nothing since. No one is authorized to speak for him." All of this would have been correct even if Davis had promised Cabinet appointments. But as the convention ended, Davis also wired Lincoln, "Don't come here for God's sake," and, "Write no letters and make no promises till you see me."[19]

Other factors may have played a role. For one thing, political logic dictated that Pennsylvania have a seat at the Cabinet table, meaning that if Davis made any promises, they were promises that Lincoln would keep under any circumstances. Also, Thomas Dudley, a New Jersey delegate, later claimed that the delegations from his state, Illinois, Indiana, and Pennsylvania met at the behest of the New England delegates, led by Governor John Andrew of Massachusetts. Andrew told them that "they had it in their hands to name the candidates," but if they failed to unite on one man, "Seward would be nominated and the party defeated." New Jersey agreed to drop its favorite son, William Dayton, if Pennsylvania would drop Cameron—"after the complimentary voting was over."[20]

Whatever the merit and accuracy of Dudley's recollections, the complimentary votes on the first ballot included a surprise. Lincoln ran second to Seward's 173½ votes with 102. Other delegations began moving toward Lincoln: on the second ballot, his total rose to 181, whereas Seward could gain only eleven more. The third ballot brought a stampede and a nominee: Lincoln, eventually chosen unanimously, thanks in large part to the delegates he had sent to the convention or cultivated beforehand. Not only did they maneuver well on his behalf, but they also avoided mistakes such as promising spots on the ticket to other aspirants or offering up Lincoln's name to more prominent candidates for the presidency.

With the nomination his, Lincoln entered a new phase of the election. Campaigning openly remained taboo, and he clearly chafed at the need to remain silent, but this marked the first time that he was dealing with a true national party apparatus. Granted, some questioned its value: the eternally cranky Horace Greeley wrote, "As to that good for nothing national committee, it seems incapable of doing any thing, even resigning," although that may have been because Weed's allies had more influence than he did. Whatever the merits of Greeley's criticism, being part of a

Fig. 8. The Lincoln Quick Step. (Library of Congress) The candidates in 1860 all published sheet music and encouraged voters
to sing rousing songs supporting their man for the presidency.
As shown on this Lincoln publication, symbolism on the cover
mattered, as the Republican was surrounded by images of hard
work in rural America.

larger, nationwide campaign required him to be involved—but cautiously.
Greeley's caution ran into two channels: in not being seen as campaigning for the office and in dealing with better-known national figures who
already were often at loggerheads. His background and inclinations were
at odds with necessity and reality: as he told Senator Henry Wilson of

Massachusetts, "I do what I can in my position, for organization; but it does not amount to so much as it should."[21]

In a reversal of form from the divisions afflicting Illinois Republicans, Lincoln immediately benefited from his party's national feuds. Because Greeley had sought another candidate and worked his way into the convention as a delegate from Oregon, Seward and Weed blamed him for engineering their defeat. Because his delegation had failed to stand behind him at the convention, Chase felt that his fellow Ohioans had abandoned him and viewed Wade as the culprit. Absolving Lincoln of blame for their losses was not quite correct, because he had done more than it appeared to cause them, but his actions were neither overt nor personal. Accordingly, Lincoln's fence-mending began with a meeting with Weed, whom Davis and Swett urged to stop in Springfield before returning to Albany to lick his wounds. After five hours in Springfield, Weed left with much more respect for Lincoln than he had brought with him, while Lincoln reported that "he showed no signs whatever of the intriguer." Lincoln subsequently wrote a letter to him under Davis's name and, indeed, as Davis, reassuring Weed that he would distribute patronage fairly.[22]

Lincoln demonstrated his grasp of campaign politics in how he dealt with runners-up who might be upset and who occupied opposing ends of the party's ideological spectrum. Chase had written to Lincoln soon after the nomination to assure him of his support. Lincoln's response appealed to Chase's eminence and commitment to "service in the common cause," all of which struck the right tone. Bates was hardly likely to create trouble, because he had refused to leave his St. Louis home even on his own behalf, but his support could be vital. At the urging of other Illinois Republicans, Browning visited Bates and left with a strong letter endorsing Lincoln. In turn, Lincoln smoothed relations with Bates's supporters.[23]

Smoothing relations within state parties occupied Lincoln's attention and time, too. Dispatching Davis to referee disputes between Cameron's forces and his opponents in Pennsylvania, Lincoln provided him with copies of his speeches from two decades before in favor of a protective tariff, which would soothe most Pennsylvania Republicans' nerves. Indiana Republicans divided along more ideological lines, and Lincoln did a great deal to win over their most conservative wing by working through an old Whig friend, Richard W. Thompson, who helped him make inroads there and in Illinois with ex-Whigs still loath to join the newer antislavery party. Lincoln also conferred with and directed Swett in dealing with Republicans he knew in Illinois and former Whig friends in New York.[24]

Lincoln also acted on his own or at others' behest. He helped prepare his official campaign biography, written by the *Chicago Press & Tribune* editors John Scripps and Horace White—and thereby assured that voters would read the version of Lincoln's life that he wanted them to know: his years as a common laborer, his reasons for opposing the Mexican-American War, and his dedication to the antislavery cause. He advised the national party chair, Edwin Morgan, on how Illinoisans would vote. He proposed where to send speakers and which speakers to send. Notwithstanding his reputation for melancholy and pessimism, he frequently provided pep talks to fellow Republicans in his letters to them, encouraging them to keep working. He studied what his opponents did; the analyses he provided to fellow Republicans did no damage to his cause, even when he was wrong.

Neither Lincoln nor his fellow Republicans proved wrong very often during the 1860 campaign. Lincoln's opponents hoped that if they lacked the votes to defeat him, they might have enough votes to deprive him of an Electoral College majority and send the election into the House. They had no such luck. Lincoln won just under 40 percent of the national vote and an electoral majority, gaining 180 votes while his three opponents combined for 123. Six weeks after the November 6 election, South Carolina announced its secession. Six other Southern states followed before Lincoln took office on March 4, 1861.

Lincoln's election triggered secession, and that election resulted from a combination of factors. It was a perfect political storm. Party division played a role—and not just the split among Democrats. Conservatives without a party came together in the Constitutional Union Party, further dividing the electorate. Southern intransigence obviously contributed to the outcome. Republicans managed their campaign well enough and tamped down the many differences that could have divided them irreparably: former Democrats versus former Whigs, radicals versus conservatives, East versus West, and North versus border states, to name a few. Douglas's dedication to keeping Southern Democrats out of the White House, whether out of loyalty to the Union or determination to run the Democratic Party or a combination of both, had the unintended effect of aiding his longtime Illinois adversary.

Ultimately, though, credit should go where it is due. As Richard Carwardine points out in his political biography of Lincoln, "An instinctive electoral strategist, as well as a salient campaigner in every president contest since 1840, he had no intention of placing his future exclusively in the hands of others." Accordingly, with varying degrees of depth and attentiveness,

Lincoln mapped out his road to the nomination and contributed to his election through both what he did and what he did not do. A variety of factors explain Abraham Lincoln's election as president in 1860. Perhaps the most crucial one of all was Abraham Lincoln.[25]

1. Cassius M. Clay to Caleb B. Smith, n.p., March 8 and 16, 1860, Box 1, Smith-Spooner Collection, Henry E. Huntington Library, San Marino, Calif.

2. Henry Steele Commager, "Introduction," in William H. Herndon and Jesse W. Weik, *Herndon's Life of Lincoln* (New York: Da Capo Press, 1983), xxxix; Eric Foner, *The Fiery Trial: Abraham Lincoln and American Slavery* (New York: Norton, 2010), xv. On Lincoln's image, see Merrill D. Peterson, *Lincoln in American Memory* (New York: Oxford Univ. Press, 1994); Barry Schwartz's two volumes, *Abraham Lincoln and the Forge of National Memory* (Chicago: Univ. of Chicago Press, 2000), and *Abraham Lincoln in the Post-Heroic Era: History and Memory in Late Twentieth-Century America* (Chicago: Univ. of Chicago Press, 2008); and Harold Holzer, Gabor S. Boritt, and Mark E. Neely, Jr., *The Lincoln Image: Abraham Lincoln and the Popular Print* (New York: Scribner Press, 1984), among Holzer's many works on this and closely related topics. See also Michael Davis, *The Image of Lincoln in the South* (Knoxville: Univ. of Tennessee Press, 1971).

3. David M. Potter, *The Impending Crisis: 1848–1861* (New York: Harper and Row, 1976), 428.

4. David Herbert Donald, *Lincoln* (New York: Simon & Schuster, 1995), 14–15.

5. David Herbert Donald, *"We Are Lincoln Men": Abraham Lincoln and His Friends* (New York: Simon & Schuster, 2003), xiii–xv.

6. Richard Hofstadter, *The American Political Tradition and the Men Who Made It* (New York: Alfred A. Knopf, 1948), 92–134, quotation at 93; "Autobiography Written for John L. Scripps," in Roy P. Basler, ed., *The Collected Works of Abraham Lincoln* (New Brunswick, N.J.: Rutgers Univ. Press, 1953–55), 4:60–62.

7. Michael S. Green, *Freedom, Union, and Power: Lincoln and His Party During the Civil War* (New York: Fordham Univ. Press, 2004), 76–78.

8. Francis P. Blair, James H. Van Alen, Horace Greeley, John D. Defrees, John C. Vogel, James B. Eads, Dr. A. Hammer to Republicans, Chicago, May 14, 1860, Thomas H. Dudley Papers, Mar.–Oct. 1860, Huntington Library. The most recent summary of the backgrounds of these candidates is Doris Kearns Goodwin, *Team of Rivals: The Political Genius of Abraham Lincoln* (New York: Simon & Schuster, 2005).

9. Donald, *Lincoln,* 45–53.

10. Donald, *Lincoln,* 78–80; "Lincoln's Plan of Campaign in 1840," c. January 1840, in Basler, ed., *Collected Works,* 1:180–81. On Lincoln's party, see Daniel Walker Howe, *The Political Culture of the American Whigs* (Chicago: Univ. of Chicago Press, 1979); and Michael F. Holt, *The Decline and Fall of the American Whig Party: Jacksonian Politics and the Onset of the Civil War* (New York: Oxford Univ. Press, 1999).

11. *Chicago Weekly Journal,* August 5, 1850, in Basler, ed., *Collected Works,* 2:83–90; *Illinois Weekly Journal,* July 21, 1852, in ibid., 2:121–32; Donald, *Lincoln,* 162–67.

12. William C. Harris, *Lincoln's Rise to the Presidency* (Lawrence: Univ. Press of Kansas, 2006), 151–52; Lincoln to Trumbull, Springfield, April 29, 1860, in Basler, ed., *Collected Works,* 4:45; Michael Burlingame, *Abraham Lincoln: A Life* (Baltimore: Johns Hopkins Univ. Press, 2008), 1:558. See also Lincoln to Thomas J. Pickett, Springfield, April 16, 1859, in Basler, ed., *Collected Works,* 3:377; Richard Carwardine, *Lincoln* (London: Pearson, 2003), 91–92.

13. Lincoln to Dr. Anson S. Henry, Springfield, November 19, 1858, in Basler, ed., *Collected Works,* 3:339; David J. Leroy, *Mr. Lincoln's Book: Publishing the Lincoln-Douglas Debates with a Census of Signed Copies* (New Castle: Oak Knoll Press, 2009); Harold Holzer, *Lincoln at Cooper Union: The Speech That Made Abraham Lincoln President* (New York: Simon & Schuster, 2004).

14. Trumbull to Lincoln, Washington, April 24, 1860, Abraham Lincoln Collection, Library of Congress, http://memory.loc.gov.

15. Donald, *Lincoln,* 242; Lincoln to Norman B. Judd, Springfield, December 9, 1859, in Basler, ed., *Collected Works,* 3:505; December 14, 1859, in ibid., 3:509; and February 5, 1860, in ibid., 3:516; Lincoln to the editor of the *Central Transcript,* Springfield, July 3, 1859, in ibid., 3:389–90; Gary Ecelbarger, *The Great Comeback: How Abraham Lincoln Beat the Odds to Win the 1860 Republican Nomination* (New York: St. Martin's Press, 2008), especially 123–26.

16. Donald, *Lincoln,* 244–45.

17. Burlingame, *Lincoln,* 1:599–600; Reinhard Luthin, *The First Lincoln Campaign* (Cambridge, Mass.: Harvard Univ. Press, 1944), 65.

18. Burlingame, *Lincoln,* 1:603; Ecelbarger, *The Great Comeback,* 192, 204–5; Reinhard H. Luthin, *The Real Abraham Lincoln: A Complete One-Volume History of His Life and Times* (Englewood Cliffs, N.J.: Prentice-Hall, 1960), 217.

19. Ecelbarger, *The Great Comeback,* 196–97, 213–14; Luthin, *The First Lincoln Campaign,* 158; David Davis to Thomas H. Dudley, Bloomington, September 1, 1860, Thomas H. Dudley Collection, Henry E. Huntington Library; Davis to Lincoln, Chicago, May 18, 1860, Abraham Lincoln Collection, Library of Congress, http://memory.loc.gov.

20. Thomas Haines Dudley, "Report on Republican National Convention of 1860; caucuses &C. leading to nomination of Abraham Lincoln," ca. 1875, Thomas Haines Dudley Papers, Henry E. Huntington Library. See also John L. Stratton to Dudley, Washington, May 23, 1860, ibid.

21. Horace Greeley to Thomas Haines Dudley, New York, September 5, 1860, in Dudley Papers, Henry E. Huntington Library; Lincoln to Henry Wilson, Springfield, September 1, 1860, in Basler, ed., *Collected Works,* 4:109.

22. Lincoln to Trumbull, Springfield, June 5, 1860, in Basler, ed., *Collected Works,* 4:71; Willard L. King, *Lincoln's Manager, David Davis* (Chicago: Univ. of Chicago Press, 1960), 144–45.

23. Lincoln to Salmon P. Chase, Springfield, May 26, 1860, in Basler, ed., *Collected Works,* 4:53.

24. King, *Davis,* 150–53.

25. Carwardine, *Lincoln,* 112.

2

The 1860 Southern Sojourns of Stephen A. Douglas and the Irrepressible Separation

James L. Huston

On the evening of Saturday, August 25, 1860, a crowd numbering between four and six thousand people gathered before the steps of the Court House in Norfolk, Virginia. Standing before them, the Little Giant of Illinois, the first presidential candidate in American history to stump personally for elevation to the chief magistracy, defended the idea of popular sovereignty as a means of overcoming the sectional division that was threatening to rip the nation into two countries. Already Stephen A. Douglas had toured the New England states and New Jersey, giving speeches almost daily, all of them concentrating on his vision of the policy of popular sovereignty in the territories—letting the residents of a territory determine the existence of slavery for themselves and mandating that Congress should have no say in the subject, a course of action most often referred to as nonintervention. The five-foot, four-inch Douglas tore into his subject in his usual style: punctuating his points with sweeping gestures and radiating an intensity that swept audiences into his grasp.

After one hour, he was interrupted by William Lamb, the editor of the Norfolk *Southern Argus* and a supporter of the Southern Democratic nominee, John C. Breckinridge; he gave Douglas a note with two questions. Then came one of the most famous moments in the campaign of 1860, as Douglas read the note and then told the crowd:

> I am not in the habit of answering questions propounded to me in the course of an address, but on this occasion I will comply with the request and respond very frankly and unequivocally to these two questions.

The first question is, if Abraham Lincoln be elected President of the United States will the Southern States be justified in seceding from the Union?

To this I emphatically answer no. (Great applause.) The election of a man to the Presidency by the American people, in conformity with the Constitution of the United States, would not justify any attempt at dissolving this glorious confederacy. (Applause.) Now I will read to you the next question and, and [*sic*] then answer it.

Question—If they, the Southern States, secede from the Union upon the inauguration of Abraham Lincoln, before he commits an overt act against their constitutional rights, will you advise or vindicate resistance by force to their secession?

Mr. Douglas.—I answer emphatically that it is the duty of the President of the United States and all others in authority under him, to enforce the laws of the United States as passed by Congress and as the courts expound them. (Cheers.)[1]

Douglas's response was a stunner, but historians have not drawn out of Douglas's 1860 Southern sojourns all the interpretive weight they possess. General histories of the antebellum decade make reference to the Douglas trips—the excursion into Virginia and North Carolina in August and then his last one in late October and early November through Missouri, Tennessee, Georgia, and Alabama—and authors praise Douglas for his valiant attempt to dilute the secessionist fervor gripping the slaveholding states.[2] Historians of the South, however, have not dealt with Douglas's Southern invasions at any great length; Lincoln's biographers have ignored it entirely.[3]

More can be gleaned from Douglas's 1860 forays into the South than from his attempt to discredit secession. Douglas's speeches demonstrated that the expansion issue was still alive and productive of sectional ill will. The response of Northerners to Douglas's remarks also point to a failure encountered historically in electioneering: electoral strategy in 1860 stifled serious debate on the question of secession. Moreover, Douglas's comments in Virginia and North Carolina were sufficiently pointed that Southerners should have realized that the North would unite against secession; thus, secession was likely to lead to war. A close look at Northern Democratic opinion indicates that on the question of the Union and the right to revolution, Republicans and Northern Democrats were strikingly similar. Finally, an analysis of the way Douglas changed his set speech on popular

Fig. 9. Hon.
Stephen A.
Douglas of Il-
linois: National
Democratic
candidate
for sixteenth
president of the
United States.
(Library of
Congress)

sovereignty as he went from one region to another reveals that the division of the nation over the extension of slavery was ultimately grounded
in a Southern demand that property rights in slaves be accepted as the
sovereign fact of national existence and that anything less demanded a
dismantling of the country. The road to disunion was no strange string of
occurrences impinging on one another, no bizarre coincidences of people
and places. Rather, it was the product of two forces, one demanding recognition of property rights in slaves, the other fearing the upheaval of society
from that recognition. Douglas was powerless against these forces.

Central to the dilemma that Democrats faced in the election of 1860 was
the division of the party into Southern and Northern factions. Northern
Democrats largely backed Douglas's presidential aspirations and agreed
with his policy of popular sovereignty in the territories. The Douglas version permitted this decision to be made in each territorial legislature prior
to statehood by the passage of laws enforcing or not enforcing rules that

made slavery possible. This position was known as the Freeport Doctrine, which Douglas enunciated in his 1858 debates with Abraham Lincoln.

Southerners detested the Freeport Doctrine because it threatened to enable the first settlers to a territory to exclude slavery immediately, before slaveholders had the chance to settle on the land with their slaves. Given the population advantages of the North—where, in 1860, two-thirds of the population resided—Douglas's version of popular sovereignty seemingly gave all the territories to Northerners and denied them to slaveholders. That hostility to "squatter sovereignty," as Southerners called the Douglas doctrine, was amplified by their anger at Douglas for deserting the Buchanan administration over the admission of Kansas under the proslavery Lecompton Constitution later in 1858. In response to Douglas's ideas, Albert Gallatin Brown and Jefferson Davis produced a set of congressional resolutions labeled the "territorial slave code." These resolutions demanded that slaves must be recognized as property, that Southerners had equal rights with Northerners to carry their property into the territories, that the federal government must protect all forms of property in the territories, and that the only moment the settlers could determine the existence or nonexistence of slavery was the moment they held a constitutional convention.[4]

These two contrasting views of the power of settlers over the slavery issue created the grand division among the Democrats. At their nominating convention, held in Charleston during the last week of April 1860, the delegates divided over platforms. Northerners stood behind the platform that reaffirmed the Cincinnati platform of 1856, which called for congressional nonintervention in the territories (effectively the popular sovereignty plank), whereas Southerners voted for the one advocating a plank that embodied the territorial slave code. Because Northerners outnumbered Southerners, the convention adopted congressional nonintervention (popular sovereignty) as the Democratic Party standard. Representatives from the cotton states bolted and left the convention. Under the party rules, which required a nominee to receive the support of two thirds of the delegates, the remaining delegates could not make a nomination for the presidency and vice presidency. Therefore, they agreed to reassemble at Baltimore in late June to complete their task. At Baltimore, the Douglas managers controlled the convention, thereby causing another division; this time, most delegates from the Border South left the proceedings. They joined with the original seceding Gulf state delegates at Richmond, reassembled shortly thereafter at Baltimore, and nominated John C. Breckinridge for the presidency and Joseph Lane of Oregon for the vice presidency on a platform touting federal protection of slavery in the territories. At the main party convention in Baltimore, Douglas's supporters awarded him the nomination for the presidency; eventually, they chose Herschel V. Johnson of Georgia as his running mate.[5]

Why the party became so divided has been a bone of contention, because the split almost guaranteed that a Democratic victory in 1860 would be impossible. Moreover, the Democrats seemed to have little reason to agitate the question of slavery's status in the territories, because there were few if any places where slave labor and free labor would collide; the issue, it seemed, would not be confronted again for decades.[6] What stood out about the two Democratic nominating conventions was the clash of powerful personalities and rivalries. Douglas's revolt against acceptance of the Lecompton Constitution made him the enemy of President James Buchanan and many in his Cabinet. Senate supporters of Buchanan marked out Douglas for retribution, the most obvious form being to ensure that he did not become the Democratic presidential nominee. At Charleston, several Buchanan supporters worked against Douglas's nomination, manipulated some delegates into false strategies, and helped cause the rupture between the Northern and Southern Democrats.[7]

The clash of personalities operated in two distinct ways to hinder the Democrats' electoral appeal. First, each Democratic camps spent an inordinate amount of time belittling the other and appealing to the party faithful to support only itself. Sometimes, each faction had precious little time to woo conservatives to its side, the strategy that, it was widely acknowledged, could lead to victory over the Republicans.[8] The second way personal animosities interfered with the Democratic electoral appeal was the leadership's inability to fuse the warring factions into a united body. Only in New York City and in New Jersey could it bring the Breckinridge and Douglas forces together, both agreeing that presidential electors should cast their ballots in such a way as to secure a defeat of Lincoln. Douglas personally rejected fusion in all cases, especially in the key states of New York and Pennsylvania. He did so formally on the basis that the Breckinridge camp housed disunionists who should never be recognized. He also understood that any agreement with the people who caused the Charleston rupture would send his supporters into the Republican Party. Thus, fusion attempts among the anti-Lincoln elements failed.[9]

All kinds of problems in obtaining financial contributions and favorable endorsements from newspapers—the pervasive media of the day—beset the Douglas campaign, but Douglas and his supporters initially had some hopes of victory.[10] The Republican surge in 1854–55 had been repulsed in the presidential election of 1856, with the states of Illinois, Indiana, Pennsylvania, New Jersey, and California voting Democratic. Furthermore, most Democrats were aware that only a decade before, their party had strength in Wisconsin, Michigan, Maine, Connecticut, and Rhode Island. A spark of optimism had resulted from the split of the Rhode Island Republicans in that state's spring election, enabling a nominal Democrat to win the gubernatorial seat. The key to that electoral victory was wooing the conservative elements of the state and stressing the dire economic future if the nation should elect Republican radicals. If Douglas could convince the conservative element—the Fillmore voters of 1856—to stick with him in 1860, he could repeat the 1856 Buchanan vote and perhaps improve on it. Of course, this strategy depended on the South's voting for him. In late June, this was not an inconceivable outcome, though the strategy badly underestimated the strength of the Republican appeal as well as Southern loyalty to the regular party.[11]

Douglas left Washington, D.C. in late June and in early July resided in New York City, organizing his campaign. There he ran into financial and organizational difficulties, forcing him to recognize that his candidacy was not doing well. On the advice of his young wife, Adele, and from numerous invitations to speak, Douglas determined to break the precedent of presidential candidates' refraining from campaigning during an election. Instead, he would go on a speechmaking tour. He could at first plausibly argue that he intended to visit his mother in upstate New York and to attend the graduation ceremony of Adele's brother, James Madison Cutts, Jr., from Harvard. This became Douglas's New England tour, which ran from mid-July to the third week in August. As he went from city to city, crowds gathered at railroad stations or near his hotel, and he gave speeches. No one was deceived; Douglas was defying precedent and openly campaigning for the highest office in the land.[12]

The Little Giant made lengthy speeches at Boston, Lexington, Concord, Springfield, Manchester, Augusta, Newport, Albany, Saratoga, Troy, and finally Newark before he plunged into Virginia. His remarks in the North are an interesting backdrop to his Southern excursion. Douglas praised past New England Unionists, such as the "god-like Webster," in an ef-

STEPHEN FINDING "HIS MOTHER."

Fig. 10. Stephen Finding His Mother. (Library of Congress) Douglas's insistence that he was just visiting his mother instead of campaigning for the presidency led to many satirical cartoons and parodies. Here "Mother" Columbia, seated in a chair adorned with an eagle and shield, holds Douglas over her knee and spanks him with a switch labeled "Maine Law," as the prohibition legislation supported by temperance advocates was called. In addition to this blatant reference to the Little Giant's reputation as a drinker, Columbia also scolds him for his most famous legislative work: "You have been a bad boy Steve, ever since you had anything to do with that Nebraska Bill and have made a great deal of trouble in the family and now I'll pay you for it." Douglas weeps, "Oh! Marm let me off this time and I'll never do so any more." To the left stands Uncle Sam, encouraging Columbia to " . . . lay it on him . . . give him the Stripes till he sees Stars."

fort to woo conservatives to his standard. He constantly reiterated that in Congress the slavery issue shoved aside other matters of pressing concern to Northerners, such as the tariff and the transcontinental railroad. As in his debates with Lincoln in 1858, he reminded his audiences that in "his opinion, this government is the white man's government. ['That's so.'] It was made by white men for the benefit of white men, and it ought to be administered by white men." He frequently denounced the Breckinridge faction for disunionism.[13]

The bulk of his speeches focused on popular sovereignty or congressional nonintervention in the domestic concerns of the territories. At Troy, New York, he made it explicit: both Republicans and States' Rights Democrats were centralizing interventionists who wanted to force settlers to adopt or not adopt slavery. He explained the misguided notion of the interventionists in numerous ways. At Manchester, New Hampshire, the rule was "Mind your own business." In Rhode Island, he attended a clambake near Providence and used it as an example of a local practice shaped by climate and geography and that no central government should interfere with—it was something that had to be left to the people concerned. When in Maine, he used Maine law (specifically, the prohibition against production of alcoholic beverages) as an example of popular sovereignty. If Maine people wanted a temperance law, then that was their prerogative. Adding a little humor, he said in Illinois that the Northern part of the state was for a Maine Law, but in southern Illinois, known as Little Egypt, "among the Democrats, where they were temperate, moral, and religious, they had no necessity for the law, and they didn't vote for it. [Laughter.]" So if some people thought slavery might be a bad thing with evil consequences, that was for the people in a locality to decide for themselves. If the people have good laws, "let them enjoy the benefit of them; if they are evil, let them bear the burden and the evils they entail until they become wise enough to make better ones."[14]

The last stop of this phase of his campaign was in Newark, New Jersey, on August 22. Douglas reiterated his usual themes with one addition, and the fact that he was heading south may have had some influence on why he included it. Douglas indicated an expansionist future that did not preclude additional slave states. His example was the territory of New Mexico. Two years before, Douglas said, the territorial legislature of New Mexico had passed a slave code: "if the people of New-Mexico desire a slave code, they have a right to it." Congress should not interfere because "It is no argument to say that slavery is a good thing, or that it is a bad thing. The first principle of free government is, that the people most interested must decide for themselves whether a law is good or whether it is a bad thing." In fact, slavery expansion was not dead. Before Douglas spoke in Newark, a local Democratic politician had argued that Northerners should agree that where climate and geography allowed slavery to be profitable, there slavery should be established. Indeed, among some Democrats, designs on Mexico and Cuba were still very much alive. An Indiana Democrat and former representative had written Douglas back in February, "The acquisition of Cuba and the absorption of Mexico, at the proper time, could be carried in the north west."[15]

Douglas turned south partly because of invitations informing him that his presence would help numerous Douglas conventions in Virginia and North Carolina. According to Allan Nevins, he had also determined to denounce what he saw as a conspiracy among Southern fire-eaters to engineer a coup d'état. Whatever exactly was in his mind, he traveled to Norfolk, Virginia—a stop on his way to Raleigh, North Carolina—and arrived there on Saturday, August 25.[16]

Although Douglas's address at Norfolk concentrated on popular sovereignty as a means of quelling the rancorous debate about slavery in the territories, political attention became focused on his repudiation of state secession. His reasoning deserves careful examination. First, secession would be illegitimate if based on the election of a person "in conformity with the Constitution of the United States." In other words, the country had been founded on the acceptance of the results of legitimate elections; secessionists would be traitors to the founding agreement if they acted to dissolve the compact because they disliked the outcome of a legitimate election. Second, any elected official would have to move against a community attempting secession because officials were entrusted with "enforc[ing] the laws of the United States passed by Congress." For a nation to survive, its citizens had to acknowledge "the supremacy of the laws against all resistance to them." Douglas's example of an executive who moved against lawbreakers was Andrew Jackson in the Nullification episode of 1832–33. Third, he reminded his audience that it was "the duty of every citizen of every state . . . to preserve, maintain and vindicate the rights of every citizen and the rights of every State in the Union." This idea of obedience to the law was a major theme in Northern Democratic writing on secession. Fourth, no drastic action should be taken until every avenue of redress of grievance was explored, and Douglas believed that the Constitution gave "a remedy" for all grievances. This recourse to available means of redress was tied to a fifth point, revolution. Douglas recognized "the inherent and inalienable right of revolution," but "[t]hat is a right . . . never to be resorted to until the operations of the government become more grievous than the consequences of the revolution." Sixth, there could be no oppression without an "overt act," and without an overt act of oppression, there was no legitimacy in resorting to revolution.

Douglas then supplemented these remarks about the constitutionality of secession by expounding on his idea of congressional nonintervention in the territories and by insisting that the situation of 1860 was a purposeful mess created by the Charleston seceders, who had divided the Democratic party "so as to give Lincoln every one of those [Northern] States, so that I tell you if Lincoln be elected President, it will be the secessionists whom you will have to blame for it."[17]

After Norfolk, the Little Giant spoke at Petersburg on August 28, then addressed a gathering at Raleigh, North Carolina, on August 30. He reiterated his ideas about popular sovereignty and added that the American Revolution was about the right of home rule. In this connection, he restated his belief that climate and geography determined the establishment of slavery, which depended on the "climate, the soil, the productions and the self-interest of the people where it exists." In a hot climate where the white man cannot work, you must have slaves "or you will abandon the country to the crocodile." He added a warning to Southern secessionists by reminding them of Northern self-interest, arguing that the people of the Old Northwest would never allow the Mississippi River to be controlled by a foreign power. During his address, he affirmed his support for the Dred Scott decision and argued that secession because of distaste for the outcome of a legitimate election was criminal. Showing his nationalism, he argued that there was no reason to break up "this glorious Union . . . [W]e are the greatest nation on earth in many respects," and "we are the admiration of all who love free institutions, while we are the terror of all tyrants."[18]

In the Raleigh speech was an argument that was especially intended for Southern ears. The territorial slave code had as its constitutional foundation the guarantee of property rights in slaves. The question of property rights in slaves—a hornet's nest of trouble in the North—was vital to Southerners. Douglas answered it by throwing State's Rights theory back at State's Rights supporters: I will accept no privileges for Illinois that I will not guarantee to North-Carolina; and I claim no right in the territories for my citizens or for my property that I will not guarantee for every other State in the Union. I believe in the absolute and unconditional equality of all the States of the Confederacy. (Applause.) But I claim that I have the right to go into the territories and to carry my property with me and hold it there, and to have it protected on the same terms that you have in the slaveholding States. ("Good.") But upon what terms, I ask, can I carry my property into the territories? I carry it there subject to the local law.

Douglas's point was that only local government defined property rights, not Congress. States defined property rights for their own citizens within their boundaries and could not project their laws of property beyond their boundaries. Thus no person, Northern or Southern, carried property rights with them into the territories but had property only in accordance with local—in this case, territorial—law.[19]

On August 31, Douglas spoke at Richmond, Virginia, giving his standard noninterventionist, popular-sovereignty speech. He paraded his pro-Southern credentials—he stood with Southerners in voting down the Wilmot Proviso in 1846 and 1847—and he lumped the Republicans and the Breckinridge supporters together as extremists. He again forcefully pointed out that only local law established property rights, and that states could not project their laws beyond their borders. As he moved by railroad toward Baltimore between September 1 and 5, he gave speeches at various Virginia and Maryland towns. In Baltimore on the 6th, he addressed a crowd and explained the philosophy behind nonintervention, asserted that local conditions determined whether slavery would exist or not, and charged that the Breckinridge camp was filled with secessionists: not all Breckinridge men were secessionists, but all secessionists were Breckinridge supporters. He then added, "Secession means revolution." Secessionists were in truth trying to deceive the public. The American revolutionaries seceded from the British empire, but they did not fool themselves into thinking that their departure would be peaceful; they knew they were enacting a revolution and would be hanged if defeated. The disunionists of 1860, Douglas implied, should learn from their example.[20]

In many ways, the last stop of the Douglas Southern tour was not Baltimore but New York City on September 12, where a massive Democratic rally of twenty thousand to thirty thousand people took place in Jones's Woods, near the East River. Douglas responded to some of the Southern detractors who denounced his Norfolk answers, and he produced an interesting and concise explanation for his repudiation of secession. "We live . . . under a government of law. Our rights, our liberty, our property, our lives are dependent upon the laws of the land for protection." When "we" performed "all of our duties, according to law and according to the Constitution, then we have a right to demand that every other man shall obey the same laws and the same constitution." He then flatly declared that "this Union is a perpetual bond."[21]

The first observation to make about Douglas's sojourn into the South in August and September is that the reasons he gave for disallowing secessionism were strikingly similar to those that Abraham Lincoln would enunciate in his first inaugural address. Though Douglas did not use the word, his emphasis on obedience to the law is striking and implies a dread of the consequences of "anarchy."[22] Both Lincoln and Douglas had a geographical argument against secession as a practical matter, and both denounced any group that planned to implement disunion because they were displeased with the outcome of an election. Douglas did not mention majority rule specifically, but his reasoning that the outcome of a legitimate election was no justification for secession embodied the idea. Both men emphasized the practical fact that the president had to enforce the laws. Both stated the Union was perpetual. The key differences lay in the way the two considered the territorial issue. Douglas felt the constitutional means of handling it was by congressional nonintervention, whereas Lincoln bluntly said that some matters were not specifically addressed by the Constitution and were therefore legitimate subjects of legislation. But their similarities were the reasons that during Lincoln's inaugural address, Douglas was heard to mutter, "Good."[23]

Lincoln had several months to prepare his inaugural after South Carolina's declaration of separation on December 20, but Douglas only had several seconds. Undoubtedly over the course of a decade of sectional strife, he had time to do some ruminating about the doctrine of secession. There had been much discussion about it among Southerners, but for Douglas to compose such a nearly complete answer to the problem at a moment's notice was astounding. More important, some Southerners should have recognized this unanimity among Northerners about the illegitimacy of secession. Republicans were, of course, known to be hostile to the idea; now Douglas, as the spokesperson for the vast majority of Northern Democrats, added his agreement. One would have thought that Southerners and others would have readjusted their political calculations to recognize that the Southern idea of secession—to wit, the Calhoun process by which an elected state convention could sever participation in the Union—was absolutely rejected by the vast majority of Northerners. After Douglas's Virginia and North Carolina trip, armed hostility was highly probable if a state tried this means of secession. Some Southerners might have thought about alternative ways of exiting the Union other than by separate state action.

But no one did. Indeed, Douglas's trip was furthermore unusual because it did not spark a widespread debate about secession. Breckinridge supporters excoriated Douglas and called him a Black Republican for denying the constitutionality of separate state secession. Even his few Southern supporters tried to avoid the issue and find alternative ways of explaining his intentions. After answering the questions at Norfolk, he challenged William Lamb to get the other candidates to respond as forthrightly as he had. They never did. In early September, Breckinridge made a speech in Ashland, Kentucky, but did not answer the questions; Bell did not reply; and Lincoln remained cocooned in Springfield.[24]

What was surprising about the incident at Norfolk—although perhaps in retrospect not so unexpected—was the lack of Northern debate over secession. Certainly Southerners responded to Douglas's rejoinders, but the Northern Democratic press did not. Northern Democratic editors reprinted Douglas's speech dutifully but not with any editorializing. Highly unusual was the *Cleveland Daily Plain Dealer:* "HE TAKES THE SOUTHERN BULL BY THE HORNS. THE SECEDERS SLAUGHTERED IN THEIR OWN CAMP." Likewise, the *Cincinnati Daily Enquirer* added that Douglas had "the courage to face the Disunionists in the South with the same intrepidy [*sic*] that he has found the Abolition Fugitive-Slave Law Nullifiers of the North." A Breckinridge paper, the *Boston Post,* handled the Norfolk address by calling Douglas's journey a failure, although several weeks later the editor added that the idea of coercing a state was treason against the states' rights doctrine. Republicans ignored Douglas. The *New York Times* did report on Douglas, but the editorial staff at the *New York Tribune* admitted that they were snubbing Douglas and certainly were not about to print his speeches in their paper; one of the editors made the sarcastic comment, "Mr. Douglas has made some forty or fifty speeches of like tendency since he commenced his unfortunate search for his mother."[25]

Normally one might think that when one party raised an issue of importance, the other parties would respond, but such was not the case in the North following Douglas's Norfolk address. Rather, an uncomfortable silence over secession enshrouded political discourse. Historians usually

"TAKING THE STUMP" OR STEPHEN IN SEARCH OF HIS MOTHER.

Fig. 11. Taking the Stump. (Library of Congress) In this, another cartoon poking fun at Douglas for campaigning, the Northern Democrat is a hampered by a wooden leg while speaking with John Bell of Tennessee, Constitutional Union presidential candidate (far left), and influential Democrat Virginia governor Henry A. Wise. Douglas insists, "Gentlemen I'm going to see my mother,' and solicit a little help, for in running after a nomination, I fell over a big lump of Breckenridge and have been very lame ever since." Bell says to Wise, "I think I'll give him a trifle in New York currency," a reference to fusion attempts in that state. Wise responds, "He looks like a smart little man, and if I were not Wise I'd go my pile on him." At right, the incumbent president, James Buchanan, offers a stump to Breckinridge: "Here Breck, as Dug has taken the stump you must stump it too." Breckinridge replies, "Well old Buck, if you say so, I suppose I must, but I know it will be of no use, for I feel that I have'nt got a leg to stand on." His bandaged right foot further illustrates the point that the divided Democrats have crippled themselves. Abraham Lincoln, symbolically leaning on a rail fence, calls out, "Go it ye cripples! wooden legs are cheap, but stumping wont save you."

are at a disadvantage when confronting the lack of action or evidence, and explaining why something did not happen in the past is a perilous exercise, yet the need for an answer in this case overrules caution. Secession needed to be discussed—especially the idea of separate state secession—so that both Northerners and Southerners understood well in advance of 1860 the dangers involved. But that discussion belonged in Congress; in an electoral campaign, strategy cut off the discourse. Northern Democrats, whether regular or State's rights, relied on painting the Republicans as harbingers of Southern secession; they shied away from agreeing that secession was illegitimate because it took away one of their strongest arguments to conservatives for not voting for Lincoln. But Republicans could hardly hold up Douglas as a worthy candidate for opposing secession because it made Douglas as "anti-Southern," if not as antislavery, as Lincoln, thereby obscuring the differences between the two candidates and enabling conservatives to vote for the Little Giant. Thus Northerners did not openly confront what their actions might be in the event of attempted state separation until after the presidential election, when the Southern machinery of dissolution was put into motion.[26]

Another feature of press coverage during the election was the provincialism of the editors. Most newspapers focused on state activities and local elections, especially attempts at fusion among the anti-Republican groups. Papers did print lengthy speeches by visiting dignitaries from other states and from the prominent figures in their own states, but they did not necessarily pay much attention to activity beyond their regions. Much of Douglas's performance in the South stayed in the South. Much of what he said, if newspaper reports were the main source of information, did not penetrate the rest of the country. Newspapers gave Douglas much space when he came to their states and their cities but otherwise did not follow his movements. And before long, the attitude became that his speeches were one vast repetition of the theme of popular sovereignty. Even a friendly New Jersey paper said of his Baltimore speech on September 6 that "it was similar to those previously delivered." More pointed was a Detroit Republican paper, whose editor wrote—with some truth—that "'Douglas is coming,' shrieks his organ in this city. What is he coming for? Everybody has read that same old speech of his, so that we cannot be expected to hear anything new."[27]

After the Southern tour, Douglas went through New York, Pennsylvania, Ohio, Indiana, and finally to Illinois, giving lengthy speeches to massive crowds and exhausting his voice and straining his physical stamina. He added local issues where they might benefit his campaign, but his basic themes did not change.[28] Two particular features of his post-Virginia excursion are worthy of note. First, when in Cleveland Douglas spoke briefly about the Republican fear of a "slave power." It must be underlined how seldom any Democrat, Northern or Southern, ever confronted the major oratorical weapon of the Republicans, the Slave Power conspiracy theory.

The Republicans rampaged the field of oratorical battle with the sword of the Slave Power, driving the Democrats from the field—and almost no one ever challenged them. Douglas rarely brought it up. In the short reference he made to it, he simply asked, Where was it? If the Slave Power existed, how was it that in 1860 there were more free states than slave states?[29] The second aspect of his trip is a distinct absence of argument. He did not mention property rights in slaves and the status of those rights in the territories. In front of a Southern audience, most of whom believed in property rights in slaves, Douglas had to explain why the territorial slave code was a false concept. But in front of a Northern audience, most of whom believed the old abolitionist idea that there could be no property rights in people, Douglas probably felt it best to avoid that aspect of the controversy.[30]

Tuesday, October 9, was a telling day in the election campaign of 1860 because the large Northern states of Pennsylvania, Indiana, and Ohio voted for congressional representatives and state officials; these were key states that would accurately forecast the November presidential poll. Douglas had already been hurt in early September by a Republican sweep in Maine and Vermont, for these were New England states where in past days the Democrats had fared well. Then came the surge to the Republican Party in Indiana, Pennsylvania, and Ohio, with Republican majorities in the tens of thousands. Throughout the nation, people read those results to mean Abraham Lincoln would be the next president. As William H. Trescott of South Carolina wrote to Senator James H. Hammond, "The elections in Penn. have fairly settled the Presidential campaign." Thomas H. Seymour wrote to the former president Franklin Pierce that "Pennsylvania has floored us." Although some looked to New York for salvation, he did not: "It's no use. The rip tide of abolitionism is flowing over everything North and West." Talk of secession in the South began in earnest. Douglas, who was campaigning in Iowa when news of the elections reached him, told his secretary, James B. Sheridan, "Mr. Lincoln is the next President. We must try to save the Union. I will go South."[31]

Douglas's second journey into the slaveholding states would again emphasize the doctrine of congressional nonintervention on the issue of slavery's status in the territories—and therein lies an interpretive dilemma. Anyone who followed Douglas's long two- to three-hour speeches immediately would have believed that slavery in the territories was the principal issue in this election. In the South, the subject was discussed with some regularity but often was subsumed in two questions. The first was whether

Northerners would ever allow slavery to expand beyond the South's existing borders. The second involved the ultimate fate of slavery, and the practical form in which this question was posed was whether Northerners would observe the rights of Southerners to their slave property. In the North, most Democratic papers and Republican speakers mentioned the subject of slavery in the territories only tangentially. The topics of the Slave Power and free labor engulfed the oratory of the Republicans, while the Democrats constantly warned about the fate of the Union, the inferiority of blacks, and the dire results that would befall Northern laborers.

And as numerous historians have mentioned, many contemporaries believed that the troubles emanating from the territorial question winding down because no territory existed where slavery could go. Alexander Hamilton Stephens, a widely respected Georgian politician, announced on September 1 that he was supporting Douglas. Stephens said Douglas was known to be a friend of the South, and although he disagreed with the Little Giant over popular sovereignty, he could excuse Douglas on that question "because I look upon the matter as involving no principle of any vital importance."[32] Revisionist historians and many since have declared the territorial issue an "abstraction" not involving actual material interests. For that reason, many historians have viewed the battle between territorial popular-sovereignty and slave-code advocates as really about personalities: Douglas supporters versus his detractors.[33]

However, neither the issue of expansion nor that of popular sovereignty had lost its potency. Expansionism still lived in the minds of Douglas and Northern Democrats, taking concrete form in the desire to annex Cuba. Because Cuba allowed slavery, if the United States acquired the island it potentially would become a slave state and thereby spark off another sectional confrontation between North and South.[34]

But by the election of 1860, the territorial question had taken a particular form that explained its saliency to the South and the route Douglas had to take to combat it. In his speech endorsing Douglas, Alexander H. Stephens made it clear that Douglas recognized property in slaves, a fact of enormous significance. The territorial slave code was vital to many Southerners, because the foundational idea behind it was that Southerners had property rights in slaves and that Northerners must acknowledge that right. Not to acknowledge property rights in slaves was tantamount to declaring that the powers of government would not be used for the protection of rights in slaves; it foretold abolition by one means or another. At

Democratic rallies for Breckinridge in the North, the resolutions adopted often mentioned explicitly the duty of the federal government to protect slave property.[35] Although this aspect of the campaign of 1860 has not garnered much attention, Republicans at times did explicitly deny that slaves, who were human beings, could be treated as property like "horses or oxes."[36]

Douglas took his wife, Adele, and his personal secretary James Sheridan for a tour into the cotton South to argue for Union and not for his own presidential aspirations. In Illinois he went to Springfield and Centralia, then journeyed to St. Louis, Memphis, Huntsville, Kingston, Atlanta, Macon, Columbus, Montgomery, and Selma. He finally reached Mobile on November 5, the day before the election. He was given courteous and at times friendly receptions; the crowds were—as they had been elsewhere—numerous, with thousands of citizens pouring out to hear him. Not everything went smoothly, however. In Montgomery, someone threw rotten eggs at him and Adele as they went to a hotel, and a deck gave way on the steamer *Virginia,* delaying his departure from that city. It is almost that with the exception of a few papers, Northerners did not follow his October–November Southern trip at all.[37]

When in Illinois and Missouri, Douglas gave his standard popular sovereignty speech, as he would do at all his stops throughout the South. In these talks he branded both the Republicans and the Breckinridge supporters as disunionists, declared that the regular Democracy—that is, the Democratic Party—would have won the nomination for him and the election for the party had it not been for the premeditated division of the conventions at Charleston and Baltimore. Douglas also insisted that local determination of slavery was the only way to handle that question— Congress must practice nonintervention. In his usual two- to three-hour oration, he injected humor, explained how the slavery controversy ruined the chances of passing other useful legislation such as the Pacific railroad, and appealed to the racial sentiments of the audience by stressing that the United States government was a white man's government. In both Illinois and Missouri he added from the start a view of the question of disunion unique to the West (and the Old Northwest): "We of the Mississippi Valley can never consent that this Union shall ever be dissolved." This artery of commerce simply was too important to the people in this river basin—it was a distinct economic plea for insisting that the Union was perpetual.[38]

When in Missouri, however, Douglas ventured beyond St. Louis and went to Jefferson City, where on October 22 he gave an extended address.

He was now talking to Southerners and slaveholders; his message changed in important ways, even though its gist reiterated his popular-sovereignty appeal. A large portion of his speech was devoted to property rights in the territories, a subject usually absent from his Northern talks. Here he used a telling example. If a person took a horse into the territories, what act of Congress protected the person in his property? The answer was that there was no law of Congress for any form of property in the territories; all property law was local law. That was the truth that supported his doctrine of popular sovereignty and especially his pronouncement of the Freeport Doctrine in 1858 that any territorial community could exclude or include slavery by local law.[39]

He then turned to the burning question of secession. He first reflected that the problem would not have arisen if the radicals at the Charleston Democratic convention had not seceded and had accepted majority rule—which he had done in 1852 and 1856, when he lost the presidential nominations. The seceders had actually plotted to defeat him "at all costs." Thus, if Lincoln was elected in two weeks, it would be the fault of the Breckinridge supporters. He then referred to his Norfolk answers—but in a special way. At Norfolk he had said the president and the federal government would have to suppress rebellion and those individuals breaking the law; in fact, when in Maryland, Virginia, and North Carolina, Douglas had used the example of Jackson and the threat to hang traitors. There, Douglas had been bellicose. He was not bellicose in Missouri, nor would he be so in any of the other Southern states he visited in October and November. He used his responses to the Norfolk resolutions to emphasize his firm belief that the election of a president under the rules of the Constitution was no reason for secession. He added, "I am for fighting him [Lincoln] in the Union and under the Constitution, and not in favor of breaking up the Government." He then emphasized that Congress would be Democratic and that any hostile actions Lincoln might take could be thwarted easily; that is, Lincoln posed no danger to any Southern state. If Lincoln violated the Constitution, Douglas declared, he would be thrown out of office. Trying to tie Republicans and secessionists together, Douglas ended by saying that there were no exceptions to obedience to the law as given by the Constitution.[40]

As Douglas left Missouri and went into Tennessee, arriving in Memphis on October 24, the Northern Democratic press was warming up to the potential of a Lincoln victory on November 6, and the editors and writers were not touting popular sovereignty. They wrote in horrendous racist tones, called the Republicans abolitionists, and shrieked that emancipation would produce a flood of violence and white degradation.[41] Equally, they began the drumbeat of the likelihood of Southern secession if Lincoln were elected. The *New York Herald* printed and the *Cincinnati Daily Enquirer* quoted, "THE CRISIS AT THE SOUTH. A DISSOLUTION OF THE UNION INEVITABLE in the Event of Lincoln's Election." Wrote the "negrophobic" *Detroit Free Press,* "The Crisis," and "The Impending Revulsion." The *Cleveland Daily Plain Dealer,* half the time scourging Southern secessionists, the other half pleading with Northern voters to fear secession, had as headlines, "VOTERS! If you would have Civil War, GO FOR LINCOLN" and "LABORERS: If you would be thrown out of employment and see your children begging in the streets, VOTE FOR LINCOLN."[42]

Much of the Democratic writing and oratory about "negro equality" and the fear of secession aimed at driving voters to the Democratic standard and may not have been honest reflections of attitudes toward either African Americans or white Southerners. But within these editorials, however, was an interesting sidelight about how Democrats viewed the sectional struggle over slavery. They had none of the Republicans' fears of the Slave Power or over the fate of free labor or of civil liberties. Rather, they saw the Republicans and their allies as assaulting the South, giving Southerners a valid reason for contemplating secession. The editor of the *Providence* (Rhode Island) *Daily Post* wrote, "Secession may be foolishness—resistance may be madness; the South may be the most unreasonable community on the footstool of the Creator—but we tell this Republican party in plain language, that with a feeling of deadly hostility toward an institution which exists, almost as by an act of God, in fifteen States of the American Union, you have no right to expect a peaceful reign." In the *Erie Weekly Observer,* one writer tried to reason with Republicans that when the institutions of another community were assaulted, they should expect a hostile reaction verging unto separation. He asked Northerners what their reaction would be if William L. Yancey, an Alabaman whom most Northerners branded as the leading secessionist of the day, had said slavery must go north and the president was to use all his power to achieve it. Would not the North then attempt secession? Northern Democrats saw all the aggression stemming from the antislavery side of American politics and very little from the alleged Slave Power.[43]

No one in the North was reporting on Douglas as he dove into Georgia and Alabama, and thus some of his comments elicited no Northern response. On October 30 he had another two-and-one-half-hour address at Atlanta to an estimated crowd of twenty thousand. He repeated his Norfolk answers but without the belligerence. Trying to show a softer side of the Northern attitude toward slavery, he said Northerners were just dollars-and-cents people who let climate and geography determine the establishment of slavery: in Illinois, "Slavery was not profitable. They [Illinoisans] could not make any money out of it, hence they turned philanthropists and abolished it [Laughter and applause.]" In the South, he had to touch on property rights in slaves, and he again used his horse illustration: "Suppose you go into Kansas to-day and your horse is stolen, what act of congress is violated? [Laughter.]" His doctrine of popular sovereignty thus did not discriminate against Southern property rights; under popular sovereignty (and the Freeport Doctrine) there was a perfect equality of rights among Northerners and Southerners in the territories because local legislation operated equally on all migrants who came there. He of course emphasized that only he among the candidates had responded openly to the question of secession if Lincoln were elected, and he again denounced the Charleston seceders for putting the Democracy in its perilous position by dividing the party into sectional factions.[44]

The Little Giant invaded Alabama and gave an extended address at Montgomery—again, ignored by the Northern press. Besides the usual themes of popular sovereignty and the conspiracy of the Charleston seceders to break down the Democratic party, Douglas made a strong effort to pull on the nationalist heartstrings of his listeners: The nation that the founders created was the "greatest blessing ever conferred on a free people" and could be preserved only by people obeying its rules. He charged that "there is a conspiracy on foot [sic] to break up this Union." Again he used his illustration of animal property in the territories being protected by local, not congressional, law in order to show that charges of bias against Southern property in the doctrine of popular sovereignty were untrue. In conclusion, he again stressed obedience to the laws and the substance of his Norfolk answers—without, however, the ferocity with which he had spoken them in Virginia.

He added two things of interest in his Montgomery address. First, he mentioned—as he almost never did—that in 1850 the North had been in a frenzy over being "in the hands of the slave power." He said nothing further, again leaving historians at a loss to understand how Northern Democrats understood this basic fear of the Republican Party. Second, he advocated the acquisition of Cuba and as clearly as was possible promised that it would be a slave state. That proposal should have created a furor in the North—but no one was reading or listening to Douglas's speeches in his second Southern tour.[45]

He arrived at Mobile one day before the presidential ballot was to be taken, and when giving his speech he was given two more questions by a Breckinridge supporter. These two were of much less significance than the Norfolk questions. The first inquiry was if the election went into the House of Representatives, would he support Lincoln or Breckinridge; the second was whether he would accept a position in the Cabinet if Lincoln were elected. The Little Giant brushed both outcomes aside as impossibilities. He would never support a sectional candidate—meaning that he rejected both Lincoln and Breckinridge—and he would never turn against his party by joining a non-Democratic presidential team.

He also repeated a theme that was prominent in this tour. If Lincoln were elected, he would lack a majority in both the Senate and House of Representatives; he would be totally impotent as an administrator. Thus, "he is powerless for mischief" and was really an "object of pity," not fear. Because Lincoln would be in such a weak position, why should Southerners think of secession due to his election? "[W]hy should we break up the best government that the sun in its course around the earth ever shone upon, merely because we have been defeated in a Presidential election?" Rather, the Democrats must unite, fight on, and in four years "rescue the country from those hands in which it should not have been placed."[46]

Douglas left Mobile on November 7 a depressed, disheartened man, because he saw in Alabama, even among his staunch friends, that the tide of secessionism was inundating the state. He traveled by ship to New Orleans, arriving there on November 8. In a oration to a crowd and several days later in response to a letter from concerned citizens, the Little Giant again stressed that the Constitution had means of redress for any grievance, that Lincoln had no political power in Congress and could be thwarted at every turn, and that obedience to the Constitution was the duty of every citizen.[47]

The election of 1860 was over, and after November 6 a host of new circumstances altered the debate about secession. The December 20 decision of South Carolina to leave the Union, generally anticipated but still shocking, sparked a deeper discussion of the legality of secession and its implications than had occurred during the election. South Carolina's decision also complicated the discourse by confounding the doctrine of secession with hopes of compromise, charges of intransigence against the Republicans, and outbursts of racism. These matters will not be gone into here except for two views that emerged vibrantly in the postelection period. The first was a rejection of separate state secession. The states had joined a compact, and the rules of that compact commanded the assent or at least the consultation of the other states. In a December letter to August Belmont, one of his New York lieutenants in the election campaign, Douglas wrote: "I must say however that I can never recognize or acquiesce in the doctrine that any State can secede & separate from us without our consent." For a state to take action on its own, without reference to the other states in the compact, was the destruction of government, a headlong plunge into anarchy. This deprecation of secession was strongly attached to the continuous Democratic chant during the fall of 1860 that obedience to law was the duty of every citizen. For Northern Democrats, this idea was crucial for their eventual support of the Union after the firing on Fort Sumter.[48]

But the force tugging Northern Democrats away from enforcing obedience to law was the dread of coercing a state and destroying the ideal of a country that operated by voluntary consent. The editor of the *Kenosha* (Wisconsin) *Democrat,* an individual named S. Cadwallader, explained the Democrat abhorrence of coercion as well as did anyone in the North. Unlike in the nations of Europe, he said, "The voluntary system was adopted as a substitute for the system of force. The stability of the government was to be based upon the good will of the people toward it—upon the intelligence, love of liberty, respect for order and conservative impulses of the masses. Right minds and willing hearts were substituted for the old idea of brutish power." J. C. Cabell of Virginia put the attitude more succinctly in a letter to William Rives, writing that consent was necessary for a peaceful republic: "[There] is no Union in the sense of the constitution which has to be maintained at the point of the bayonet." The two halves of the Northern Democratic mind can be best viewed in President James Buchanan's December 3, 1860, annual message to Congress. Though heavily criticized by scholars for being antisecession while offering no practical remedy to the situation, the section on the right of individual state separation is indeed an excellent illustration of the Northern Democratic mind during the winter of secession.[49]

What finally drove Northern Democrats to war was violence directed toward the Union and its property. There was no negotiated end to the stalemate between the infant Confederacy and the Union. As a Philadelphia Democrat wrote to James Buchanan, "Secession or disunion, from any cause, is unpopular with the mass of people here, and with the Democratic party." No better illustration of the Northern consensus on the error of separate state secession could be found than in the editorial comments of two Springfield, Illinois, papers, the Republican *Illinois State Journal* and the Democratic *Illinois State Register.* These two papers had engaged in bitter partisan warfare for decades. But the *Register* reprinted an editorial from the *Journal* that declared that South Carolina could not secede: "She cannot get out of this Union until she conquers this government. . . . [I]f she violates the laws, then comes the tug of war"; and, finally, "Disunion by armed force, is treason." Charles Lanphier, the editor of the *Register,* succinctly expressed the Northern Democratic attitude toward this belligerent writing: about the editorial of his political adversary, "We in the main concur."[50] Northern Democrats agreed with Republicans that individual state secession was illegitimate, that without just cause it was a willful violation of the constitutional compact. The Democrats differed from the Republicans in their dread of coercion. So the Democrats sat paralyzed atop a narrow fence rail in a fit of indecision: secession was wrong, but so was coercion of a state.

What finally pushed Northern Democrats to determine that the illegality of individual state secession and the violation of compact was more important than a noncoercive union of voluntary members was the firing on Fort Sumter. When Confederate leaders determined to remove the federal presence from Charleston harbor by military action, they convinced Northern Democrats that obedience to law was under violent assault and that anarchy beckoned—the understanding of secession that Douglas enunciated time and again during the election of 1860. The Confederate firing on Fort Sumter was a colossal blunder. So long as the Confederacy had fired no shots, the stalemate tended to make Northern Democrats more receptive to a peaceful separation of the cotton states; the goal of a noncoercive Union was triumphing over the belief of the illegitimacy of separate state secession. The New York Democrat John A. Dix, once a free-soiler but throughout the 1850s a Douglas Democrat, recalled precisely how the cannonading of the fort swung the Democrats to a war footing. He wrote that it was "by no means improbable that if a separation had

Fig. 12. Douglas Campaign Banner. (Library of Congress)

been sought by the slave-holding States persistently, and through peaceful means alone, it might have been ultimately conceded by the Northern States in preference to a bloody civil war." Instead, "the forcible seizure of arsenals, mints, revenue-cutters, and other property of the common government," culminating in the firing on Fort Sumter, "put an end to argument as well as to the spirit of conciliation." If the Union had granted independence to the Confederacy after its "aggression" on Fort Sumter, the North would have been guilty of "pusillanimity" and shorn of its "honor."[51]

The journeys of Stephen A. Douglas into the South proved ultimately fruitless in stopping the secession avalanche, but these sojourns do offer a way to see how the issues of 1860 produced an "irrepressible" separation.[52] Douglas's speeches and their reception reveal the yawning chasm that had opened up between the sections and especially the parties that represented those sections; it also explains why the reconciliationists, the moderates of 1860, stood no chance—that is, no chance of being victorious in the long run. Perhaps secession could have been avoided in 1860, but it was going to occur sometime thereafter. At the heart of this conflict was—as all now recognize—slavery, and the particular aspect of slavery that proved beyond compromise was property rights. Moderates could find no common ground on property rights between Breckinridge Democrats and Northern Republicans, and for that reason the moderates were swept aside. Understanding the election of 1860 from this angle, then, leads to the conclusion that the Southern attempt to create a slaveholding white-supremacist republic was completely rational; and the insistence of Republicans on limiting slavery's role in national affairs was rational as well. And this means that the position of moderates, such as Douglas and his Northern Democrats, as well as those Southerners wishing to stay in the Union, was ultimately irrational.

Douglas's plunge into the South carried a number of themes, but the most distinctive one, especially in comparison to his Northern speeches, was his emphasis on property rights in slaves and how popular sovereignty upheld and did not betray them. Douglas had good reason to place property rights in slaves in a prominent position in his oratory. For Southerners, this was the central point of the campaign. Although many historians have questioned whether the subject of slavery in the territories still contained any urgency by 1860, and thus have virtually trivialized all of Douglas's speeches, they generally have not dealt with the property-rights aspect of the territorial question and the way Southerners had framed the slave code for the territories.[53] Property rights were the core legal defense of slavery and a constitutional argument of merit; its employment during the election shows that Southerners were talking about the present and future existence of slavery itself, not only about its extension into new lands.

An abundance of material in newspaper reports and editorials reveal how prominent in the election of 1860 the theme of property rights in slavery was in Southern oratory. The secessionist William Lowndes Yancey, the Georgia senator Robert Toombs, the Virginia senator James M. Mason, and Douglas's running mate, Herschel V. Johnson, all used it during the campaign or immediately afterward.[54] Perhaps the best illustration of the power behind the fear for the security of slavery as expressed in property-rights terms can be seen in the 1860 experience of Richard Lathers, a South Carolinian transplanted to New York City. He argued against secession to his fellow South Carolinians and was answered in a letter by Andrew G. Magrath and Henry Gourdin, who declared, "Neither Congress nor the Supreme Court has any power to decide any question for us in relation to our property in our slaves." And then they came to Lincoln: "Mr. Lincoln denies that there is any such thing as property in slaves. . . . A President who does not believe that a negro held in servitude is property, must extend to that negro the protection which the law of the United States provides for a citizen. . . . Can you ask us to confide in this man?" Lathers then took that argument and gave it to a New York City meeting in early 1861. Besides the question of the territorial rights in the West, he said, "The next question will be whether there can be such a thing as a claim for property in slaves. . . . The South will never come back until that principle is settled."[55]

The question of staying within the Union or leaving it was a matter of figuring out the best strategy for preserving slavery. For two reasons secession was the logical choice. First, Southerners were very much aware that the "war" on slavery had started thirty years earlier and had never receded but had only grown stronger. A letter by "G" to the Augusta, Georgia, *Constitutionalist* put the matter succinctly: "Gradually, steadily, surely, the Northern Democrats are being cut down, and disappear from the halls of Congress." J. F. H. Claiborne, the antebellum author of a biography of the Mississippi fire-eater John A. Quitman, also testified to the obvious path of history: "One by one the staunchest of them [Northern conservatives] must give way, or be trampled down by the overwhelming masses of Black Republicans." The conservatives in the North were a dying breed and destined for extinction. At the same time, the zeal of the Republicans was the zeal of religious bigots—of the old intolerant Puritans. Against that religious fortress, no reason or softening of heart could be expected.[56]

This combination of the fear of Northern religious radicalism with the constant augmentation of antislavery sentiment in the North destroyed Douglas's plea to the Southern states to stay in the Union. All Douglas really offered was a chance in two or four years to defeat the Republicans. But it is likely that many Southerners were taking a longer view of the subject. It made no real difference what Lincoln could or could not do in the short run; the long-run reality was that antislavery feeling in the populous North would continue to grow and gain electoral strength. What realistic chance was there of a reversal of the antislavery sentiment? Southerners knew there was none, and they were undoubtedly correct. If the objective of Southern civilization was the continuation of slavery, then remaining in the Union was a sure means of defeating that goal. Separation certainly meant acceptance of risks and possible defeat; but over the decades it offered more possibilities for continuation than staying cojoined with Northerners in the Union. If the cotton states had not seceded in 1860, they would have made the attempt later. Any victory Douglas would have had in 1860 was destined to be only temporary.[57]

The forces driving Southerners to secession, especially in the cotton South where slavery was most profitable and slaves most numerous, was thus composed of two acknowledged realities. The first was how strongly Southerners wanted, for economic reasons and as a means of race control, to maintain the peculiar institution.[58] The second was the realization that antislavery sentiment had been ever growing in the North and nothing was going to stop it. Eventually, antislavery sentiment would capture the federal government and somehow the federal government would be used against slavery. The exact mechanism of federal attack was a matter of considerable conjecture in 1860, but the idea that antislavery leaders would forgo the chance to use the powers of the government to undermine property rights in slaves was, for them, ludicrous. This is why explanations of secession based on the idea of contingency are deeply flawed. It was not the case that unusual incidents combined to lead Southerners to disunion, and it was not a matter of each separate step on the road to separation led to multiple next steps, only a few of which would end in secession. Rather, behind each decision and enactment of Southern leaders was the force of a determination to maintain slavery and a realization of a growing antislavery Northern sentiment; prescient Southerners realized that the United States of America was becoming a dangerous environment for the health of Southern slavery. This force pushed Southerners, eagerly or remorsefully, to disconnect the slaveholding states from the Union. At best, Douglas's arguments could only delay the timing of the inevitable decision; nothing he said could diminish the forces acting on the Southern mind.[59]

At the same time, Douglas could have no effect on the other part of the sectional problem—convincing the Republicans, or simply those with an antislavery disposition, to give up their crusade. Douglas and most Southerners ascribed Republican motivation to an unreasonable emotional embrace of racial egalitarianism and an unbounded moral righteousness that found slavery an evil. (Other rationales were mixed in, of course, including anti-Southernism and Northern greed for federal power.) The Democrats were the individuals who most saw the moral question of slavery as the primary force generating sectional division, as do now a number of current historians.[60] Yet in the election of 1860, Republicans campaigned on fears of the Slave Power and apprehensions about the future of free labor, not on the morality of slavery. These were the two pillars of Republican argument that led them to assemble a majority out of the Northern electorate. Rather than the Democrats' stress on antislavery emotionalism, the Republicans exhibited a deep, abiding fear that the vitality of the Southern slave-labor system was eroding all the essential goodness of the American republican experiment: civil liberties, equality of citizens before the law, an educated public, a peace-loving nation, the ability of common people to obtain economic competence, and appropriate federal policy were dying because of slavery. For Republicans, slavery was dragging the nation back into the system of aristocracy, a society that gave all its rewards to an undeserving few and pressed impoverishment on its multitudes.[61] Republicans saw, and would ever see, slavery as the enemy of the American experiment in self-government; it simply must be curtailed and eventually eliminated.

Douglas and the Democrats seldom answered the free-labor concerns of Northerners adequately, and almost never responded to the assertions that the nation had fallen into the hands of the Slave Power. Indeed, in all of Douglas's speeches in the election of 1860, he mentioned (so far as I can tell) the Slave Power charge only twice, only in one sentence, and with a flippancy that ignored the apprehensions of vast numbers of Northern people.[62] In particular, Douglas denied that the system of slavery had any ill effects on Northern freedoms and Northern society. But Northern apprehensions had a basis in reality; in their mania to maintain and extend slavery, Southerners were actually demanding Northern subservience to the interests of slavery. The election of 1860 was proof of the case: Northern Republicans had to sacrifice their legislative agenda, or the South would leave the Union. Republicans considered that demand blackmail. One of the first historians of the election of 1860, Emerson Fite, caught that attitude when he quoted the New Hampshire senator John P. Hale's view of the Southern demand on policy for the territories: "You must give in, for we [Southerners] cannot; you are used to it and we are not."[63]

Few crusades in American history have had a higher probability of failure than those of Stephen A. Douglas in 1860. The forces acting to produce disunion were real and monumental in their strength. Northerners were convinced that slavery was undermining, distorting, and ruining the republican experiment; Southerners were obsessed with preserving and enhancing slavery, concentrating their political energies on obtaining an ironclad agreement that the federal government would observe property rights in slaves in every field of its operations. The joint of the conflict was slavery: for Republicans, it was the source of national ruination, for Southerners, it was the fountain of proper race relations and prosperity. Both sides were growing in their convictions about the effects of slavery.

Against those convictions stood Stephen A. Douglas, arguing that Southerners had to sacrifice their doctrine of property rights in the territories while telling Northerners that slavery had no effects whatsoever on their lives. Against these forces, his arguments were totally ineffective. Stephen A. Douglas was the Don Quixote of politics in the election of 1860, but he was not tilting at windmills.

1. The proceedings at Norfolk were taken down by a reporter from the *New York Herald;* that version then passed throughout the country as the standard record of Douglas's response. The quote here comes from the *Cleveland Daily Plain Dealer,* August 28, 1860, 2. A note on references: for newspapers, after the first citation, the "daily" will be dropped; only if the paper is a weekly or semiweekly will the frequency of publication be included in the title.

2. Douglas R. Egerton, *Year of Meteors: Stephen Douglas, Abraham Lincoln, and the Election that Brought on the Civil War* (New York: Bloomsbury Press, 2010), 199–206; David M. Potter, *The Impending Crisis, 1848–1860,* ed. and completed by Don E. Fehrenbacher (New York: Harper, 1976), 440–41; Allan Nevins, *The Emergence of Lincoln: Prologue to Civil War, 1859–1861* (New York: Charles Scribner's Sons, 1950), 2:290, 293; Robert W. Johannsen, *Stephen A. Douglas* (1973: repr., Urbana: Univ. of Illinois Press, 1997), 791. Lionel Crocker argued that Douglas's arguments against secession bore fruit in the Border South, enabling Unionists there to stem the secessionist tide: Lionel Crocker, "The Campaign of Stephen A. Douglas, the South, 1860," in *Antislavery and Disunion, 1858–1861: Studies in the Rhetoric of Compromise and Conflict,* ed. J. Jeffrey Auer (New York: Harper and Row, 1963), 277–78. For other Douglas biographers, see George Fort Milton, *The Eve of Conflict: Stephen A. Douglas and the Needless War* (Boston: Houghton Mifflin, 1934), 492–99; Damon Wells, *Stephen Douglas: The Last Years, 1857–1861* (Austin: Univ. of Texas Press, 1971), 252–54. For purposes of brevity, reference will be made only to the works most pertinent to the election of 1860 and Douglas's role.

3. There is no need to list all the Lincoln biographers who did not mention Douglas's Southern trips; Lincoln and his campaigners simply ignored the Little Giant in the South. The historians of the antebellum South who deal with the subject include William A. Link, *Roots of Secession: Slavery and Politics in Antebellum Virginia* (Chapel Hill: Univ. of North Carolina Press, 2003), 199–200; Ollinger Crenshaw, *The Slave States in the Presidential Election of 1860* (Baltimore: Johns Hopkins Univ. Press, 1945), 77–88; Donald E. Reynolds, *Editors Make War: Southern Newspapers in the Secession Crisis,* 2d ed. (Carbondale: Southern Illinois Univ. Press, 2006), 79–80, 135–36; Craig M. Simpson, *A Good Southerner: The Life of Henry A. Wise of Virginia* (Chapel Hill: Univ. of North Carolina Press, 1985), 234–35; William C. Davis, *Breckinridge: Statesman, Soldier, Symbol* (Baton Rouge: Louisiana State Univ. Press, 1974), 237–40.

4. This is a standard interpretation; see Potter, *Impending Crisis,* chaps. 15–16; Johannsen, *Douglas,* chaps. 23, 24, 28, 29.

5. Egerton, *Year of Meteors*, 51–82, 149–75; Potter, *Impending Crisis*, 409–16; Johannsen, *Douglas*, chap. 28.

6. Charles W. Ramsdell, "The Natural Limits of Slavery Expansion," *Mississippi Valley Historical Review* 16 (September 1929), 151–71; Crenshaw, *Slave States*, 87–88. On the importance of the slavery issue in 1860, see Nevins, *Emergence of Lincoln*, 2:279–84; Dwight Lowell Dumond, *The Secession Movement, 1860–1861* (New York: Macmillan, 1931), 44–47.

7. Senators working against Douglas included Jefferson Davis (Mississippi), Judah P. Benjamin (Louisiana), and Graham Fitch (Indiana); Buchanan operatives in Charleston included John Slidell (Louisiana), William Bigler (Pennsylvania), James A. Bayard (Maryland), and Jesse D. Bright (Indiana). Personality conflict is the essential interpretation of Roy F. Nichols, *The Disruption of the American Democracy* (New York: Macmillan, 1948), 4–7, 224–26, 290–305; Elbert B. Smith, *The Presidency of James Buchanan* (Lawrence: Univ. Press of Kansas, 1975), 102–9; Egerton, *Year of Meteors*, 52–55. Robert Johannsen called Charleston "a tragedy of miscalculation": Johannsen, *Douglas*, 759.

8. For example, speech of Ben Butler, *Boston Post*, October 5, 1860; speech of Jesse D. Bright, *New York Times*, September 17, 1860, 1; (Washington, D.C.) *Constitution*, August 31, 1860; (Concord) *New Hampshire Patriot and State Gazette*, October 3, 1860; ratification meeting of Douglas Democrats in *Philadelphia Evening Bulletin*, June 5, 1860, 8; E. Read to John G. Davis, May 22, 1860 and J. R. Briggs to John G. Davis, August 21, 1860, John G. Davis Papers, State Historical Society of Wisconsin, Madison.

9. Johannsen, *Douglas*, 792–93; Smith, *James Buchanan*, 125–26; Nichols, *Disruption*, 341–44; Crenshaw, *Slave States*, 59–72. Stephen B. Oates questions the wisdom of Douglas's refusing to fuse; see Oates, *With Malice Toward None: The Life of Abraham Lincoln* (New York: Harper and Row, 1977), 200.

10. On Douglas's difficulties, see Nevins, *Emergence of Lincoln*, 2:290–93. It seems that the older historians believed that the Southern managers of the Breckinridge campaign hoped that Northern Democrats would finally cave in to Southern demands on the platform and accept a new compromise presidential candidate, all others withdrawing from the race. This, of course, never happened. Smith, *James Buchanan*, 125–26; Dumond, *Secession Movement*, 108–10.

11. Stephen A. Douglas to Nathaniel Paschall, July 4, 1860, and Douglas to Charles H. Lanphier, July 5, 1860, in *The Letters of Stephen A. Douglas*, ed. Robert W. Johannsen (Urbana: Univ. of Illinois Press, 1961), 496–98; Allen Johnson, *Douglas*, 429; Robert W. Johannsen, "Stephen A. Douglas' New England Campaign, 1860," *New England Quarterly*, 35 (June 1962), 162–86; James L. Huston, "The Threat of Radicalism: Seward's Candidacy and the Rhode Island Gubernatorial Election of 1860," *Rhode Island History*, 41 (1982), 86–99.

12. Johannsen, *Douglas*, 775–79.

13. Quote from Douglas speech at Concord, *Boston Herald*, August 1, 1860, 4; see speech at Boston, *Boston Herald*, July 18, 1860, and in *Harper's Weekly*, July 28, 1860, 470; speech at Troy, N.Y., in *New York Times*, July 28, 1860, 2.

14. Quotes from Augusta, Maine speech in *Cleveland Plain Dealer*, September 3, 1860, 1; quote on benefit of laws from speech in Lexington, Mass., in *New York Times*, July 21, 1860, 5; Rhode Island clambake episode in *New York Times*, August 16, 1860, 1, *Boston Herald*, August 3, 1860, 2; "A Few of Douglas' Sage remarks in his Speech delivd at Augusta, August 16, 1860," in John F. Potter Papers, State Historical Society of Wisconsin.

15. First quote on Newark meeting from *New York Daily Tribune*, August 23, 1860, 5; second Newark quote from (Trenton, N.J.) *Daily True American,* August 25, 1860; speech of Jacob Vanatta at a Douglas Democratic meeting, *Newark* (N.J.) *Daily Advertiser,* August 23, 1860, 2; Daniel Mace to Stephen A. Douglas, February 22, 1860, Addenda, Box 2, Douglas Papers, Univ. of Chicago.

16. Announcement of Southern journey in *New York Times,* August 16, 1860, 4; Nevins, *Emergence of Lincoln,* 2:293. Johannsen does not report this entry in Charles Francis Adams's diary as motivation for the Southern trip; Johannsen, *Douglas,* 779, 786–88.

17. Norfolk address in *Cleveland Plain Dealer,* August 28, 1860, 2.

18. (Raleigh, N.C.) *Semi-Weekly Standard,* September 5, 1860, 2.

19. Ibid.

20. Douglas speech at Baltimore in *Lynchburg Virginian,* September 11, 1860, 1; *Lexington* (Va.) *Valley Star,* September 20, 1860, 1; *New York Times,* September 7, 1860, 1. Remarks at other cities are truncated as editors recognized the amount of repetition in his speeches; *Staunton* (Va.) *Spectator,* September 4, 1860; *New York Times,* September 1, 3, 5, 1860; *Harper's Weekly,* September 8, 1860, 566.

21. Douglas speech in New York, (Chicago) *Daily Times and Herald,* September 18, 1860, 1; *New York Times,* September 13, 1860, 1.

22. Lincoln's first inaugural in James D. Richardson, ed., *A Compilation of the Messages and Papers of the Presidents, 1789–1902* (New York: Bureau of National Literature and Art, 1903), 6:5–12. On anarchy, see Philip Paludan, "The American Civil War Considered As a Crisis in Law and Order," *American Historical Review* 77 (October 1972), 1013–34.

23. Richardson, ed., *Messages and Papers of the Presidents,* 6:5–12; Daniel Farber, *Lincoln's Constitution* (Chicago: Univ. of Chicago Press, 2003), 105–11; on Douglas's muttering during the inaugural, see Johannsen, *Douglas,* 844. A brief note will be interjected here about the historical treatment given to popular sovereignty. Harry Jaffa has written that Douglas believed in the right of the majority to rule that bordered on majoritarian tyranny and destruction of natural rights. This is an obvious overstatement. One notes that in 1860, amid all his popular-sovereignty addresses, Douglas denied citizens the right to vote themselves out of the Union. See Harry V. Jaffa, *A New Birth of Freedom: Abraham Lincoln and the Coming of the Civil War* (Lanham, Md.: Rowman and Littlefield, 2000), 473–87.

24. James L. Abrahmson, The *Men of Secession and Civil War, 1859–1861* (Wilmington, Del.: Scholarly Books, 2000), 75–77; Crenshaw, *Slave States,* 77–80; Don Reynolds, *Editors Make War,* 16, 77–94; Crocker, "Campaign of Stephen A. Douglas," 264. Breckinridge's Ashland speech, September 5 (Milledgeville, Ga.) *Federal Union,* September 25, 1860; see William C. Davis, *Breckinridge,* 237–40.

25. Quote from *Cleveland Plain Dealer,* September 6, 1860, 1); *Cincinnati Daily Enquirer,* August 28, 1860, 2); *New York Tribune,* September 4, 1860, 4). *New York Times* coverage September 12, 1860, 3); comments of *Boston Post,* September 6, 12, 1860; see editorial, *Boston Post,* October 11, 1860, 1. Democratic newspapers that contained the Douglas responses in Virginia with little or no editorial comment include (Albany, N.Y.) *Atlas and Argus,* August 28, 29, 1860, 1; (Wilkes-Barre, Pa.) *Luzerne Union,* September 5, 1860; *Detroit Daily Free Press,* September 8, 1860; (Philadelphia) *Public Ledger,* August 30, 1860, 2; *Boston Herald,* August 28, 30, 1860, 4; (Philadelphia) *Press,* August 28, 1860, 2; (Trenton, N.J.) *True American,* August

28, 1860, 2; *Pittsburgh Morning Post,* September 4, 1860, 4; *Daily* (Springfield) *Illinois State Register,* August 28, 1860.

26. Potter, *Impending Crisis,* 433; Nevins, *Emergence of Lincoln,* 2:305; Kenneth M. Stampp, *And the War Came: The North and the Secession Crisis, 1860–1861* (Baton Rouge: Louisiana State Univ. Press, 1950), 7–8; Michael A. Morrison, *Slavery and the American West: The Eclipse of Manifest Destiny and the Coming of the Civil War* (Chapel Hill: Univ. of North Carolina Press, 1997), 265.

27. Quotes from (Trenton) *True American,* September 8, 1860, 2; *Detroit Weekly Tribune,* October 16, 1860, 4.

28. Extended reports on Douglas's speeches can be gleaned from *New York Times,* September 8, 10, 1860, 8; *Cleveland Plain Dealer,* September 22, 24, 1860, 2; (Columbus) *Ohio State Journal,* September 26, 1860; (Indianapolis) *Indiana State Journal,* September 29, 1860; speech at Syracuse, *Lexington* (Va.) *Valley Star,* October 11, 1860, 1; speech at Milwaukee, (Albany) *Atlas and Argus,* October 23, 1860; speech at St. Louis, *Chicago Times and Herald,* October 24, 1860, and (St. Louis) *Daily Republican,* October 20, 1860, 2. Reports on Douglas's movements with pithy comments about his speeches can be found in *New York Times,* September 15, 18 19, 20, 21, 24, 26.

29. Speech at Cleveland, *Cleveland Plain Dealer,* September 24, 1860, 1. The moments when any Democrat ever challenged the Republicans or Free Soilers about the Slave Power were precious few. Yet it was partially by exploiting fear of the Slave Power that the Republicans rose to prominence. On the Slave Power, see Michael F. Holt, *The Political Crisis of the 1850s* (New York: Wiley, 1978), 151–54; William E. Gienapp, *The Origins of the Republican Party, 1852–1856* (New York: Oxford Univ. Press, 1987), 357–65; Leonard L. Richards, *The Slave Power: The Free North and Southern Domination, 1780–1860* (Baton Rouge: Louisiana State Univ. Press, 2000). For a speech by a Democrat who did respond to the Slave Power, see John M. Belohlavek, *Broken Glass: Caleb Cushing and the Shattering of the Union* (Kent, Ohio: Kent State Univ. Press, 2005), 293.

30. On the abolitionists and property rights in man, see James L. Huston, "Abolitionists, Political Economists, and Capitalism," *Journal of the Early Republic* 20 (Fall 2000), 505–6; James L. Huston, *Calculating the Value of the Union: Slavery, Property Rights, and the Economic Origins of the Civil War* (Chapel Hill: Univ. of North Carolina Press, 2003), 108–9.

31. Quotes from William H. Trescott to James H. Hammond, October 14, 1860, James H. Hammond Papers, Library of Congress, Washington, D.C.; Thomas H. Seymour to Franklin Pierce, October 18, 1860, Franklin Pierce Papers, Presidential Papers, Manuscript Division, Library of Congress, Washington, D.C., microfilm; quote by Douglas in Johannsen, *Douglas,* 797–98. Election results also in *Harper's Weekly,* September 15, 1860, 582, and September 22, 1860, 598; *New York Tribune,* September 6, 11, October 11, 12, 1860; (New Orleans) *Daily Picayune,* October 10, 11, 13, 14, 16, 1860; letter of Benjamin H. Hill in (Milledgeville, Ga.) *Southern Recorder,* October 23, 1860; (Huntsville, Ala.) *Southern Advocate,* October 24, 1860, 2; *New Orleans Daily Crescent,* October 13, 1860, in Dwight Lowell Dumond, ed., *Southern Editorials on Secession* (New York: Century Co., 1931), 187; *Nashville Union and American,* October 12, 1860, in ibid., 181.

32. Speech of Alexander H. Stephens in (Augusta, Ga.) *Daily Constitutionalist,* September 4, 1860, 2. For other such expressions, see editorial *Staunton* (Va.) *Spectator,* September 4, 1860, 2; editorial, *Detroit Free Press,* September 20, 1860,

2; speech of Fernando Wood, *New York Times,* September 18, 1860, 1; (Lexington) *Kentucky Statesman,* January 6, 1860, in Dumond, ed., *Southern Editorials,* 1; John A. Gilmer to Stephen A. Douglas, March 8, 1861, Box 36, Douglas Papers, Univ. of Chicago. See Reynolds, *Editors Make War,* 33–35.

33. On the vitality of the issue of slavery in the territories, see the revisionists, such as Avery O. Craven, *Civil War in the Making, 1815–1860* (Baton Rouge: Louisiana State Univ. Press, 1959), 66–67; Johannsen, *Douglas,* 701, 731, 766; Potter, *Impending Crisis,* 403–4; William W. Freehling, *The Road to Disunion: The Secessionists Triumphant* (New York: Oxford Univ. Press, 2007), 282, 285. Michael M. Morrison finds that the expansion issue was the determinative one in national politics; however, it was symbolic of concerns such as equality in the Union and the future of the nation; see Morrison, *Slavery and the American West,* 221, 229–30, 232–33, 255–60, 276–79.

34. Speech of William H. Richardson, *New York Times,* May 23, 1860, 1; Robert E. May, *The Southern Dream of a Caribbean Empire, 1854–1861* (Baton Rouge: Louisiana State Univ. Press, 1973), 232–41.

35. Stephens speech, (Augusta Ga.) *Daily Constitutionalist,* September 4, 1860, 2; Breckinridge meetings, *Philadelphia Evening Bulletin,* July 3, 1860, 2, and August 21, 1860, 3; *New York Tribune,* July 17, 1860, 7. See "Popular Sovereignty," *DeBow's Review* 27 (December 1859), 627, 641. Avery O. Craven, one of the revisionist historians, had written that the North-South battle was over moral values, not concrete matters, and that the territorial slave code was really the product of pride rather any pressing need; see Craven, *Civil War in the Making,* 86. Paul Escott saw Davis's role in producing the territorial slave code as a way to salvage his reputation in Mississippi after he had inadvertently approved a version of the Freeport Doctrine while vacationing in Portland, Maine; see Paul D. Escott, "Jefferson Davis and Slavery in the Territories," *Journal of Mississippi History* 39 (May 1977): 97–116. William J. Cooper Jr. also believes that Davis held to a watered-down version of the territorial slave code that was not that distant from the creed of noncongressional intervention; see Cooper, *Jefferson Davis, American* (New York: Alfred A. Knopf, 2000), 328–29.

36. Quote from "Property in Slaves," *New York Times,* September 8, 1860, 4; see also editorial, *New York Tribune,* January 11, 1860, 4; *Lewistown* (Pa.) *Gazette,* September 20, 1860, 2; see speech of Cassius M. Clay in Ottawa, Ill., *Chicago Press and Tribune,* September 13, 1860, 2.

37. On the itinerary, see Crocker, "Campaign of Stephen A. Douglas in the South," 271; Johannsen, *Douglas,* 799–803; Crenshaw, *Slave States,* 83–88; Wells, *Douglas,* 253–57. Newspapers announcing the second Douglas trip are *Pittsburgh Morning Post,* November 1, 5, 1860; *New York Times,* November 15, 17, 18, 1860; *New York Tribune,* October 24, 1860, 4; *Boston Herald,* October 30, 1860; (Philadelphia) *Press,* October 29, 1860.

38. Remarks at St. Louis, Springfield, and Centralia in *Daily* (St. Louis) *Missouri Republican,* October 20, 1860 (quote, p. 2); October 19, 1860, October 24, 1860; St. Louis remarks also in (Chicago) *Times and Herald,* October 24, 1860.

39. Speech in (St. Louis) *Missouri Republican,* October 22, 1860.

40. Ibid. Note the comment of Russell McClintock that Douglas was bellicose only in August; see McClintock, *Lincoln and the Decision for War: The Northern Response to Secession* (Chapel Hill: Univ. of North Carolina Press, 2008), 39.

41. The racism of the antebellum Democrats is well known. Jean H. Baker, *The Political Culture of Northern Democrats in the Mid-Nineteenth Century* (Ithaca,

N.Y.: Cornell Univ. Press, 1983), 177–211, 348–49. The attitude of the Democrats is best summed up by the title of an editorial in the primary Douglas paper in the nation: "'Negro Equality the Only Universal Principle of the Republicans," *Daily* (Springfield) *Illinois State Register,* September 11, 1860. Lately, the emphasis on Democratic racism has been softened, but in the election of 1860 it was ferocious. For mitigation of the Democracy's racism, see Jonathan H. Earle, *Jacksonian Antislavery and the Politics of Free Soil, 1824–1854* (Chapel Hill: Univ. of North Carolina Press, 2004); and Daniel Feller, "A Brother in Arms: Benjamin Tappan and the Antislavery Democracy," *Journal of American History* 88 (June 2001): 48–74.

42. *New York Herald,* quoted in *Cincinnati Enquirer,* October 31, 1860, 1; *Detroit Free Press,* November 3, 1860, 1, 2; *Cleveland Plain Dealer,* November 3, 1860, 2. For other examples, *Erie* (Pa.) *Weekly Observer,* October 20, 1860; *Pittsburgh Post,* October 31, 1860.

43. *Providence Daily Post,* November 8, 1860, in Howard Cecil Perkins, ed., *Northern Editorials on Secession* (New York: American Historical Association, 1942; repr., Gloucester, Mass.: Peter Smith, 1964), 1:84; *Erie* (Pa.) *Weekly Observer,* November 17, 1860, 2; see also *Hartford* (Conn.) *Daily Times,* October 27, 1860, 2; *Boston Post,* November 15, 1860, 1; (Indianapolis) *Indiana Daily State Sentinel,* November 3, 1860, in Perkins, ed., *Northern Editorials on Secession,* 1:72–73; *Pittsburgh Post,* October 11, 1860, 4.

44. *Daily* (Atlanta) *Southern Confederacy,* November 1, 1860; and *Augusta Constitutionalist,* November 1, 1860, clippings found in Box 44, folder 3, Douglas Papers, Univ. of Chicago.

45. David R. Barbee and Milledge L. Bonham, Jr., eds., "The Montgomery Address of Stephen A. Douglas," *Journal of Southern History* 5 (November 1939): 527–52, quote on Slave Power, 536; on Cuba, 543–44; on conspiracy, 551; on animals in the territories, 545.

46. Douglas at Mobile, *New York Times,* November 15, 1860, quoted in Crocker, "Campaign of Stephen A. Douglas in the South," 277; Johannsen, *Douglas,* 801–2.

47. *New York Times,* November 15, 1860, 1; To Ninety-Six New Orleans Citizens [November 13, 1860], in Johannsen, ed., *Letters of Douglas,* 499–502; Johannsen, *Douglas,* 805–7.

48. Stephen A. Douglas to August Belmont, December 25, 1860, in Johannsen, ed., *Letters of Douglas,* 505. Many in both the North and the South recognized the implications of separate state secession for government stability; e.g., *New York Times,* November 15, 1860, 4. On the South, see *New Orleans Daily Picayune,* October 31, 1860, in Dumond, ed., *Southern Editorials on Secession,* 199–201; *Daily Nashville Patriot,* September 19, 1860, ibid., 167–68; letter of Amos Kendall in *Lynchburg Virginian,* September 26, 1860, 1. See Stampp, *And the War Came,* 22–24.

49. *Kenosha* (Wisc.) *Democrat,* May 31, 1861, 2; J. C. Cabell to William Rives, November 13, 1860, William C. Rives Papers, Library of Congress; Buchanan's annual message in John Bassett Moore, ed., *The Works of James Buchanan Comprising His Speeches, State Papers, and Private Correspondence* (1908–11; repr. New York: Antiquarian Press, 1960), 9:12–19. See also Potter, *Impending Crisis,* 519–21.

50. George M. Wharton to James Buchanan, November 16, 1860, James Buchanan Papers, Historical Society of Pennsylvania, Philadelphia, microfilm; (Springfield) *Illinois State Register,* December 21, 1860, 2.

51. John Adams Dix, *Memoirs,* comp. Morgan Dix (New York: Harper and Brothers, 1883), 1:345. The presentation here indicates that Democrats and Republicans had more

in common than most have recognized; all historians acknowledge the centrality of the Fort Sumter episode. Treatment of the Northern Democrats in Stampp, *And the War Came*, 33, 42, 211–12; Baker, *Affairs of Party*, 326–30; Hubert H. Wubben, *Civil War Iowa and the Copperhead Movement* (Ames: Iowa State Univ. Press, 1980), 22–28; Frank L. Klement, *The Limits of Dissent: Clement L. Vallandigham and the Civil War* (Lexington: Univ. Press of Kentucky, 1970), 42–45; Joel H. Silbey, *A Respectable Minority: The Democratic Party in the Civil War Era, 1860–1868* (New York: Norton, 1977), 34–39; Jennifer L. Weber, *Copperheads: The Rise and Fall of Lincoln's Opposition in the North* (New York: Oxford Univ. Press, 2006), 4–18; James L. Huston, *Stephen A. Douglas and the Dilemmas of Democratic Equality* (Lanham, Md.: Rowman and Littlefield, 2007), 184–95. For the problems of Stephen A. Douglas after the election, there is no better source than Johannsen, *Douglas*, chaps. 30–31. For Republicans, among a huge outpouring of Lincoln scholarship, see Stampp, *And the War Came*, 8–33; William C. Harris, *Lincoln's Rise to the Presidency* (Lawrence: Univ. Press of Kansas, 2007), 240–41; Richard J. Carwardine, *Lincoln: A Life of Purpose and Power* (Edinburgh Gate: Pearson Education, 2003); David M. Potter, *Lincoln and His Party in the Secession Crisis*, 2d ed. (New Haven, Conn.: Yale Univ. Press, 1962). The crucial aspect of Fort Sumter is given in Allan Nevins, *The War for the Union* (New York: Charles Scribner's Sons, 1959), 1:74; Stampp, *And the War Came*, 287–88.

52. The phrase "irrepressible conflict" comes from William H. Seward's speech in 1858, and many have used it to mean an irrepressible war. Actually, it means two sides at loggerheads and in constant dispute; it may mean war but not necessarily. I am using the phrase "irrepressible separation" to illustrate my belief that secession actually was inevitable and that it was fruitless to try to keep this Union of slaveholding and nonslaveholding states together over time.

53. Crenshaw, *Slave States*, 51–53, 57–58, 87–88; Smith, *James Buchanan*, 108–11; Daniel W. Crofts, *Reluctant Confederates: Upper South Unionists in the Secession Crisis* (Chapel Hill: Univ. of North Carolina Press, 1989), 96–98. See Roger L. Ransom, *Conflict and Compromise: The Political Economy of Slavery, Emancipation, and the American Civil War* (New York: Cambridge Univ. Press, 1989), 167.

54. Yancey speech at Louisville in *Louisville Daily Courier*, October 24, 1860, 1; Robert Toombs to Robert Collins, et al., May 10, 1860, (Augusta, Ga.) *Daily Constitutionalist*, May 19, 1860; James M. Mason to Nathaniel Tyler, November 23, 1860, in Virginia Mason, *The Public Life and Diplomatic Correspondence of James M. Mason, with Some Personal History* (New York: Neale Publishing Co., 1906), 157; speech of Herschel V. Johnson at Cooper Institute, New York, in (Trenton, N.J.) *True American*, October 27, 1860.

55. A. G. Magrath and H. Gourdin to Richard Lathers, December 8, 1860, in Richard Lathers, *Reminiscences*, ed. Alvan F. Sanborn (New York: Gafton Press, 1907), 89–90; Pine Street Meeting, 1861, in pamphlet contained in Richard Lathers Papers, Library of Congress, Washington, D. C. .

56. "G." in (Augusta, Ga.) *Daily Constitutionalist*, April 11, 1860; J. F. H. Claiborne, *Life of and Correspondence of John A. Quitman* (New York: Harper and Brothers, 1860), 2:267. On religious influence, Benjamin N. Wilson to Richard Lathers, February 3, 1861, in Lathers, *Reminiscences*, 116; Craven, *Civil War in the Making*, 31; Klement, *Limits of Dissent*, 1; W. F. Herring to Alexander H. Stephens, November 9, 1860, Alexander H. Stephens Papers, Library of Congress, Washington, D. C. On the idea of a bleak future within the Union, see Marc W. Kruman, *Parties and Politics in North Carolina*,

1839–1863 (Baton Rouge: Louisiana State Univ. Press, 1983), 201; Potter, *Impending Crisis*, 475–79; Don E. Fehrenbacher, *The Slaveholding Republic: An Account of the United States Government's Relations to Slavery,* completed and ed. Ward M. McAfee (New York: Oxford Univ. Press, 2001), 301–6; Marc Egnal, *Clash of Extremes: The Economic Origins of the Civil War* (New York: Hill and Wang, 2009), 263.

57. Of course, other interpretations for Southern secession exist. On racial fears, Charles B. Dew, *Apostles of Disunion: Southern Secession Commissioners and the Causes of the Civil War* (Charlottesville: Univ. Press of Virginia, 2001); Steven A. Channing, *Crisis of Fear: Secession in South Carolina* (New York: Norton, 1970). On fear of the loyalty of nonslaveholders, Abrahamson, *Men of Secession and Civil War*, 82–83; Michael P. Johnson, *Toward a Patriarchal Republic: The Secession of Georgia* (Baton Rouge: Louisiana State Univ. Press, 1977). On Southerners' fear for their liberty, William J. Cooper, *Liberty and Slavery: Southern Politics to 1860* (1983; repr., Columbia: Univ. of South Carolina, 2000), 267–69. One must not forget the revisionist belief that everyone in 1860 had taken leave of their senses and had given in to fear; Craven, *Civil War in the Making,* 199–216. Roy Nichols thought the reason for Southern secession was simply the loss of national power by the leadership; this was later refined by Barry Weingast to be a loss of power in the only part of the government that evenly balanced Northern states against Southern states, the U.S. Senate; Nichols, *Disruption,* 353; Barry R. Weingast, "Political Stability and Civil War Institutions, Commitment, and American Democracy," in Robert Bates et al., *Analytic Narratives* (Princeton, N.J.: Princeton Univ. Press, 1998), 148–93. Both Michael Morrison and Lacy Ford Jr. have stressed republicanism—the political ideology rooted in agrarian philosophy—as the principal division between Northerners and Southerners, a rather updated version of the states' right versus centralization interpretation of the coming of the Civil War; see Morrison, *Slavery and the American West,* 6–10, 258, 276–78; Lacy Ford, Jr., *Origins of Southern Radicalism: The South Carolina Upcountry, 1800–1860* (New York: Oxford Univ. Press, 1988), vii–viii and chap. 10.

58. William C. Davis, *The Cause Lost: Myths and Realities of the Confederacy* (Lawrence: Univ. Press of Kansas, 1996), 182–83; Channing, *Crisis of Fear,* 289–90.

59. The theory of contingency in Civil War causation has been most prominently forwarded by Edward L. Ayers, *What Caused the Civil War? Reflections on the South and Southern History* (New York: Norton, 2005), 133–36, more generally 117–43; Freehling, *The Road to Disunion,* 423–26, 531–34. As an aside, if one wants to delve into the rationality of the situation, there is only one way to consider it in terms of the slaveholding South. Southerners should have recognized that slavery was a doomed institution and should have brought up the question of emancipation with Northerners, arguing that if Northerners were serious they should then compensate slaveholders in the same way Great Britain had compensated slaveholders in the West Indies emancipation. They could raise the money through bonds. At the same time, Southerners could have argued that Northerners should let white Southerners determine race relations, thus satisfying their fears for white supremacy. It must be realized that in this scenario, there would have been no Fourteenth or Fifteenth Amendments to the Constitution, and in all likelihood to this day the United States would have either an "apartheid" division of the races or continued Jim Crow segregation—quite a monstrous price to pay to avoid a civil war.

60. The moral question of slavery and its hyperemotional quality led the revisionist historians of the 1930s—James G. Randall, George Fort Milton, and Avery O.

Craven—to single it out as the principal cause of secession and civil war. Part of that analysis has been resurrected lately; see Michael F. Holt, *The Fate of Their Country: Politicians, Slavery Extension, and the Coming of the Civil War* (New York: Hill and Wang, 2004). Present historians have danced gingerly around the moral issue of slavery, but the tendency to elevate it has been observable, especially in Lincoln studies. The ethno-cultural interpretation emphasized the religious element in the Republican crusade against slavery: see Paul Kleppner, *The Third Electoral System, 1853–1892: Parties, Voters, and Political Cultures* (Chapel Hill: Univ. of North Carolina Press, 1979), 55–56, 58–60; Joel H. Silbey, "The Surge of Republican Power: Partisan Antipathy, American Social Conflict, and the Coming of the Civil War," in *Essays on American Antebellum Politics, 1840–1860*, ed. Stephen E. Maizlish and John J. Kushma (College Station: Texas A&M Univ. Press, 1982), 213–26. Robert W. Fogel, after finding Southern slavery to be a profitable institution, determined that religious hysteria was the only force available to drive the nation to civil war; see Fogel, *Without Consent or Contract: The Rise and Fall of American Slavery* (New York: Norton, 1989), 269–387. Currently, many scholars combine New England religious imperialism and a narrow sense of nationalism—meaning only the nation that New Englanders inhabited—produced the emotional state leading to sectional hatred; see Susan-Mary Grant, *North Over South: Northern Nationalism and American Identity in the Antebellum Era* (Lawrence: Univ. Press of Kansas, 2000), 30–36; Peter J. Parish, *North and Nation in the Era of the Civil War*, ed. Adam I. P. Smith and Susan-Mary Grant (New York: Fordham Univ. Press, 2003), 113–28, 132–39.

61. The central works that explore the Republican dread of slavery are Eric Foner, *Free Soil, Free Labor, Free Men: The Ideology of the Republican Party before the Civil War*, 2d ed. (New York: Oxford Univ. Press, 1995); Holt, *The Political Crisis of the 1850s;* Gienapp, *Origins of the Republican Party;* and Richards, *The Slave Power.* How slavery promoters in Kansas attacked Northern liberties can be found in Nicole Etcheson, *Bleeding Kansas: Contested Liberty in the Civil War Era* (Lawrence: Univ. Press of Kansas, 2004), 2–3, 75. John Ashworth holds that sectional antagonism arose over the Northern shift in production from craft to machine, making wage labor a crucial dimension in the moral outlook of the North and thus delegitimizing Southern slavery; see John Ashworth, *Slavery, Capitalism and Politics*, vol. 2: *The Coming of the Civil War, 1850–1861* (New York; Cambridge Univ. Press, 2007), 3–7, 167–71, 329, 435. A works that stresses the anti-Southernism of the Republicans is Ronald P. Formisano, *The Birth of Mass Political Parties: Michigan, 1827–1861* (Princeton, N.J.: Princeton Univ. Press, 1971), 5–8, 239. For the impact of slavery on foreign diplomacy, see Fehrenbacher, *The Slaveholding Republic*, chap. 4. For domestic concerns, see the older but still highly pertinent Russel B. Nye, *Fettered Freedom: Civil Liberties and the Slavery Controversy, 1830–1860* (1963; repr., Urbana: Univ. of Illinois Press, 1973); Elizabeth Varon, *Disunion! The Coming of the American Civil War, 1789–1859* (Chapel Hill: Univ. of North Carolina Press, 2008), 147.

62. In all my notes of thirty years of research into congressional speeches and election speeches from 1846 to 1860, I can count almost on one hand the number of times Democrats responded to the Slave Power argument of their opponents. Most of the time, the response was that the North, and particularly its antislavery elements, warred on the South. See speech of Yancey, *Richmond Enquirer*, September 25, 1860, 2. For an example of Democrats talking about the Northern war on the South, see *Hartford Times*, October 29, 1860, 2. See Richards, *The Slave Power*, 1–2.

63. Emerson David Fite, *The Presidential Campaign of 1860* (New York: Macmillan, 1911), 189; see also speech of Moses Grinnell at Cooper Union, *New York Times,* September 28, 1860, 1; Seward speech at Seneca Falls, ibid., November 2, 1860, 1; Henry J. Raymond at Rochester, ibid., November 3, 1860. The question of how, in concrete terms, Southern slavery could have reshaped the North has generally been dismissed by historians, especially Southern historians. For example, in the older works of Eugene D. Genovese, the throbbing dynamism of Northern capitalism was destined to roll over and smash the pathetically slow, retarded, slovenly economy of the slave South; see Genovese, *The Political Economy of Slavery: Studies in the Economy and Society of the Slave South* (New York: Random House, 1967), 3–5. For an alternative view, see Fehrenbacher, *Slaveholding Republic;* and Huston, *Calculating the Value of the Union,* chap. 3. On Douglas's inability to respond to the Slave Power conspiracy thesis, see Huston, *Douglas,* 70, 77, 99–100, 182–85.

3

A Forlorn Hope

Interpreting the Breckinridge Campaign
as a Matter of Honor

A. James Fuller

The campaign of John C. Breckinridge, the Southern Democratic candidate for president, remains one of the most puzzling aspects of the election of 1860. Why did the vice president of the United States, a young man with a bright political career and future, choose to accept the nomination of the Southern Democrats, splitting his party and almost certainly ensuring its defeat in the presidential election? What did the Southern Democrats (and some Northerners) hope to achieve in supporting Breckinridge? It seemed unlikely that Breckinridge could win the election. He himself admitted as much when he told Mrs. Jefferson Davis, "I trust I have the courage to lead a forlorn hope."[1]

So why did he run? Historians remain divided but offer several different interpretations of the Breckinridge campaign. One traditional argument holds that Breckinridge and his supporters hoped to win by ensuring that the election would be thrown into the House of Representatives, where Democratic dominance would deliver him the presidency. Related to this approach is the idea of "fusion," wherein the three main opponents of Abraham Lincoln would agree to instruct their electors in the various states to cast their votes in such a way as to deny the Republican a majority and send the election to the House. Another interpretation sees the Southern Democratic campaign as aimed at forcing Stephen A. Douglas to withdraw and uniting the entire party behind a compromise candidate. A more sinister motive is seen in the argument that Southern fire-eaters hoped to divide the Democrat party in hopes of electing Lincoln in order to bring about secession and achieve their goal of a Southern Confederacy.

Fig. 13. Hon.
John C.
Breckinridge
of Kentucky:
Democratic
candidate for
sixteenth presi-
dent of the
United States.
(Library of
Congress)

Then there is the position that the Southern Democrats had no real plan but were confused, disorganized, and adrift.

Reconciling these interpretations seems unlikely. Each view seems logical given certain criteria. Further, the chaos of the Democratic conventions in Charleston and Baltimore and the resulting division of the party made not only for high drama and historical consequence but also for disagreement about what actually happened, then and now. If we examine the campaign from the perspective of the candidate himself and the white Southerners who voted for him, a resolution to the historiographical debate emerges. A brief account of the Breckinridge nomination and campaign and a summary of each of the major scholarly interpretations allows for a reconsideration of the motives of the candidate and his supporters. In the end, the concept of honor provides a means of reconciling the competing views.

When Democrats gathered for their 1860 national convention in Charleston, South Carolina, Stephen A. Douglas of Illinois stood ready to secure the party's nomination for president. A favorite in the Northern states, Douglas had built a powerful political organization and confidently prepared to achieve the goal toward which he had worked for many years. But he lacked critical support. His bitter disputes with President James Buchanan had cost him the backing of the party's patronage. More important, he had lost much of his Southern support. Once the darling of Southerners who had enthusiastically supported his doctrine of popular sovereignty for resolving the issue of the territorial expansion of slavery, Douglas now faced acrimonious opposition from many in the South who saw him as a traitor to their cause. In the years between the Kansas-Nebraska Act and the Democratic convention in 1860, the debate over the expansion of slavery had only intensified. Proslavery advocates now saw Douglas's position as restricting slavery, because his Freeport Doctrine, expressed in 1858, would allow each territorial legislature to decide the question of slavery. Southerners insisted that the Constitution protected their property rights—an argument upheld by the Dred Scott decision in 1857—and wanted a slave code providing federal protection for slavery in the territories. They denounced Douglas's plan as "squatter sovereignty" that would effectively limit the expansion of slavery by encouraging Northerners to use their superior population numbers to control territorial legislatures and exclude the peculiar institution.

Thus, in 1860, Douglas faced the harsh reality that his party was deeply divided along sectional lines. He did have some Southern support, but opposition to him was strong and well organized. Indeed, some delegates, such as those from Alabama, came with instructions to walk out of the convention if the party platform did not include the slave code. Other candidates hoped to win the nomination if and when Douglas faltered, but the sectional divisions made it unlikely that the party could unite behind any candidate. In the ensuing struggle, a large Southern contingent did indeed bolt from the convention, leaving Douglas with a majority of votes, but not enough to be nominated. The Democrats adjourned, agreeing to meet again in Baltimore. The battle grew more embittered, because Douglas and his supporters refused to readmit all of the bolters and moved to replace them with delegates who would vote for the Little Giant. Of course, his enemies fought back. Again, the convention divided along sectional lines. Eventually, Douglas was nominated, but the Southern Democrats met and nominated John C. Breckinridge as their candidate. The Democracy had split, unable to overcome the sectional division.[2]

An obvious rival to Douglas for the nomination in 1860, John C. Breckinridge held to the traditional code of honor that required candidates to remain aloof and deny their ambitions for office. Furthermore, his genuine loyalty got in the way of his candidacy, because he would not allow his supporters even to cast votes for him in the convention as long as his fellow Kentuckian James Guthrie stood any chance of being nominated. Still further, as a young man, only thirty-nine, with several future election possibilities ahead of him, Breckinridge did not want to jeopardize future presidential runs by alienating any particular faction in 1860. Still, he hoped for the nomination and took his wife with him to Charleston for the Democratic convention. After the second day of balloting, the Breckinridges dined with a number of other prominent politicians who supported the Kentuckian for president. During the meal, a messenger brought the news (ultimately proven false) that Douglas had withdrawn and Guthrie was on the verge of victory. During the shocked silence that followed the announcement, a man seated near the vice president and his wife thought that he could hear the beating of Mrs. Breckinridge's racing heart and noted that her husband's face went ashen white. The report seemingly dashed his hopes for the nomination. He and his wife, who shared his aspirations, were visibly shaken by the news. Although he certainly had ambitions for the presidency, his personality, future possibilities, and sense of honor prevented him from maneuvering in such a way as seriously to challenge the front-runner in the early stages of the process. But he and those closest to him held out hope for 1860, thinking that perhaps he might win the nomination as a second-line candidate, one on whom the various sides could agree when their first choices did not prove able to secure the necessary two thirds of the votes. Going into the election, then, Breckinridge remained publicly patient, biding his time in the background, even while enjoying widespread support, especially among Southerners.[3]

Who was John C. Breckinridge? A native Kentuckian born in 1821, he hailed from a prominent Bluegrass family. His grandfather had served as a U.S. senator before becoming attorney general of the United States under Thomas Jefferson, and his father had been a state legislator and secretary of state of Kentucky. His uncle and surrogate father, Robert Breckinridge, gave up a promising legal and political career following his conversion to Christianity, which led him to statewide fame as a minister, educator, and antislavery activist. Well educated at Center College in Kentucky, then at the College of New Jersey (now Princeton University), John C. Breckinridge returned to his home state to continue his studies at Transylvania University in Lexington. He received his degree in law in 1841 and was admitted to the bar. His path to success in law and politics lay open before him and he set out on it.[4]

An attorney with a bright future, Breckinridge also won praise as an orator, delivering a well-received Fourth of July speech shortly after he graduated. But when a young lady he courted rejected him in favor of another suitor and his funds ran low, he decided to leave Kentucky for the Iowa Territory. On his way to the West, he stopped briefly in Illinois to inspect a small piece of land he had inherited. He was tempted to stay and begin his career there, but he continued on to Iowa when he learned that there were already enough lawyers practicing in the area, including Stephen A. Douglas and Abraham Lincoln. He began his law practice in Iowa but returned to Kentucky for good in 1843 when he allowed his sister to persuade him to come for a visit. She introduced him to Mary Cyrene Burch, with whom he fell in love. After a short engagement, the couple married in December 1843 and settled in Georgetown, where he established a law office with a partner in Lexington and entered politics by supporting the candidacy of James K. Polk.[5]

Breckinridge moved his family to Lexington to meet the demands of his growing legal practice but soon took another course. His support for the Democratic Party led to a commission as an officer in a volunteer regiment and service in the U.S.-Mexican War. Major Breckinridge and his men arrived too late to march with Gen. Winfield Scott on his victorious route from Vera Cruz to Mexico City, moving to join the occupying forces in the aftermath of the campaign. Although the Kentuckian spent more time as a lawyer arguing before military courts than in actual combat, he served well and with distinction, earning praise from both his superiors and the men in the ranks. Upon his return to Kentucky, he threw himself into politics. He initially supported Zachary Taylor for president, seeing him as a man above party. But when it became clear that Taylor was a Whig, Breckinridge worked hard for Old Rough and Ready's Democratic opponent. Still, the young lawyer won a reputation for being bipartisan and earned the respect of many Whigs, including longtime family friends such as Senator John Crittenden.[6]

In 1849, he proved himself an able candidate when he won election to the state legislature, even though he ran as a Democrat in a predominantly Whig district. During his term, he introduced a series of resolutions on slavery and the Union. He supported popular sovereignty, an idea that would soon be championed by Douglas of Illinois, but argued that property rights in the territories had to be protected by the federal government. Slavery might be excluded, but only at the time of statehood, not before. In addition, Breckinridge strongly opposed the abolition of slavery in the District of Columbia, arguing that Southerners had a right to their property in all areas shared by all of the states, whether territories or the federal district. At the same time, he strongly supported the Union and denounced those who called for secession. His legislative motions were not that different from those of Henry Clay, who was the architect of the Compromise of 1850 adopted just a few months after Breckinridge introduced his resolutions. Despite their party differences, in Kentucky, at least, Breckinridge was often seen as taking on the mantle of Clay. He certainly seemed to do so when he supported some economic policies favored by the Whigs, such as internal improvements. To be sure, as a Democrat, he argued that he did so because these particular policies stood to benefit his constituents rather than being a reflection of his ideological principles. Still, he did nothing to discount his connection to Clay and would spend more time with the aging statesman, even being with him near the time of his death and enjoying widespread support among Kentucky Whigs as that party collapsed at the national level.[7]

A rising star in the Democracy, Breckinridge went on to great heights, exploiting his bipartisan reputation in twice winning election to the U.S. House of Representatives from a district where Whigs held an advantage, first in 1851, then again in 1853. Observers often associated him with the Young America movement, and it seemed a fitting description for the thirty-year-old congressman, but his support for expansion differed from theirs and he detested the movement's open disrespect for the older political generation. He also staunchly opposed the Know-Nothings of the American Party and their anti-Catholic, anti-immigrant policies. Breckinridge also aligned himself with Franklin Pierce and became one of the president's most trusted congressional allies. Throughout his career, his loyalty, adherence to honor and tradition, and generally conservative politics made him an orthodox Democrat. He supported state's rights, free trade, limited government, and fiscal responsibility. Never an innovator, he earned respect as a man who could get things done and won praise from across the nation for his eloquence as a speaker, both on the stump and on the floor of Congress.[8]

The Kentuckian's loyalty, adherence to Democratic orthodoxy, and political skills paid off in 1856 when he was the party's nominee for vice president at the age of thirty-five. Running with James Buchanan, Breckinridge campaigned vigorously, making a series of widely publicized speeches, helping the ticket carry the election. He became the country's youngest vice president when he took office at just thirty-six. Unfortunately, his loyalty hurt him, because Buchanan resented the fact that Breckinridge had supported Pierce at first, hoping that the incumbent president would seek reelection. This led to other difficulties between the two men and, as a result, Breckinridge followed the typical path of vice presidents, playing a minor role in the administration. This actually was an advantage to him later, when the corruption of the Buchanan administration became public during the 1860 campaign and severely hurt the Democrats, especially anyone close enough to be targeted by those pointing out the scandalous behavior. Although he did use his position to help himself in real estate schemes, Breckinridge remained far enough removed from the administration to escape the brunt of the charges, but close enough to be smeared by those who painted the picture of corruption with a broad brush. Furthermore, he had always enjoyed a friendly relationship with Stephen A. Douglas, a matter of great importance when the Northern Democracy split into Douglas and Buchanan factions. If any Southerner stood a chance of reaching across that divide, it was Breckinridge. Buchanan would support him, albeit reluctantly. If Douglas could not take the nomination himself, he might be persuaded to throw his support to the Kentuckian.[9]

Well positioned for the presidency by 1860, Breckinridge could afford to wait for a better opportunity if he thought he needed to do so. The Kentucky legislature elected him to the U.S. Senate in late 1859, enabling him to continue his political career and ready himself for a later run for the presidency. But he stood ready to seize the chance in 1860 if it presented itself. Orthodox on policy, he had a record of compromise and practicality that enabled him to reach across party lines on some issues. But the issue of slavery mattered most in 1860, and there Breckinridge faced a harsh reality. He had owned slaves himself, although he apparently owned none in 1860. But he quickly denied that he had ever opposed the institution and challenged anyone to prove that he had ever shared his uncle Robert's abolitionist views. Clearly a supporter of slavery, he was not known as a fire-eater, having always couched his defense of the peculiar institution in more moderate terms. But his position remained quite clear and was the

Fig. 14. President James
Buchanan, 1860. (Library of
Congress)

same one he had held since the controversy of 1850 and his resolutions
in the Kentucky legislature: he believed that popular sovereignty required
federal protection of slave property in the territories and meant that slaveholders could not be forbidden to take their slaves into territories before
statehood. This put him at odds with Douglas, whose Freeport Doctrine
called for the possible exclusion of slavery by the territorial legislatures.
Despite his moderate reputation, then, Breckinridge could not hope to
garner much support among Northerners bent on a free soil policy. However, he did enjoy widespread support among Southerners and was well
liked by some Northern Democrats as well, especially the "doughfaces,"
most of whom were aligned with the Buchanan faction of the party.[10]

This, then, was the man who ended up accepting the nomination of
the Southern Democrats. As a presidential candidate, he followed the tradition of not campaigning for himself. He and his supporters looked on
Douglas's speech-making and public maneuvering with disdain. A proven
campaigner who had served his party well on numerous occasions, including the 1856 election, Breckinridge might have helped himself a great
deal by taking the more modern approach to electioneering. But he could
not. Honor dictated that a gentleman deny his ambitions and make the

pretense of reluctantly accepting the call of the people to duty. It was one thing to make speeches in the traditional oratorical fashion when one sought lower offices, but not when running for the presidency. Although he enjoyed the support of the Buchanan administration and its federal patronage and had the help of some important Northern Democrats who disliked Douglas (such as Senator Jesse D. Bright of Indiana), Breckinridge lacked the political organization to run a truly national campaign. Douglas had been working for years to build such an organization, but not even he could match the Republicans in the North. Democratic machines in certain areas proved helpful, such as those parts of Pennsylvania where Buchanan held sway, but were not enough to overcome the huge advantages of both Douglas and Lincoln. Refusing to campaign like Douglas, without an organization to rival Lincoln's, supported only by a handful of Northern Democrats, and opposed in the South by the Constitutional Union candidate, John Bell, what chance did Breckinridge really have?

The numbers tell the story. Breckinridge finished third in the popular vote, with his 848,000 trailing Lincoln's 1,866,000 and Douglas's 1,383,000 votes, but coming in ahead of the 593,000 cast for Bell. He finished second in the Electoral College with 72 votes to Lincoln's 180, Bell's 39, and Douglas's 12. Lincoln won the seventeen free states, Breckinridge took eleven slave states, Bell took three slave states (Virginia, Tennessee, and, much to Breckinridge's chagrin, Kentucky), and Douglas managed to win only Missouri and a portion of electors in New Jersey.[11]

A closer look at the numbers is telling: Breckinridge won higher percentages of the vote in those Southern counties that had fewer slaveholders than in those where slavery dominated. Historians continue to debate why this was so, but it probably indicates that party loyalty and traditional voting patterns remained important in the election. He did better in rural areas than in the cities, which seemed to support Unionist sentiment whether they were Northern or Southern municipalities. And the outcome was clear. Even if Lincoln's three opponents had united, the Republican still would have won the election. Of course, to unite the opposition, one has to begin making assumptions about how the voters would cast their ballots, and that opens the door to all sorts of possibilities and raises even more questions. Rather than engage in counterfactual speculation about alternatives, it is better to try to explain what actually did happen and look at why Breckinridge ran and why so many Southern Democrats supported him, considering each of the major interpretations of his campaign in turn.[12]

Perhaps the most traditional interpretation of the Breckinridge campaign holds that the Southern Democrats hoped to win the election by throwing the contest into the House of Representatives. This argument has been made by many scholars, but arguably the most influential statements of it came from the Progressive historians in *The Disruption of American Democracy,* a classic work by Roy F. Nichols, and in Allan Nevins's volume *The Emergence of Lincoln.* Other writers who support this position include Frank H. Heck, a biographer of Breckinridge, and, more recently, Bruce Chadwick. The argument centers on mathematical calculations based on the reality that presidential elections are not truly national contests but rather a series of state-level competitions. The winner does not need a majority of popular votes, but rather an Electoral College majority determined by taking the right states with the right numbers of electors. Thus, the Republican victory depended on carrying the Northern states in order to achieve their majority in the Electoral College. To be sure, these authors also outlined the push for a fusion ticket in the various states, with all of the votes for Douglas, Bell, and Breckinridge being given to the candidates in such a way as to deny Lincoln a majority of electoral votes. In the House, all of these candidates could hope for victory, because each state cast one vote; thus, no candidate had a clear majority of states in such calculations. This would lead to a deal-making compromise. All three camps had voices arguing that their candidate could emerge victorious if the fusion scheme was carried out. If the House became deadlocked, the election would go to the U.S. Senate, which would elect the vice president, who would become the acting president. There it was likely that Breckinridge's running mate, Joseph Lane of Oregon, would be elected, and the Southern Democrats would have their victory.[13]

The mathematical calculations for victory went along the following lines. In 1856, the Republican candidate, John C. Frémont, had carried eleven of the sixteen Northern states for a total of 114 electoral votes. Lincoln needed 35 more to secure a victory in 1860. Since the election of 1856, Minnesota and Oregon both had entered the Union as free states. The Republicans could be confident of Minnesota, reducing the necessary number of electoral votes to 34. California, with a national delegation of Democrats, seemed lost to them, and they could write off the entire South. Lincoln still could achieve his victory by taking Pennsylvania (27 electoral votes) and any one of the remaining Northern states that Frémont had lost: New Jersey (7 electoral votes), Indiana (13), or Illinois

(11). But all of these states had been Democratic bastions. The corruption of the Buchanan administration, the Panic of 1857 and the resulting depression, and the growing tension over slavery in the territories put these states within reach for the Republicans, but the outcome was not certain. If Buchanan could deliver Pennsylvania and Senator Bright could help Breckinridge in Indiana, it might be possible to throw the election into the House of Representatives. Alternatively, a fusion of the candidates might achieve the same end. Such calculations seem strange today, even in the wake of the disputed 2000 election, when the possibility of the presidency's being decided by Congress again emerged on the American political scene. But it was a very real possibility in 1860. After all, John Quincy Adams had become president in the 1824 contest when the election was thrown into the House. This congressional decision still was within living memory. And for Southerners used to wielding national power in such a way as to protect their rights and property against the growing population of the North, such a plan seemed perfectly legitimate as well as possible.[14]

Of course, Lincoln took all of the Northern states, splitting only New Jersey with Douglas. Fusion occurred in only a handful of states, because the Little Giant refused to go along with the plan. When asked about such a scheme in order to send the election to the House, Douglas had replied, "By God, sir, the election shall never go into the House—before it shall go into the House, I will throw it over to Lincoln." Those who counted on fusion discounted Douglas's own sense of honor. In his mind, he deserved the nomination of the entire Democratic Party. He would not sell out to the Slave Power but held to his own version of popular sovereignty. Douglas saw himself as the only truly national candidate, the only one able to save the country from the extremists of both sections. As he put it in a letter to a friend during the campaign, "We must make the war boldly against the Northern abolitionists and the Southern Disunionists, and give no quarter to either." When the Deep South delegates led the bolters out of the convention, they all but slapped Douglas in the face. To knuckle under and accept some sort of scheme in order to defeat the Republicans was as impossible for him as it was for the fire-eaters to accept him as their candidate. In the end, complete fusion among all three of Lincoln's opponents was achieved only in New York, New Jersey, and Rhode Island; Breckinridge's and Douglas's supporters fused only in Pennsylvania.[15]

No doubt some Breckinridge supporters thought he might be able to win the election outright. Although not usually considered likely by scholars, it occasionally appears in the literature. This view points out that the opposition was also divided. The Constitutional Unionists, made up mostly of old-line Whigs and former members of the American Party, might very well take votes away from the Republicans. Still further, Breckinridge might achieve an Electoral College victory. To do so, he would have to carry all of the slave states, which was not outside the realm of possibility. With a total of 303 electoral votes, 152 were needed for election. The fifteen slave states totaled 120. That meant that if he could carry all of the slave states, Breckinridge would need only 32 additional electoral votes. James Buchanan might deliver Pennsylvania, long a Democratic stronghold, and its 27 electoral votes. That would leave only five more votes for Breckinridge to win. Californian and Oregon were likely choices, with a total of seven electoral votes. If not won on the Pacific Coast, victory might be possible in Indiana, Illinois, Ohio, or New York, although most Southern Democrats thought that the states of the Old Northwest were certain to support the Republican in 1860. Still, with Breckinridge's popularity and national reputation and the support of Buchanan, it did not seem impossible that he might win the election outright. Ultimately, it became clear well before November that he would not win. Buchanan proved too weak to carry all of the slave states and failed to deliver even his home state, because Kentucky turned away from the Democracy in the wake of the economic crisis brought on by the Panic of 1857. California and Oregon went Republican. And the states of the Old Northwest did indeed vote for Lincoln, with Douglas, not Breckinridge, attracting the opposition votes. But such results were not certain at the outset of the campaign.[16]

Other scholars, such as Emerson Fite, William C. Davis, and Thomas Alexander, offer yet another interpretation, insisting that the Breckinridge campaign, far from wanting to divide the Democracy, aimed at uniting the Democrats behind a compromise candidate. But in order to do this, the Southern Democrats first had to destroy Douglas. Thus, they bolted from the convention in Charleston and refused to support the Little Giant. Then they supported Breckinridge, all in order to keep the party divided so they could force Douglas to withdraw from the race when he realized that he could not win and that the party would lose. The Southerners then offered the Illinois senator a deal in which Breckinridge also would withdraw and the party would come together behind a different candidate, probably Horatio Seymour of New York, who had remained outside the sectional debates and whose views on slavery satisfied the Southerners.

Even if he did not withdraw, the Southerners hoped to win concessions from Douglas, especially support for a territorial slave code.[17]

This argument centers on the hatred of Southern fire-eaters for Douglas, whom they saw as a sell-out, a traitor, and a man nearly as dangerous to them as a Republican. As Emerson Fite put it, "The death of the party was not sought; the Southerners were too good party men for that." The Southern Democrats wanted "Not the death of the Democratic party, then, nor yet the dissolution of the Union of the states was the compelling force back of the Charleston and Baltimore secessions; the true motive was a desire to vindicate Southern principles, by securing the abasement of Stephen A. Douglas and his principles." According to Fite, "It was a question of how best to serve slavery. . . . [T]he institution was in great and immediate danger. The Northern Democrats would give aid in one way, the slaveholders sought it another." To Southerners, Douglas and his Northern supporters, once considered staunch allies, now stood as a threat to the peculiar institution. Douglas's refusal to accept the implications of the Dred Scott decision and the Southern demand for a slave code protecting slavery in the territories made him a bitter foe, and many of the Southern radicals aimed at his destruction. In Fite's analysis, the fire-eaters' plan aimed at denying Douglas the nomination and the presidency at all costs. Indeed, as Sean Wilentz put it, "the Breckinridge campaign could never quite decide whether its chief aim was to win the election or lambaste Stephen Douglas." Although Eric Walther, a recent biographer of William L. Yancey, does not completely agree with every aspect of this interpretation of the Breckinridge campaign, his work certainly supports the notion that the fire-eaters hated Douglas and were bent on destroying his campaign. It was Yancey who engineered the Southern secession from the Democratic convention; he also became one of the most visible supporters of the Breckinridge campaign.[18]

According to these scholars, once the Southerners had destroyed Douglas's chances for election, they would offer him the opportunity to save the Democratic Party and the Union by agreeing to a mutual withdrawal and a reunification of the Democracy behind a compromise candidate such as Seymour. The evidence for this hypothesis rests almost entirely on the word of Jefferson Davis. According to his account, written many years later, after all of the other parties involved were dead, Davis approached Douglas, Breckinridge, and Bell with a plan for their mutual withdrawal in favor of Seymour. In fact, Davis claimed that he and several other Southern

Fig. 15. William L. Yancey. (*Harper's Weekly*, September 15, 1860)

HON. WILLIAM L. YANCEY.

Democratic leaders, including Robert Toombs, actually persuaded Breckinridge to accept the nomination on the basis of this plan. Toombs supposedly argued that if the Kentuckian accepted, "Douglas would be forced into withdrawal within forty days." According to the Confederate president, the plan fell apart when Douglas refused to go along with it. Whether or not this was the sole motive for their maneuvers and whether or not Breckinridge saw it as the primary purpose of his campaign, the Southern fire-eaters clearly hated Douglas and hoped to defeat him. That alone lends merit to this interpretation, even if it does not satisfactorily explain every aspect of the contest.[19]

Another major interpretation is offered by scholars who argue that Breckinridge actually ran to lose. In this view, held by the political scientists Jeffery Jenkins and Irwin Morris as well as historians such as Douglas

Egerton and William Freehling, a handful of fire-eaters plotted to divide the Democrats and used the Southern Democratic candidate to guarantee a Republican victory, thus paving the way for secession and the Southern Confederacy for which they had long dreamed and worked. According to this hypothesis, Breckinridge was a tool (knowing or unwitting) of masterful politicians such as William L. Yancey and Jefferson Davis, who used him for their own purposes. A unified "slavocracy" arrogantly and aggressively destroyed the Democratic Party and the nation to achieve their ends. This interpretation actually began with Douglas himself, who pointed to the way that the fire-eaters such as Yancey moved so openly to oppose him and divide the party. As Georgia's Alexander H. Stephens, one of Douglas's strongest Southern supporters put it, the fire-eaters "intended from the beginning 'to rule or ruin.'" Historian Douglas Egerton argued that "Stephens was wrong. Yancey and the "seceders" who used Douglas's ambitions against him were not motivated by "envy, hate, jealousy, [or] spite.'" Instead, "Their calculations were eminently rational; they planned to ruin so they could rule."[20]

The problem with this interpretation is that it insists that political leaders always act rationally, that their plans are always clear cut, and that they can strategically implement those plans over time. Frankly, this smacks of conspiracy theory by requiring a level of organization and planning that simply did not exist at the time. It holds that a handful of Southern radicals controlled the situation and pulled the strings to carry out their master plan. To refute competing theories, those who argue for Breckinridge's running to lose often employ counterfactual analysis and make arguments about what certain individuals *should* have known. To be sure, some fire-eaters did long for secession and worked many years for Southern independence. And even some of those who did not hope for secession did not see it as a terrible alternative to be avoided at all costs. Still, to argue that the Breckinridge campaign intentionally aimed to lose and that hundreds of thousands of voters went along with the plan to break up the Union is to take things a bit too far. A more useful way of interpreting the role that secession played in the Breckinridge campaign is explained by Eric Walther in his biography of Yancey: "In fact, Yancey had several motives and many potential goals." Rather than being masterminds and powerful political puppet masters, the fire-eaters had mixed motives and reacted tactically to events while trying to achieve multiple aims and carry out several strategies. With an overall goal of defending slavery and state's

Fig. 16. Jefferson Davis
between 1858 and 1860.
(Library of Congress)

rights, they hoped to defeat Douglas and win Democratic support for a territorial slave code in the party platform. They hoped to unite the Southern states politically the better to wield power and defend their principles. They hoped to nominate a strong Southern candidate and, if possible, win the election for him. If that was not possible, they hoped to carry out a fusion plan and throw the election to the House. If that did not work and Lincoln won the election, they would move toward secession. As always, history proved more complex than allowed for by a linear interpretation that assumes purely rational and clearly defined motives and previously established, unchanging plans.[21]

One useful corrective to the "running to lose" interpretation can be found in the work of Ollinger Crenshaw, who argued that the Southern politicians, far from being a "united aggressive slavocracy," were actually "by turns confused, indifferent, despondent, and defeatist," and that "many gave up the fight long before election day." Although some welcomed Lincoln's election and worked for secession, in general, the Southern Democrats were disorganized. Part of the confusion stemmed from the "Texas Troubles," a series of slave insurrections in the fall of 1860 that spawned hysteria and reports of abolitionist plots across the South. Some observers at the time wondered if proslavery advocates might not have created the "Texas Troubles" to rally voters, whereas others thought that abolitionists caused the slave rebellions as part of a systematic plan to destroy the peculiar institution. However real or imagined or widespread they actually were, the insurrections added to the chaotic situation that plagued Southern Democratic political strategies. Indeed, Crenshaw argued, "the entire picture is one of confusion and drift."[22]

Perhaps historians would be better off incorporating all of the major interpretations into their analysis of the Breckinridge campaign, allowing for the mixed motives and confusion of the politicians acting in the context of 1860. Some of the best accounts of the election lean in that direction, including several different theories, even if the author decides that one better explained the campaign than the others. Nichols, for example, outlined numerous alternatives in his book. Crenshaw raised several possibilities including "emotionalism," which he decried as a method by which the radicals were able to create confusion. David Potter incorporated several of the major theories into his analysis and pointed to the need to analyze the situation in context: "Arguments about whether the bolters wanted to throw the election into Congress, or to wring concessions from the Douglas forces, or to break up the Union all suffer from one common defect: They are too rational." The context of the day, the highly charged atmosphere, the excitement, the emotion, created turmoil. Different men had different agendas and mixed motives and wanted different things at the same time: "men took positions which led on to consequences that they did not visualize." And voters cast their ballots in context, thinking different things at different times, with mixed motives and mixed feelings.[23]

Nearly all of the authors interpreting the Breckinridge campaign have missed the importance of honor in the thinking of the candidate and his Southern supporters. As Bertram Wyatt-Brown has shown, honor was reputation and respect, but it was also tied to hierarchy and power relationships; it involved self-worth and the views of others, social standing and the avoidance of shame. When considered as an ethic that lay at

Fig. 17. Progressive Democracy—Prospect of a Smash Up. (Library of Congress) This cartoon depicts the Republican locomotive about to smash into the Democratic wagon caught on the tracks. The Democrats in the wagon are headed in different directions, with a Native American driver symbolizing New York's Tammany Hall machine driving the Douglas/Johnson ticket one way while President Buchanan tries to take the Breckinridge/Lane ticket the other way. The Native American cries, "Now then little Dug! put in and pull, while I cry Tammany to the rescue,' for I hear a rushing sound that bodes us no good." Buchanan urges, "Come Jack, and Joe, pull up! and don't let the other team stir the wagon I'd rather the Machine would be smashed than have them run away with it." Meanwhile, Abraham Lincoln and his running mate Hannibal Hamlin warn, "Clear the track!" and "Look out for the Engine, when the bell rings!"

the very heart of Southern society, the concept of honor provides a new lens for understanding the Southern Democratic candidate and his supporters in 1860. In fact, honor offers a means of reconciling the various existing interpretations and making sense of events in ways that refute David Potter's assertions and make the actions of Southern leaders seem quite rational when seen in the context of a very different worldview. Ultimately, Breckinridge's hope that he had "the courage to lead a forlorn hope" neatly defined his candidacy in the vocabulary of Southern honor.[24]

Throughout the antebellum period, Southern politicians used the language of honor to explain the sectional conflict. One aspect of this vocabulary of honor was the denunciation of corruption. Kenneth S. Greenberg argued that honor was an important component of the political culture of slavery, a culture that was often contradictory and fraught with tensions. Sometimes expressed in noble action, honor also brought violence, including duels or other physical rituals like the whipping of slaves and the caning of men beneath a gentleman's social standing. The man of honor derived his right to wield such violent power from his virtue. Corruption meant dishonor. In the sectional conflict, then, Southern leaders appealed to an important part of the culture of honor when they denounced political corruption. They argued that political parties and politicians "could no longer resolve disputes because they had become hopelessly perverted." According to Greenberg, the view that corruption had grown so acute as to render existing political structures hopeless was the hallmark of Southern radicals such as the fire-eaters. "By the eve of the Civil War the vision of a corrupt American politics had triumphed in the South." In Greenberg's analysis, this view of corruption combined the high-minded virtue of republicanism with honor's sense of duty and respect, allowing Southerners to depict themselves as the guardians of political purity while denouncing Northern Yankees as corrupt, vulgar, and beyond the hope of redemption.[25]

The corruption of the Buchanan administration only underscored honor's rejection of political debasement. The Pennsylvania Democrat had seemed an ally of the South and had tried to protect slavery in his machinations in Kansas and his support for the Dred Scott decision. But corruption had pervaded his term in office and he had ultimately only exacerbated the sectional tension over slavery instead of resolving it. If a "doughface" president backed by the dominant party could not protect the South and corruption meant that his administration put money and power before principles, what chance did Southerners have? Although Greenberg's argument centers on the move toward secession, this fear of corruption lends credence to Southern fears of Douglas in the 1860 campaign. In their view, the Little Giant had sold them out. He was too corrupt, a man willing to do anything to get power, saying one thing and then another, all in the name of winning the presidency. To many Southerners, Douglas was a liar who claimed to be defending property and the Constitution but who in reality hoped to make the territories free and deny Southerners equal rights under the law. Willing to say whatever it took to win elections, Douglas lacked honor and his campaign smacked of the political corruption that Southern radicals saw as the problem with the North as a whole.

To the Southern radicals, the election of 1860 was a final opportunity for purification through the political process, a last chance to cleanse

Fig. 18. The Undecided Political Prize Fight. (Library of Congress) A pro-Breckinridge cartoon in which Lincoln and Douglas box one another in the ring while the Southern Democrat thumbs his nose at them and heads for the White House. The other corners in the ring feature stereotypical imagery as an Irishman supports Douglas and a black man helps Lincoln. Such images made obvious reference to Douglas's pro-immigrant/pro-Catholic reputation and Lincoln's antislavery views. The bottles of liquor in the ring remind us that temperance remained an important issue.

American politics. Electing an honorable statesman such as Breckinridge, enacting a territorial slave code, and cleaning up the graft and scandalous behavior of the past might yet save a nation too far gone in its venality. If the Southern Democrats failed to win the election, they might reject the system outright and seek purification outside the Union. Indeed, according to the radicals, the election of Lincoln would mean the outright triumph of corruption and a threat to the very fabric of the South. The "Black Republicans," Southern Democrats charged, were out to destroy society. As the pro-Breckinridge *New York Herald* put it, Republicans were socialists, ready to push "socialism in its worst form," complete with "women's rights, the division of land, free love and the exaltation of the individual" over the community. The campaign focused on gender, with women at the center of the contest. The Breckinridge camp promised a manly defense of Southern womanhood against Northern heresies and painted specters of radical destruction of tradition, complete with appeals to racist fears and class divisions. According to the *Herald,* Lincoln and his supporters wanted to destroy the family and institute "the forced equality of all men in [socialist] phalansteries." All of it was "part of the logical chain of ideas" that flowed from "the soul of black republicanism." Lincoln's victory would bring subservience, even enslavement. For decades, Southern leaders had cast the sectional conflict in such terms, arguing that it was a question of liberty versus slavery. The irony of slaveholders arguing against being enslaved was not lost on some at the time or on later historians. But Southerners chafed at the idea of being subservient to the national government or to the North in the Union. Honor dictated independence and mastery, not servile dependence. Slaves had no honor. Therefore, gentlemen had to defend their honor or become slaves.[26]

The specter of John Brown clarifies this view of the election. That many Northerners celebrated the abolitionist raider as a martyr appalled Southerners. The Southern radicals argued that Lincoln's election would create many more John Browns; the fear of abolitionist attacks on property and the lives of slaveholders demanded a manly defense of honor. Thus, Brown's raid at Harper's Ferry made the "Texas Troubles" all the more significant in 1860. Although some claimed that traditional honor called for stoicism in the face of trouble, primal honor called for violent action against the threat. In 1860, primal honor carried the day in what Bertram Wyatt-Brown called "a classic example of the contest between raw honor and Stoic precept." Although his argument, like Greenberg's, focused on secession, Wyatt-Brown's analysis fits the election that preceded the dissolution of the Union. He, like Potter and Crenshaw, notes the emotionalism surrounding the events of 1860. But, unlike them, Wyatt-Brown does not see this emotionalism as irrational. Rather, it was an expression of honor. "Honor trumped sober reflection. Its will had to be done. . . . [T]he civil conflict in the United States had to be fought, regardless of the enormous costs in treasure and blood." That defeat seemed likely did not deter men of honor, whether campaigning in an election or fighting in a war. Death before dishonor was not a mere cliché for Southerners.[27]

When considered in such a light, the election of 1860 becomes a ritual of honor, nothing short of a duel, with the Southern Democratic candidate challenging the North as a whole, defending the very identity of Southerners against those who would deprive them of honor and make them slaves. The language used in the campaign reflects clearly how a sense of honor motivated Breckinridge and his supporters. Adhering to the traditional code of the gentleman candidate, an expression of honor in its own right, the Kentuckian made only one major speech during the campaign. His speech came only after a multitude of attacks by his opponents obliged him to defend himself against their charges, and he delivered it late in the campaign. But his chief surrogate on the national scene was William L. Yancey, the Alabama politician who led the Southern secession from the Charleston convention. Yancey's speeches during the nominating process and the campaign made him the "Voice of the South," and he employed the language of honor to explain the election and call for voters to cast their ballots for Breckinridge.[28]

On April 28, 1860, during the heated chaos of the national Democratic convention in Charleston, Yancey rose to his feet and defended the honor of the South while attacking his old foe, Stephen A. Douglas. He first denied the charges of disunion that had been leveled at him and his fellow delegates from the Deep South states. Whereas they had pushed for a territorial slave code provision in the party platform and opposed Douglas, Yancey insisted that they were merely defending the Constitution and trying to save the Democratic Party. He moved on in the language of a gentleman whose honor had been slighted: "The South is in a minority, we have been tauntingly told today." He noted the growth of the North's population and claimed that Southerners did not mind being in the numerical minority, as long as they had "the benefit of the Constitution that was made for the protection of minorities." The Alabaman fired back at the Northerners in his party: "[F]eeling conscious of your numerical power, you have aggressed upon us. We hold up between us and your advancing columns of numbers that written instrument which your and our fathers made, and by the compact of which, you with your power were to respect as to us and our rights." Yancey hinted at corruption in his next line, arguing that the founding fathers had made it so that every generation would observe the Constitution and that "the majority should not rely upon their voting numbers, but should look, in restraint upon passion, avarice, and lust for power, to the written compact, to see in what the minority was to be respected, and how it was to be protected, and to yield an implicit obedience to that compact. Constitutions are made solely for the protection of the minorities in government, and for the guidance of the majorities."[29]

But Southern rights had been trampled and Southern honor violated, Yancey charged: "Ours are now the institutions which are at stake; ours is the peace that is to be destroyed; ours is the property that is to be destroyed; ours is the honor at stake—the honor of children, the honor of families, the lives, perhaps, of all of us." The South "can yield no position until we are convinced that we are wrong. We are in a position to ask you to yield. What right of yours, gentlemen of the North, have we of the South ever invaded? What institution of yours have we ever assailed, directly or indirectly?" He asked the Northern Democrats to consider the "possessions acquired in the Mexican War, in which, gentlemen, it is but modestly stating the fact when I say that Southern chivalry was equal to Northern chivalry—that Southern blood was poured out in equal quantities with Northern blood—and Southern genius shone as bright upon the battlefield as Northern genius." But, Yancey argued, "when the battle was done, and the glittering spoil was brought forward . . . vast and disproportionate quantity was given to the North." He moved on to politics, asking why the Democratic Party was no longer dominant in the North as it once had been, while the South was "more unitedly Democratic." He thought the answer was clear: "Antislavery sentiment is dominant in the North—slavery sentiment is dominant in the South." The Northern Democrats declined "because you have tampered with the antislavery feeling of that section." The Democracy of the North had not done this "as a matter of choice," had not been "willful traitors to your convictions of duty." Instead, they had found "an overwhelming preponderance of power in that antislavery sentiment" and believed that was "the common will of .your people." Sensing that antislavery dominated, Northern Democrats had "hesitated before it; you trembled at its march. You did not triumph over the young Hercules in his cradle, because you made no direct effort to do so." The inaction of Northern Democrats had allowed the antislavery movement to grow into three distinct branches, including abolition, free soil, and popular sovereignty as defined by Douglas. The Southern fire-eater called on his Northern counterparts to root out antislavery, "this cancer, which is not only eating into your body, but into the body of the country at large."[30]

Yancey continued to couch his arguments in terms of honor throughout the campaign. Responding to Douglas's campaigning and tour of the South, the Alabama fire-eater undertook a nationwide speaking tour of his own. In his speeches he carefully argued that Breckinridge and his supporters were not disunionists, but were actually pro-Union, for a "constitutional

Union" that guaranteed the rights of the Southern minority. This played well in the South, where Yancey was known for his previous activities on behalf of secession. But as he moved northward, he returned to the more defiant language of primal honor. He charged that the Republicans were the true disunionists and that the party of Lincoln intended to make slaves of the South, hoping to "make us hewers of wood and drawers of water." He claimed that the Republican marching clubs, the Wide Awakes, were the front lines of an invasion, as the antislavery movement behind Lincoln readied for enslaving Southerners by "arming itself, training its midnight bands for the purpose of forcing the Union of a mere majority upon the South." Still denying disunion, he defended slavery while accusing Republicans of being the true radicals bent on destroying the Union. He often played to Northern racism and admitted that Southern Democrats "stand upon the dark platform of southern slavery, all we ask is to be allowed to keep it to ourselves. Let us do that, and we will not let the negro insult you by coming here and marrying your daughters." Yancey insisted that slaves were property and that the Constitution protected all property. But he also admitted that Southerners viewed slaves as people as well and argued that Southern laws reflected that view, protecting the lives of slaves as well as the property rights of the slaveholders. He repeated the arguments made by many proslavery advocates, insisting that slaves were well treated, well fed, and well clothed. He argued that equality was intended only for "the dominant race, the ruling race, the Caucasian race, the white race."

Yancey combined racism and a defense of slavery with his defense of Southern honor, to which he returned time and again. Southerners "cannot afford to lose honor and equality and be treated with injustice." He begged the Republicans and Northerners in general to avoid slighting the South. "Do not destroy our self respect; do not do us that injustice, which, when done to a worm, it turns on the heel that crushes it; which, when done to the brute creation, gives evidence of some sort of resistance. Do not overtax our manliness." Southern honor and masculinity hinged on this election, and Yancey staunchly took to the field to defend his beloved South.[31]

While Yancey took the fight to the North itself, Breckinridge followed the dictates of honor by remaining largely silent throughout the campaign. He wrote the expected letters to friends that the recipients published in newspapers and made occasional brief remarks to crowds of gathered supporters. But as the charges of his opponents mounted, he finally agreed to make one lengthy address in hopes of dismissing the opposition's main

Fig. 19. Congressional Surgery. Legislative Quackery. (Library of Congress) In this pro-Southern cartoon parodying calls for compromise to save the Union, "Dr. North" tells "Patient South" that " . . . We will first, with your assistance, take off your legs, then fix you up on these constitutional amendments." The South replies, "Can't see it."

contention: that his campaign aimed at disunion. The candidate made his speech on September 5, 1860, at a barbecue held in his honor at Henry Clay's Ashland estate by the late Whig's son, who had become an ardent Breckinridge supporter. Thousands came to hear him speak; the large number of women present indicated the depth of the candidate's support, because partisan identification was a family matter. Even though they could not vote, women actively participated in campaigns. With their significance in Southern honor, their presence at the barbecue meant that Breckinridge was seen as a man worthy of trust, a hero who would protect the ladies and the South as a whole. Although he was ill, the candidate held forth for three hours. He began by denying the many charges against him, taking each in turn. First, he refused to talk about whether or not he was a slaveowner, a charge that had been made against him by Constitutional Unionists trying to discredit him in the slave states by pointing out that he did not own any slaves. Because it was a personal matter, he argued that he did not have to go into it, itself an indignant defense of honor that brought a voice from the crowd saying, "That is manly." The fact that he did not own slaves at the time did nothing to dampen his defense of the institution. Secondly, Breckinridge denied that he had abandoned his position on slavery in the territories. He argued that Douglas was the one who had changed positions and that he and the Southern Democrats held firmly to the correct constitutional interpretation of the issue. The Kentuckian also denied that he had ever been antislavery, although he clearly respected his relatives who held to such views.[32]

Although the crowd received the speech with careful attention and rewarded the candidate's efforts with plenty of applause, it was widely considered a disappointment. A Breckinridge campaign manager in Norfolk asked the Illinois senator (1) if the Southern states would be justified in secession if Lincoln was elected; and (2) if they did secede, should the Republicans use force against them. Douglas had answered no to the first question and yes to the second without any hesitation. But Breckinridge did not address the questions in his long speech. Furthermore, his arguments that he loved the Union did little to dismiss the charges that his campaign aimed at the ultimate separation of the Southern states. Too many Americans agreed with Douglas when the Little Giant said that although not every Breckinridge man was a disunionist, every disunionist was a Breckinridge man. If the purpose of the speech was purely political, then, it did little to help the cause. Few voters were swayed.[33]

But when viewed as a ritual of honor, Breckinridge's speech can be interpreted quite differently. Although the Kentuckian certainly hoped to win over voters, especially in his home state, his primary purpose was to defend his personal honor as well as that of his campaign, and of the South as a whole against the charges made against them. In fact, his address was an oration, not a speech. As such it was a ritual of honor that displayed his independence, his mastery, his dignity, his reputation. Breckinridge was not begging for votes, he was standing on the field of honor, displaying his superior character, challenging anyone to deny that he was worthy of his position. Throughout the address he used the masculine language of honor. Such gendered vocabulary was laden with meaning in a culture of honor, where manliness meant respect, independence, and power. The crowd at Ashland recognized this and applauded the listener who called out that Breckinridge was manly when he refused to answer questions about personal matters, such as whether or not he owned slaves.

The candidate also often referred to duty, a term that later observers simply saw as a matter of public service. But in the Old South, duty meant honor. So, too, did Breckinridge's several verbal challenges to those who made charges against him. When he called on anyone who could confirm such charges or had ever heard him say what his enemies claimed he had said to step forward and "now speak, or forever hold his peace," Breckinridge was not simply using a rhetorical device to fend off political attacks. Instead, such words were the language of honor, the challenge of a duelist, the wounded response of a slighted party who had at last taken too much. His refusal to address the questions about secession and the government's response to it were, of course, a political sidestep. But they were readily accepted by the Kentuckian's listeners, because to engage them would have been outside the realm of dignified honor. In the culture of honor, the speaker's demeanor, the way he handled himself, meant as much as his words. For Breckinridge to deny that he was a disunionist, then turn to answering questions about secession, would have been unthinkable.[34]

Near the end of his address, he stated, "I am not ashamed of the principles upon which I stand. I am not ashamed of the reasons by which they are sustained. I am not ashamed of the friends that support me. I am not ashamed of the tone, bearing, and character of our whole organization." At that point, amid applause, someone in the crowd called out, "The truth will prevail." Breckinridge went on, "Yes, the truth will prevail. You may smother it for a time beneath the passion and prejudices of men, but . . . the truth will reappear as the rock reappears above the receding tide." He believed that "this country will yet walk by the light of these principles. Bright and fixed, as the rock-built lighthouse in the stormy sea, they will abide, a perpetual beacon, to attract the political mariner to the harbor of the Constitution." He appealed to his fellow citizens by saying, "People of Kentucky, you never abandoned a principle you believed to be right."

As the crowd showed its agreement with this sentiment by its applause, Breckinridge closed his oration, "For myself, conscious that my foot is planted on the rock of the Constitution . . . with a spirit erect and unbroken, I defy all calumny, calmly await the triumph of truth."[35]

In the terminology of honor, the candidate was projecting himself, his truth, and daring anyone to give the lie to it. The Ashland address was nothing less than a defense of Breckinridge's honor. It was as clearly a ritual of honor to the candidate and to the crowd that heard him as a duel would have been. He did not denounce his enemies as liars but called them out to prove that he was anything less than what he said he was. To "give the lie" to something or someone meant showing that appearance was different from reality. In this case, Breckinridge's oration was a public appearance, a ritual by which he showed himself to be what he said, a means of establishing that his true nature was different from what had been claimed in political attacks.[36]

But honor did not deliver a political victory in 1860. Defeated for the presidency, Breckinridge tried to remain in the U.S. Senate even as his home state remained in the Union while eleven Southern states broke away and formed the Confederacy. However, his support for state's rights now made Breckinridge vulnerable to charges of treason, and he soon resigned his seat and joined the Southern cause. He served as a general and, later, as secretary of war for the Confederacy. After the war, he returned home to Kentucky, where he worked hard as a spokesman for reconciliation between the North and South. Throughout the rest of his life, no matter the particular circumstances, he explained himself in the language of honor.[37]

How does honor change our understanding of the Breckinridge campaign of 1860? Certainly, it allows each major interpretation to stand on its historical strengths and weaknesses, although it may encourage scholars to look for ways to bring all of the theories together in a more complex analysis. But David Potter already offered such a move toward complexity by inviting his readers to consider the context within which events occurred. Instead of bolstering one argument or another, honor allows us to rethink the entire Breckinridge campaign and every action taken within it. Rather than employing modern theories and models of political science taken from the twentieth or twenty-first century and using them as a template to explain 1860, using the lens of honor affords us an opportunity truly to come to terms with the context in which Southerners operated. Political addresses were not only speeches but also rituals of honor, orations that might express the same meaning as duels. Words were not simply political rhetoric; they were also coded expressions of respect and power in a society based on race, slavery, and honor. What seems rational or irrational to us today did not necessarily seem that way to Southerners involved in the election of 1860. To be sure, Southerners had multiple and mixed motives and faced very real tensions and contradictions in their society and culture and in their thinking. They certainly understood modern meanings and political devices. But they also understood their own cultural and ethical traditions. To take up the interpretative lens of honor is not to entirely dismiss all other motives. After all, motives often mix. Rather, it offers a means of reconciling very different and very complex ideas by providing a worldview within which to frame the many different explanations historians have offered. Thus, in its own right, honor stands as the most significant interpretation of the Southern Democratic campaign of 1860.[38]

John C. Breckinridge aptly used the language of honor when he accepted the nomination of the Southern Democrats and told Mrs. Jefferson Davis, "I trust I have the courage to lead a forlorn hope." He used a military term of honor to describe what he was doing. The "forlorn hope" referred to those soldiers who took the riskiest and most dangerous role in a military operation. In the nineteenth century, in a society steeped in the terminology of Napoleonic warfare, a forlorn hope meant an infantry assault against a fortified position. The first troops to advance took the greatest risk and suffered the greatest number of casualties. To be chosen for such an attack was considered a great honor; officers and men alike often volunteered for the duty. To lead a forlorn hope was the ultimate way to do one's duty; it was the very height of honor. To be killed while undertaking a forlorn hope was to win a lasting reputation as a man of courage, a man of honor. Southerners extolled such courage and valued such honor. For Breckinridge, a veteran himself, accepting the nomination in the face of almost certain defeat was tantamount to being chosen to lead the hopeless infantry charge. The chances of winning or losing in such a situation did not necessarily mean that the candidate was motivated by any particular idea or plan. It was not about winning or losing the presidency. It was not even really about slavery or secession, although those issues mattered. Instead, it was about honor, which brought together all of the various motives and couched them in terms that Southerners clearly understood. Thus, Breckinridge went forward. Thus, a majority of voters in most of the Southern states cast their ballots for him. That he probably could not win did not matter to them. Understanding the election and all of its various meanings in terms of honor, Breckinridge's supporters were truly following him into a forlorn hope.

1. Varina H. Davis, *Jefferson Davis, Ex-President of the Confederate States of America: A Memoir by His Wife* (New York: Belford Co., 1890), 1:685.

2. For detailed accounts of the intricacies and dramatic events of the Democratic convention in 1860, see Roy Franklin Nichols, *The Disruption of American Democracy* (New York: Macmillan, 1948), esp. 288–322; Allan Nevins, *The Emergence of Lincoln: Prologue to Civil War, 1859–1861* (New York: Charles Scribner's Sons, 1950), 203–28; Douglas R. Egerton, *Year of Meteors: Stephen Douglas, Abraham Lincoln, and the Election that Brought on the Civil War* (New York: Bloomsbury Press, 2010), 51–82, 149–75; Bruce Chadwick, *Lincoln for President: An Unlikely Candidate, An Audacious Strategy, and the Victory No One Saw Coming* (Naperville, Ill.: Sourcebooks, Inc., 2009), 23–43; David M. Potter, *The Impending Crisis, 1848–1861* (New York: Harper & Row, 1976), 407–13. Reinhard H. Luthin, *The First Lincoln Campaign* (1944; repr., Gloucester, Mass.: Peter Smith, 1964), 120–35; Emerson David Fite, *The Presidential Campaign of 1860* (1911; repr., Port Washington, N.Y.: Kennikat Press, 1967), 92–116.

3. For the story of the Breckinridges' reaction at the dinner party, see William C. Davis, *Breckinridge: Statesman, Soldier, Symbol* (Baton Rouge: Louisiana State Univ. Press, 1974), 219.

4. David, *Breckinridge,* 3–18; Frank H. Heck, *Proud Kentuckian: John C. Breckinridge, 1821–1875* (Lexington: Univ. of Kentucky Press, 1976), 1–11; James C. Klotter, *The Breckinridges of Kentucky, 1760–1981* (Lexington: Univ. of Kentucky Press, 1986), 95–98. Davis's book remains the best and most complete biography of Breckinridge. Heck's work is much shorter and less thorough, although he differs with Davis on some points. Klotter's work places Breckinridge within the context of his illustrious family while providing a fine biographical study of the man in his own right. Rather than refer to each of these books for the biographical section of this chapter, I will note page numbers for Davis only. Those interested in Breckinridge should consult the others as well, especially in matters of interpretation.

5. Davis, *Breckinridge,* 21–31.

6. Davis, *Breckinridge,* 32–42.

7. Davis, *Breckinridge,* 42–51. Elting Morison noted that Breckinridge's attachment to Clay and nationalist sentiments continued even in the 1860 campaign; see Morison, "Election of 1860," in *History of American Presidential Elections,* ed. Arthur Schlesinger, Jr., vol. 2, *1848–1896,* (New York: Chelsea House, 1971), 1100–1101.

8. Davis, *Breckinridge,* 52–146.

9. Davis, *Breckinridge,* 147–205.

10. Breckinridge denied that there had been any kind of arrangements to secure him the seat in the U.S. Senate. See John C. Breckinridge, *Substance of a Speech by Hon. John C. Breckinridge, Delivered in the Hall of the House of Representatives, at Frankfort, Kentucky, December 21, 1859.* Davis, *Breckinridge,* 206–27;

Heck, *Proud Kentuckian,* dedicates an appendix to Breckinridge's views on slavery, 163–64.

11. Many sources provide the numerical breakdowns of the election of 1860, but these are drawn from Potter, *Impending Crisis,* 442–47.

12. Potter, *Impending Crisis.,* 442–47.

13. Nichols, *Disruption of American Democracy,* 341–48; Nevins, *Emergence of Lincoln,* 284–85; Heck, *Proud Kentuckian,* 89–90 ; Chadwick, *Lincoln for President,* 105–11. The section of Heck's biography on the election is taken from his earlier article on the subject, "John C. Breckinridge in the Crisis of 1860–1861," *Journal of Southern History* 21, no. 3 (August 1955): 316–46.

14. Potter, *Impending Crisis,* 436–37.

15. Douglas quoted in Robert W. Johannsen, *Stephen A. Douglas* (New York: Oxford Univ. Press, 1973), 802, 777; Potter, *Impending Crisis,* 437.

16. For mention of Breckinridge's possibly winning in the Electoral College, see Nichols, *Disruption of American Democracy,* 340; and Ollinger Crenshaw, *The Slave States in the Presidential Election of 1860* (Baltimore: Johns Hopkins Univ. Press, 1945), 61.

17. Fite, *Presidential Campaign of 1860,* 92–116, 205–35; Davis, *Breckinridge,* 226, 232; Thomas B. Alexander, "The Civil War as Institutional Fulfillment," *Journal of Southern History* 47, no. 1 (February 1981): 3–32. For the hope of winning concessions from Douglas, see Robert W. Johannsen, "Douglas at Charleston," in *Politics and the Crisis of 1860,* ed. Norman A. Graebner (Urbana: Univ. of Illinois Press, 1961), 88–89.

18. Fite, *Presidential Campaign of 1860,* 116; Sean Wilentz, *The Rise of American Democracy: Jefferson to Lincoln* (New York: Norton, 2005), 762; Eric H. Walther, *William Lowndes Yancey and the Coming of the Civil War* (Chapel Hill: Univ. of North Carolina Press, 2006), 232, 243–44, 253.

19. Davis, *Breckinridge,* 224–25; for other accounts of the Davis plan, see Nevins, *Emergence of Lincoln,* 285–86; Egerton, *Year of Meteors,* 170.

20. Jeffery A. Jenkins and Irwin L. Morris, "Running to Lose? John C. Breckinridge and the Presidential Election of 1860," *Electoral Studies* 25 (2006): 306–28; Egerton, *Year of Meteors,* 8–13; William W. Freehling, *The Road to Disunion,* vol. 2, *Secessionists Triumphant, 1854–1861* (New York: Oxford Univ. Press, 2007). Austin L. Venable, "The Conflict Between the Douglas and Yancey Forces in the Charleston Convention," *Journal of Southern History* 8, no.2 (May 1942): 226–41, provides a useful account of the bitter divide between the Little Giant and the Southern radicals. For the Stephens quote and Egerton's argument about it, see Egerton, *Year of Meteors,* 8. Related to this interpretation is the work of William L. Barney, who argues that the Breckinridge campaign appealed to Southern voters because of its ideology of expansion and secessionism; see Barney, *The Secessionist Impulse: Alabama and Mississippi in 1860* (Princeton, N.J.: Princeton Univ. Press, 1974). Barney takes an economic view, arguing that Southerners actually faced a crisis caused by a drought, soil exhaustion, and rising prices of rapidly disappearing cotton land. For a thoughtful review and rebuttal of Barney's work, see Michael F. Holt, *Political Parties and American Political Development from the Age of Jackson to the Age of Lincoln* (Baton Rouge: Louisiana State Univ. Press, 1992), 303–8.

21. For the most obvious statement of this interpretation in terms of rational actors and in the language of conspiracy, see Jenkins and Morris, "Running to Lose,"

esp. 324–25; Walther, *William Lowndes Yancey*, 253. William C. Davis argues, somewhat curiously, that "By and large, what Breckinridge did represent in this election was the spirit of moderation and conciliation. Those who stood most to lose by emancipation or abolition, and the most to gain by disunion, had gone for Bell." Davis, *Breckinridge*, 246.

22. Crenshaw, *Slave States in the Presidential Election of 1860*, 72–73, 92–111.

23. Potter, *Impending Crisis*, 414.

24. Bertram Wyatt-Brown, *Southern Honor: Ethics and Behavior in the Old South* (New York: Oxford Univ. Press, 1982), 14, 363, passim.

25. Kenneth S. Greenberg, *Masters and Statesmen: The Political Culture of American Slavery* (Baltimore: Johns Hopkins Univ. Press, 1985), 124–35. For more on the role of republicanism in 1860, see the arguments of Thomas E. Rodgers in chap. 6 of this book.

26. Greenberg, *Masters and Statesmen*, 141; *New York Herald*, September 19, 1860. Also see Kenneth S. Greenberg, *Honor and Slavery: Lies, Duels, Noses, Masks, Dressing as a Woman, Gifts, Strangers, Humanitarianism, Death, Baseball, Hunting, and Gambling in the Old South* (Princeton, N.J.: Princeton Univ. Press, 1996). Elizabeth Varon argued, "More so than in any previous campaign, the rhetoric of the 1860 contest focused on women"; see Varon, *We Mean to Be Counted: White Women and Politics in Antebellum Virginia* (Chapel Hill: Univ. of North Carolina Press, 1998), 144–50.

27. Bertram Wyatt-Brown, *The Shaping of Southern Culture: Honor, Grace, and War, 1760s–1880s* (Chapel Hill: Univ. of North Carolina Press, 2001), 187–91. C. Vann Woodward's classic essay on John Brown's role in Southern thinking at the time emphasized how Southern psychological insecurities and paranoia ironically played out in the election of 1860 and secession; see Woodward, "John Brown's Private War," in *The Burden of Southern History* (Baton Rouge: Louisiana State Univ. Press, 1960), 41–68.

28. John C. Breckinridge, *Speech of Hon. John C. Breckinridge, Vice-President of the United States, at Ashland, Kentucky, September 5th, 1860, Repelling the Charge of Disunion and Vindicating the National Democracy* (Washington, D.C.: National Democratic Executive Committee, 1860); Walther, *William Lowndes Yancey*, 253. Walther's biography of Yancey is one of the few scholarly works that includes any real consideration of honor in analyzing the election of 1860.

29. William L. Yancey, *Speech of the Hon. William L. Yancey, of Alabama Delivered to the National Democratic Convention, April 28, 1860, with the Protest of the Alabama Delegation* (Charleston: Walker, Evans, & Co., 1860).

30. Yancey, *Speech . . . to National Democratic Convention.*

31. For these quotations and a careful analysis of Yancey's tour, see Walther, *William Lowndes Yancey*, 252–73.

32. Breckinridge, *Speech . . . at Ashland*. For more on women and their participation in the election of 1860, see Erika Rozinek, "Trembling for the Nation: Illinois Women and the Election of 1860," *Constructing the Past* 2, vol. 1 (2001), art. 4. For two examples of the scholarship on women's participation in antebellum politics, see Elizabeth R. Varon, "Tippecanoe and the Ladies, Too: White Women and Party Politics in Antebellum Virginia" *Journal of American History* 82, no. 2 (1995): 494–521; Jayne Crumpler DiFiore, "Come, and Bring the Ladies: Tennessee

Women and the Politics of Opportunity During the Presidential Campaigns of 1840 and 1844," *Tennessee Historical Quarterly* 51, no. 4 (1992): 197–212.

33. Davis, *Breckinridge*, 237–40; Morison, "Election of 1860," 1100–1101; Johannsen, *Stephen A. Douglas*, 799.

34. On the rituals of honor involved in public speaking, see Greenberg, *Masters and Statesmen*, 12–14; Wyatt-Brown, *Southern Honor*, 330–31. For the ways in which masculinity intersected with republicanism as well as honor, see the interpretation of Thomas E. Rodgers presented in chap. 6 of this book.

35. Breckinridge, *Speech . . . at Ashland.*

36. For this understanding of the ritual, see Greenberg, *Honor and Slavery*, 8–9.

37. Davis, *Breckinridge* provides detailed analysis of the Kentuckian's service to the Confederacy and his later life.

38. Many scholars have pointed out the role of honor in the secession crisis; their work might be usefully employed in analyzing the election of 1860 as well as other events. Especially insightful on the reasons that so many Southerners went along with secession and the ways in which race and slavery were mingled with honor are Wyatt-Brown, *The Shaping of Southern Culture*, 177–202; Greenberg, *Masters and Statesmen*, 107–46; Stephanie McCurry, *Masters of Small Worlds: Yeoman Households, Gender Relations, and the Political Culture of the Antebellum South Carolina Low Country* (New York: Oxford Univ. Press, 1995), 239–304; J. Mills Thornton, *Politics and Power in A Slave Society: Alabama, 1800–1860* (Baton Rouge: Louisiana State Univ. Press, 1978), 343–461; Lacy K. Ford, Jr., *Origins of Southern Radicalism: The South Carolina Upcountry, 1800–1860* (New York: Oxford Univ. Press, 1988), 338–73.

4

The Last True Whig

John Bell and the Politics of Compromise in 1860

A. James Fuller

The election of 1860 featured four candidates for the presidency and actually became two separate races as the Republican Abraham Lincoln faced off against the Northern Democrat Stephen A. Douglas in the free states, while the Southern Democrat John C. Breckinridge ran against the Constitutional Union candidate, John Bell, in the slave states. Although the other three presidential candidates remain popular subjects for study, especially Lincoln and Douglas, John Bell has received very little attention from historians. Every study of the coming of the Civil War and the 1860 election mentions the Constitutional Unionist candidate, and nearly every survey textbook features an electoral map with his name displayed along with the others, but scholars still largely neglect Bell's campaign. Most writers dismiss the Constitutional Union Party as being a hopeless, half-hearted effort by a group of elderly conservatives that garnered a lot of respect but little actual support. Although most third parties in American history took clear stands on principle and earned a measure of scholarly esteem or at least some consideration because of that, historians have scorned the Constitutional Union platform of "the Union, the Constitution, and the enforcement of the laws," as a political sidestepping of the major issues. Thus, writers continue to find Bell's last-place finish in the popular vote and his third-place finish in the Electoral College a fitting result for a candidate who avoided the problems confronting the country. Still, in the literature as well as in 1860, Bell gets a measure of respect. Scholars note that he won several of the slave states, but like the voters of the time, the historians reject him and generally argue that his largely irrelevant campaign was doomed to fail.[1]

Fig. 20. Hon. John Bell of Tennessee: National Union candidate for sixteenth president of the United States. (Library of Congress)

John Bell deserves more. When examined more closely, his candidacy reveals the neglected reality behind the cursory dismissals of the historians who have so quickly dismissed the Constitutional Union effort. In his recent study of the election, Douglas R. Egerton, like so many other scholars before him, noted that "Bell was the first candidate to be nominated in 1860" and included "the fact that the venerable Whig Party was back under a new name indicated that there would be at least three candidates in the field that year."

John Bell was a Whig. That fact, so often stated simply and left without elaboration by historians, provides the clue to interpreting his campaign and the Constitutional Union Party. In their efforts to build on the remnant of Southern Whiggery, Bell and his supporters drew on the legacy of their old party and its most famous leader, Henry Clay. It is ironic that all four of the candidates for president in 1860 tried to claim the mantle of Clay, as even the Democrats Douglas and Breckinridge associated themselves with his name. Despite the fact that the Kentuckian had never won the presidency, all of them hoped in 1860 to save the Union as Clay had done several times. But Lincoln, Douglas, and Breckinridge all planned to save the Union, as they each defined it, on their own terms. Only John Bell held fast to the political principle that had worked so well for Clay and the Whigs in the past. The Constitutional Unionists promoted compromise as the means of saving the country and averting civil war. What many observers saw in 1860 and many historians have seen since as equivocation and avoiding the issues actually was a call to compromise. To Henry Clay and to Bell after him, the United States was a compromise between the Union, on the one hand, and the Constitution, on the other. In 1787 compromise created the Union, and Clay had saved it several times since with compromises. In 1860, the country needed another compromise. Bell ran as the last true Whig candidate for president under the label of the Constitutional Union Party, urging Americans to set aside their opposing views in favor of everyone's conceding something in order to save the Union and avoid a crisis. Unfortunately for Bell, compromise proved to be a political liability in the context of 1860.[2]

Voters in 1860 knew who John Bell was and respected him, even if they were not enthusiastic about his presidential candidacy. Since few remember him today, a brief biography is necessary to show how he came to be his party's nominee. A native of Tennessee born in 1796, Bell came of age along with his state, which entered the Union in the year of his birth. His grandfather fought in the American Revolution before moving to Tennessee to settle a farm. Bell's father lived as a farmer and blacksmith, and young John grew up working both on the land and in the blacksmith shop. That early mixture of agriculture and mechanical pursuits set a pattern for his future; he later invested in both planting and industry, a mixed financial style that mirrored the economy of the Upper South whence he came. But Bell chose to pursue a career in the law following his graduation from Cumberland College (later the now defunct University of Nashville).[3]

He practiced law for only a short time before turning to politics, winning a seat in the state senate in 1817. Even in this first office he supported the kinds of policies that would become typical of the later Whig Party, voting for the creation of state banks and calling for an investigation into the ways "squatter's rights" had deprived the state of much-needed education funds. After completing his two-year term in the senate, he returned to the law and built a lucrative practice. He married and started a family with his wife, Sarah Dickinson Bell. By 1822, his family lived in Nashville, where he continued his practice and also served as director of the Nashville Bank and on the Board of Trustees of his alma mater. In 1826, Bell ran for Congress and defeated Felix Grundy, a close friend of Andrew Jackson, while expressing support for the national government's paying for internal improvements and denouncing the abuses of power and the corruption of the spoils system—rhetoric befitting an era dominated by republicanism and foreshadowing the politics of the Whig Party. Although Jackson's active support for Grundy during the campaign offended Bell, the young politician continued to support Old Hickory for the presidency. This was an important matter in the aftermath of the election of 1824, which so many in Tennessee saw as having been stolen through the "corrupt bargain" between Henry Clay and John Quincy Adams.[4]

During his congressional career, which lasted until 1841, Bell was the chairman of the House Committee on Indian Affairs and was a member of the Judiciary Committee as well. Despite his affiliation with policies supported by the later Whig Party, in his early years in Congress he allied himself with President Andrew Jackson, a fellow Tennessean with whom Bell agreed on a number of issues. His Jacksonian leanings included Indian removal; as chairman of Indian affairs, Bell supported and signed the bill that forced the tribes off their lands. Breaking with his earlier stand on banks and internal improvements, he thought it best to give Jackson's financial schemes a chance during the Bank War and supported the president's veto of the Maysville Road Bill. In the early 1830s, then, Bell was a Democrat allied to Jackson. But labeling him a Jacksonian Democrat may overstate the actual case, because it makes him out to be an ideological member of a party. Instead, both his personal connection to a fellow Tennessean and his view of the Constitution motivated Bell during Jackson's tenure. Bell respected Jackson, and the two shared views on many issues important to their state. When the congressman thought that the anti-Jackson opposition to the president's bank policies was personal, he rallied to defend Old Hickory. But his motivations stemmed from more than personal politics. Bell's views of the Constitution also shaped his actions; he accepted much of the president's interpretation of executive power and agreed with him on the constitutionality of some issues. This all fitted well within the broader ideology of republicanism that dominated the revolutionary era and the early Republic and persisted even as the Second American Party System began to emerge. As long as Jackson did not overstep constitutional bounds, Bell could support him, especially if the opposition to the president seemed less about principle and more about

politics and personality. But Bell disagreed with Jackson on many important matters, and that meant that a break inevitably came.[5]

Bell's split with Jackson began during the 1834 controversy over the
speakership of the House of Representatives. The president wanted his
close friend and fellow Tennessean James K. Polk to take the Speaker's
chair. Instead, John Bell won the election and held the leadership position
in the House for a term. That broke his personal connection to Jackson.
When Bell's views on banking made it clear that he did not fully support
the president in the ongoing Bank War, the separation became complete.
By 1836, the Jacksonians derisively called Bell the "Great Apostate" and
jeered him for joining the opposition led by Henry Clay. Thereafter, John
Bell was a Whig. Jackson seethed with anger at Bell's defection, but also
took it personally when other Tennessee politicians such as David Crock-
ett and Hugh Lawson White joined the Whigs. For the president, especially, loyalty and friendship mattered deeply. When those he had considered friends from Tennessee allied with his political enemies, it slighted
his sense of honor. Old Hickory never forgave such acts, and his vitriol
only drove the defectors like Bell and White closer to Clay and the Whigs.[6]

Led by Bell and White, the Whigs of Tennessee won a great victory over
the Jacksonians by sweeping the elections in 1836, capturing a majority
of the state's congressional seats. From then on, Bell served as one of the
top Whigs in the state. His work in Congress and during the presidential
campaigns made him a national leader of the party as well. In 1840, he
helped the Whigs win the presidency, and William Henry Harrison chose
him to be secretary of war. He held that post under John Tyler following
Harrison's death shortly after he took office. Bell liked the job and had
sought it even while still affiliated with the Democrats, but he resigned
his Cabinet post shortly after assuming it as part of a Whig protest against
Tyler's veto of legislation creating a new national bank. Bell returned to
private life, taking up his law practice again and expanding his business
interests. His first wife had died in 1832, and he left the raising of his five
children to her family. He married a wealthy widow, Jane Erwin Yeatman,
in 1835, and this brought interests in a Nashville bank and a substantial
iron works. This second marriage coincided with Bell's defection from the
Democrats, leading his critics to note that his new wife's family and business benefitted from the kinds of economic policies now promoted by the
Whigs. He supported Henry Clay in 1844 and helped the Whig candidate
beat the Democrat James K. Polk in his home state of Tennessee. Polk, of

course, won the election by a narrow margin. Bell returned to politics in 1847 when he won election to the U.S. Senate, where he served two terms, leaving office in 1859. Throughout all of these years, he remained an important Whig leader, whether in office or not.[7]

The Whig Party took its name from the traditional use of the term "Whig" as a label for those who opposed tyranny. From its inception, the party claimed that its main principle was to safeguard liberty against the concentration and abuse of power by corrupt men. Thus, the Whigs defended republicanism. Although not all Whigs agreed on the exact definition of republicanism, many held to a version of this ideology that viewed the Union as limited by the Constitution, which provided for dual sovereignty in a federal system. This meant that although they were nationalists, they recognized that some powers lay with the states. Still, they took up the nationalist mantle first worn by Alexander Hamilton and the Federalists and then carried on by the National Republicans; thus, the Whigs usually promoted a stronger national government. The new party also typically supported government intervention in the economy to promote business interests. Whig support for moral and social reform attracted many evangelical Protestants to the party, although religious support was rarely monolithic. Generally adhering to the party's platform, Bell sometimes differed on key issues. The most obvious example of his breaking with the party line involved internal improvements. Although he consistently supported the distribution of federal money for the building of roads, canals, harbors, and railroads, he disagreed with the methods of Clay's American System, which put the building of such infrastructure under congressional control. Bell held to a strict constitutional interpretation that allowed the national government to distribute funds for such projects but saw congressional control as going beyond the legal bounds of dual sovereignty. Here, his views clearly reflected the idea that the Constitution limited the power of the Union.[8]

Throughout his career, Bell often took moderate positions between the parties and the extremists on many issues but held to a consistent view of defending the Constitution, promoting compromise, and fighting against corruption. Thus, Bell's Whig Party stood for a republican vision of ordered liberty against the abuse of power and demagoguery. Above all, it stood for defending both the Union and the Constitution through compromise. Although Bell toed the party line on most issues, his moderate politics enabled him to reach out to many on the other side of the political aisle. His alliance with Clay included economic matters, for Bell supported the national bank and wanted federal money used for internal improvements. However, the strongest point of agreement that he shared with Clay beyond the party's first principle of defending liberty was the spirit of compromise that enabled the Whig leadership to forge agreements along practical lines and promote national unity.

Bell's views on slavery stood as the most significant example of his moderate politics and devotion to compromise and allied him closely to Clay. Like the Kentuckian, Bell owned slaves, including many laboring in his coalfields as well as his iron works. He denounced abolitionism and believed that the Constitution protected the property rights of slaveholders like himself. Yet he also disagreed with those proslavery extremists who wanted to extend the institution at all costs. Holding to an interpretation of the Constitution that allowed for state's rights, he believed that the Union could continue while divided between free and slave states. He repeatedly walked the fine line of compromise and moderation on the issue of slavery and its territorial expansion. This meant opposing the so-called gag rule during the 1830s, when Congress voted to table automatically abolitionist petitions regarding slavery. Bell opposed abolitionism, but argued that "whether the petitioners had strict right on their side or not, sound policy dictated the reception and reference of their petitions." This not only defended the constitutional rights of citizens, Bell asserted, it might also diminish further abolitionist agitation made possible by sympathy with the restriction of free speech.[9]

In the 1840s, the Tennessee Whig led a small number of Southern members of his party in joining those Northern Whigs who opposed the U.S.-Mexican War. This made Bell an ally of Abraham Lincoln, as the two men joined to criticize President Polk and his policies. Because the Whig opposition painted the conflict as a war for slavery, Bell found himself once again cast in the role of opposing slavery. In this case, his choice stemmed as much from personal politics as from philosophical principles. Polk remained Bell's archnemesis, and the Whig's natural reaction was to oppose anything his Democratic rival supported. Despite his opposition to his old enemy's war policy, Bell still managed to vote for the ratification of the Treaty of Guadalupe Hidalgo, which brought peace and added vast amounts of territory to the United States. This demonstrated his moderate course of compromise but also reflected a stand on principle. Bell claimed that he supported the treaty because he feared "that if the war went on, we would be compelled to take all Mexico and incorporate it into this confederacy." Bell argued that would surely ruin the country and that "Mexico would be the grave of our liberties." Even taking California, New Mexico, and the other territory acquired in the treaty spelled doom, because the Tennessee senator feared that the application of the Wilmot Proviso would once again raise a sectional crisis. Obvious though his prophecy may have been, it soon came true.[10]

In the bitter sectional controversy that followed on the heels of the U.S.-Mexican War, Bell stood firmly allied with Henry Clay. Throughout the complicated maneuvering that surrounded the Compromise of 1850, he once again demonstrated his moderate politics in his support for the various measures that went into the deal that eventually seemed to save the Union and calm the sectional crisis. He even offered a series of resolutions of his own in an attempt to win support for compromise when Clay's plan stalled. Perhaps his most famous provision was a call for the immediate division of Texas into five separate states, which reflected his support for slavery, because such a move would create more slave states to protect the institution politically. However, he also supported the abolition of slavery in the District of Columbia. Such seeming contradictions showed his moderation and desire to compromise and the ideological views behind such actions.[11]

In the 1850s, he opposed the Kansas-Nebraska Act and the Lecompton Constitution even as the issue of slavery in the territories helped destroy the Whig Party as a national organization. To be sure, other issues, including temperance, prohibition, and immigration played a role in this destruction. But slavery's expansion remained the crucial issue. Henry Clay had died, as had other important party leaders such as Daniel Webster. Without Clay to forge a compromise and prevent a sectional crisis, the Whigs began to split, imperiling the party. Bell tried to save his party and lead the country in another compromise by opposing the Kansas-Nebraska Act of 1854. Doing so made him a traitor to the sectional cause in the minds of many of his fellow Southerners. Still, he stood strong. One of his main arguments against Stephen Douglas's plan for organizing the new territories contended that the land in question lay close to reservations that belonged to the Indian tribes the government had removed from their homes east of the Mississippi. Opening up such territory to settlement violated the agreements with the Indians by subjecting them to renewed contact with whites, and Bell believed that the Indians "were sure to contract all the vices, without adopting any of the virtues of civilized communities." Furthermore, the northern part of the territory contained fewer Indians, meaning that more land would be open to white settlers. This made it virtually impossible for Southerners to create a new slave state while ensuring that Northerners would add to their power. Still further, he feared that the South faced great danger, because the new law would repeal the Missouri Compromise. Bell argued that instead of actually addressing the unjustness of the Missouri Compromise in limiting slavery, the new law would simply exacerbate sectional controversy and give ammunition to the abolitionists.[12]

He, like other compromisers, argued that the issue of expansion was false anyway, because slavery and plantation agriculture could not thrive in the arid climate of most of the territory in question. To destroy the Union over such a bogus issue was either foolhardy or a nefarious plan by those who actually wanted disunion. Compromise remained an attractive alternative amid what Stephen Douglas himself called "a hell of a storm." Bell's efforts fell short, Douglas won the day, and the Whigs collapsed. Despite this defeat, the compromiser opposed the proslavery Lecompton Constitution during the administration of James Buchanan, once again standing for moderation and compromise. Opposing Lecompton earned him more criticism from the South, with proslavery advocates castigating him as a traitor. He argued against the move on constitutional grounds and held his ground even though it cost him his seat in the Senate. Throughout his career, then, Bell refused to give up on Whig principles.[13]

Those principles derived in large part from Henry Clay, in whom Bell found a model of the politics of compromise. The leader of the Whig Party proved especially adept at finding middle ground, at making deals, at getting things accomplished, at saving the nation from sectional division. Clay's compromises included the Missouri Compromise of 1820, the compromise that ended the nullification crisis of the 1830s, and the Compromise of 1850.

Although Clay was not a compromiser by nature, his ideological understanding of the Union and the Constitution demanded sectional conciliation. He believed that the Constitution was a legal compact that gave sovereignty over some matters to the states rather than to the national government. In this republican vision of dual sovereignty in a Union that was partly federal and partly national, the issue of slavery required sections and individuals to make mutual sacrifices to save the compact between the

Fig. 21. John J.
Crittenden, Sena-
tor from Kentucky,
1859. (Library of
Congress)

states. For Clay, compromise stemmed from civic virtue and obligations. Compromise required that the majority conciliate rather than destroy the minority. This went far beyond practical considerations to encapsulate an ideological republicanism that was the underpinning of the Whig Party and the American political system in the years before the Civil War. In Henry Clay, John Bell found an ally and saw an example of how to save the country from disaster.[14]

Kentucky offered another model of compromise and another close friend and ally in John J. Crittenden, a longtime politician associated with the National Republicans and the Whigs. During his many years in politics, Crittenden served in the state legislature, the House of Representatives, the U.S. Senate, and governor of Kentucky. He was also twice the U.S. attorney general. A protégé of Clay, he sometimes disagreed with his party leader on minor policy issues and political tactics, but like his fellow Kentuckian, he promoted the spirit of compromise above all else. He joined Bell in opposing the Kansas-Nebraska Act and the Lecompton Constitution and, with the Tennessean, remained an influential leader of the Southern Whigs, the only remnant of the old party with a viable organization. By the late 1850s, Crittenden enjoyed a national reputation as a statesman and was Clay's heir as the symbol of the politics of compromise. When sectional crisis again threatened to destroy the Union during the election of 1860, many former Whigs and others who feared disunion looked to Crittenden to point the way and forge a compromise of some kind. Indeed, many hoped that he would help to reunite the Whig Party by running for the presidency. Perhaps a Southern Whig with a reputation as a moderate and a compromiser could deter the extremist threats to the Union from both the Republican and Democrat camps.[15]

Crittenden chose to lead the way toward compromise and averting disunion in 1860 by helping to form the Constitutional Union Party. But he did not become the new party's presidential candidate. Instead, that lot fell to John Bell. Usually neglected by historians, the Constitutional Unionists were actually the first to nominate a candidate for president in 1860. A coalition of former, mostly Southern, Whigs and American Party members, they came together during a political imbroglio over the speakership of the House of Representatives in 1859. The American Party arose in the early 1850s, following on the heels of nativist secret societies in the 1840s. Opposed to immigration and usually anti-Catholic as well, many nativists claimed to be defending republican liberty against hordes of immigrants flocking to the United States as part of a Papal Plot to take over the country. Called the Know Nothings because members always denied knowledge of the society, this semisecret movement attracted a wide following across the country in the wake of increased immigration, especially of Irish and German Catholics. Soon, the nativists formed the American Party. Dedicated to curbing immigration and securing the liberty and power of native-born, white, Anglo-Saxon, Protestant Americans, the new party developed a platform and ran candidates for office at all levels of government, including supporting Millard Fillmore for president in 1856.[16]

The American Party declined when the issue of slavery split the organization along sectional lines, just as it had the split the Whigs. The two parties shared many of the same kinds of constituents, with middle-class Protestants being an important base of their membership. Some Whigs had embraced nativism, whereas others eschewed it. Bell flirted with the American Party, hoping that it would prove to be the successor of the rapidly disappearing Whigs. He spoke at some Know Nothing meetings, and the American Party briefly considered him as a presidential candidate in 1856. But he did not wholeheartedly agree with the nativist party. Although he supported limits on immigration, he refused to advocate anti-Catholicism and denounced the secrecy of the Know Nothing movement. Still, he considered some of the former Americans allies and friends and knew that he could count on many of them as stalwart supporters. In some areas, especially in the Northern states, former Know Nothings provided the primary support for the Bell campaign in 1860.[17]

In a sense, the Constitutional Union Party could trace its roots to the compromises at the Constitutional Convention in 1787, but its real political organization for 1860 began in December 1859, during another battle over the speakership in the House of Representatives. The Democrats and the Republicans both lacked a majority in the House, a fact which left the 27 Whig and American members in a position to swing the vote for speaker. The new Republican Party counted 109 members, ten votes short of what they needed to elect their candidate, John Sherman. The Democracy had 101 members, but 13 of them had voted against the Lecompton Constitution for Kansas and had been "read out" of the party for failing to toe the Buchanan administration's line. They were still Democrats, but might easily vote against a Democratic candidate. Of the Whigs and Americans, 23 came from the South. With the widespread fear and confusion that followed John Brown's raid, these Southerners dared not vote for a Republican Speaker. At the same time, they did not want to help the Democrats, their longtime political foes. The speakership contest loomed large because the coming Congressional session would pave the way for the upcoming election: the Speaker appointed the committees, and those positions could influence the race for the presidency. Both major parties hoped to bring in the Whigs and Americans, but the result was a drawn-out fight. Between December 5 and January 11, the House cast thirty-four ballots without electing a Speaker. They then took a two-week break and, during that time, the Republicans cut a deal. Sherman withdrew in favor of William Pennington, a New Jersey Whig. The other House offices also went to Whigs or Americans or to Republicans closely affiliated with those two parties in recent years.[18]

The speakership battle convinced the Southern Whigs that compromise remained alive and well and that they might be able to save the country from the impending sectional crisis and disunion. Allied with the Americans, they had effectively walked the line between the two major parties and managed to compromise with one of them in a plan that gave power to a conservative coalition that was moderate on the issue of slavery. If they could create a coalition party of conservatives and moderates, of Unionists and party bolters and renegades, they might very well win the presidency and forge yet another compromise to avert a civil war, once again resolving the issue of slavery and its territorial expansion. Such a compromise might involve fusion with one of the other parties in the 1860 election. In 1859, even before the speakership battle, the movement's leaders thought that they might be able to ally with the Republicans. Members of that party such as William Seward seemed open to the idea until well into the campaign for the presidency. After all, many Republicans once belonged to the Whig Party, and the old connections remained strong. When it became clear that the Republicans did not need a fusion with the compromisers to win the 1860 election, they abandoned the idea. The compromisers then looked to Stephen A. Douglas and his campaign for a possible alliance. Douglas had earned a reputation for compromise during the crisis surrounding the Compromise of 1850 and had maneuvered the various pieces of legislation through the halls of Congress after the failure of Clay's omnibus bill. Convinced that the Little Giant was a good Union man who also believed in dual sovereignty, the compromisers hoped that they might fuse with the Northern Democrats in 1860. With such plans in mind, the movement began to organize and its leaders held meetings to discuss the 1860 election even while the speakership contest raged on in the House. In January 1860, they officially took their name and the Constitutional Union Party prepared for their convention scheduled for May in Baltimore.[19]

John Crittenden had been present for most of the organizational meetings and remained the guiding light of the new party. He had been working toward a compromise alternative to the Democrats and Republicans since at least 1858, and his influence with important men in both parties made it seem likely that a fusion plan could work. Indeed, the Kentuckian's reputation gave the new organization immediate credibility across the country. Urged to accept the nomination for the presidency, he refused, citing old age. At seventy-three, he believed that he was too old for the rigors of the campaign and the office. Remaining out of the race would also allow him to maintain his influence outside the party should it be necessary to try to save the Union through a last-ditch effort at compromise after the election. Although his refusal to run certainly diminished the party's chances, Crittenden's handpicked candidate, John Bell, also enjoyed a solid national reputation and a long record of compromise. A

Fig. 22. The Political Quadrille. (Library of Congress) In this parody of the political "dance," Dred Scott, the former slave involved in the famous court decision of 1857 plays the fiddle in the center. At the upper left John C. Breckinridge dances with Democratic incumbent and ally James Buchanan, depicted as a goat or (as he was nicknamed) "Buck." At the upper right Abraham Lincoln whirls with a black woman, an obvious reference to the Republican stand on slavery. At lower right John Bell dances with an Indian brave. This pairing may allude to Bell's previous work on Native American issues. At lower left Stephen A. Douglas dances with an Irishman, an allusion to his support among immigrants and allegations of his secret Catholicism.

convention of former Whigs met in Tennessee in February and nominated their native son for president.[20]

With Crittenden's support, Bell enjoyed a clear advantage, but other candidates might claim the new party's nomination. Foremost among them towered Sam Houston of Texas. A native of Tennessee and a longtime protégé of Andrew Jackson, Houston had won election as that state's governor before scandal sent him off to northern Mexico. There, he became president of the Republic of Texas and led the fight for independence. When Texas joined the Union, he served as governor and U.S. senator. Although his fame guaranteed recognition, his drinking and dueling diminished this physical giant's attractiveness as a presidential candidate. Houston's manner also hurt his chances; his refusal to allow his supporters to submit his name to the convention seemed to reflect hauteur rather than the honorable reluctance of a gentleman. And his affiliation with Jackson did not help him with the former allies of Henry Clay who made up much of the new party. Missouri nominated Edward Bates, a former congressman from that state. Bates, a native of Virginia, was a former Whig who had been mentioned for Cabinet posts and the vice presidency in the early 1850s. But he failed to gain much momentum with the Constitutional Unionists because he hedged his bets, seeming to hold out for a possible nomination by the Republicans. Indeed, Bates would go on to serve as attorney general in the Lincoln administration. Edward Everett of Massachusetts, another former Whig who had served as a governor, U.S. senator, and secretary of state under Millard Fillmore, garnered support from Northerners. Other possible candidates for the compromisers included Winfield Scott, the aging general who had headed up the unsuccessful Whig ticket in 1852, and William C. Rives, a Virginia Democrat turned Whig who had served in the House of Representatives and the U.S. Senate, and as minister to France. And despite his refusal to run, many still favored Crittenden, hoping that he would change his mind if the party nominated him.[21]

In Baltimore, Houston's supporters fought hard to win the nomination and the first ballot reflected the divisions in the new party, with Bell taking 68½ votes, Houston 57, Crittenden 28, and Everett 25, and the rest scattered among native sons such as Rives and Everett. With 128 votes needed to win, the first ballot demonstrated that Houston enjoyed enough support to be a serious challenger for the nomination, especially because first ballots rarely decided the contest and convention delegates often used their first votes to honor their state's candidate. On the next ballot, taken on the second day of the convention, the Virginia delegation asked to be allowed time for consultation before casting their votes. The rest of the states represented cast their ballots. Houston gained votes, moving up to 68, but Bell took 125, only three short of the nomination. The Virginia delegation then announced that it gave 13 votes to John Bell, giving him a total of 138 and the nomination. The Cincinnati newspaper reporter Murat Halstead, who attended all of the party conventions in 1860, reported that the hall erupted into "a great clamor of applause, a tearing roar of cheers, a violent stamping—bedlam broke loose." After a glowing speech in support of Bell by a Tennessee delegate, Edward Everett of Massachusetts won the vice-presidential nomination by acclamation.[22]

Thanks to the split in the Democratic convention, which had made it impossible for that party to nominate a candidate, the Constitutional Union nominees were the first in the field in 1860. Historians continue to insist that the Bell-Everett ticket "could not have been calculated to generate much enthusiasm" and that the candidates were too old. Indeed, even Bell's biographer argued that the nomination of Bell "was probably an unwise move." The presidential candidate was sixty-four years old and his running mate was sixty-six, confirming the taunts of opponents who called the Constitutional Union organization a party of old men. Furthermore, Bell's stands on the issues throughout the past decade meant that many of the extremists in the other parties hated and distrusted him. Proslavery Southern Democrats and abolitionist Republicans disliked him, the former because of his compromise positions, the latter because he owned slaves. That meant they would never support him. Nearly everyone agreed that Bell and Everett were solid, conservative, effective political leaders and they received their deserved respect. But they lacked the kind of charisma and influence wielded by Crittenden and, as it turned out, by the other candidates for president.[23]

But to dismiss the ticket as too old and too bland, to argue that their strengths were also their weaknesses is to miss the point that the Constitutional Union Party was an attempt to revive the Whigs and to save the Union through the politics of compromise. The candidates had to be moderate compromisers hated by the extremists in the other parties. Their appeal lay in the fact that they were not enthusiastic demagogues or radicals who would destroy the country to achieve their ends. The goal was to attract enough support to make it impossible for either the Democrats or Republicans to win the election. Once the moderates in those two parties realized that they could not elect their own candidate, cooler heads would prevail and they would turn to the compromisers to save the Union. Northern Democrats, moderate Republicans, and moderate Southern Democrats, combined with Know-Nothings and Southern Whigs, might swing the election. If Bell and Everett proved unable to win, the Constitutional Unionists would fuse with other moderates to elect the candidate of another party dedicated to compromise and the Union. Success meant compromise; it meant asking all to give up something for the virtue of the

Union. And all would win something as well, because they might deny their political enemies a victory even as they recognized that they could not win themselves. All of this fitted well within the ideology of compromise that had marked the Whigs from their inception. Far from being too old and too unexciting, the Constitutional Union ticket was perfect for the party: respectable, capable, offensive to radicals and extremists in both sections, but acceptable to moderates on all sides. Above all, the ticket solidly represented the politics of compromise.

The reception John Bell received following his nomination belied the charge that he did not generate much enthusiasm. He and his wife, Jane, had gone to Baltimore and stayed at a nearby hotel throughout the convention. On his trip home to Tennessee, large crowds greeted the candidate during his frequent stops, where he made short speeches to the cheering throngs. The large numbers of women in the audiences allowed the campaign to claim widespread support: mid-nineteenth-century political culture valued the attendance of women, and candidates who did not draw females were considered weak and undeserving of votes. Beautiful women (often interpreted along class and racial lines to mean well-to-do, white women) attending a campaign speech meant that the candidate enjoyed the support of the ideal female (usually defined as a supportive, pious, chaste, mild-mannered, submissive lady). Such notions also allowed his opponents to insult Bell because some critics thought his wife, Jane, was ugly. They also knew her to be shrewd and ambitious, which brought further criticism. Women might participate, but they had to remain within traditional bounds. Appearing to be too ambitious made Jane Bell unseemly in the patriarchal eyes of the time. In politics, appearance mattered, and Bell's own looks drew criticism as well. Balding, rather overweight, with a mouth that seemed too small for his face, he could not be called handsome. When combined with his aloof, calculating, cold manner, his appearance did little to help the Constitutional Unionist candidate.[24]

In keeping with his conservatism, Bell's campaign generally held to the traditional style of politics. The candidate did not campaign actively, letting his surrogates do most of the talking for him. Some scholars have argued that this was a political ploy, designed to keep him silent so that he could attract more votes by refusing to take a stand on the issues. This argument ignores the context of the political tradition at the time and the fact that, of the other three major candidates in 1860, only Stephen Douglas campaigned openly—and he was widely criticized for doing so. Bell's style emphasized his conservative nature, and his seeming lack of substance on the issues underscored the fact that he stood for compromise.[25]

Still, the candidate did give the obligatory speeches in response to gathered crowds outside his hotels. Shortly after the convention, he stopped in Philadelphia, where a large crowd gathered outside his hotel to hear the candidate's remarks. Bell appeared on the balcony and spoke at length about the recent convention and his privilege of serving as the Constitutional Union Party candidate. His speech struck the tone of his campaign and mostly stuck to the party line. He asked his listeners to "allow me to address a few words to you, without touching upon those questions about which there may be great differences of opinion, even in this Assembly, I would like to call your attention to the causes which have led to the assembly at Baltimore recently." Bell derided the other parties, saying that the recent convention was not that of the Democrats, was "not the Republican Party, it is not the American Party, it is not the Whig Party." No, the cause that brought that recent convention together was none of the established parties, but was rather to establish a new party. He asked the crowd, "What party is it that is to be the popular party?" Someone in the audience called out, "The Constitutional Union Party."[26]

Bell responded, "Yes, we trust it is to be the party of the country, of the Constitution. . . . It is the cause of the Union, the party of the Union, which we hope the people will inaugurate. I trust they will." Voices from the crowd cried out "They will! They have!" The candidate went on, praising his new party and arguing that they were men of wisdom and good sense who held to cherished principles. The Constitutional Unionists were sacrificing their personal interests for the good of the country, answering the call of duty out of concern for the present and future of the United States. They hoped "to allay the existing threatening dissensions and alienations to call back the country to the true objects of Government and the true purposes for which it was instituted." These true conservatives pointed to the past for the good of the future. They extolled the virtues of the American political tradition, calling for compromise "instead of exhausting their time in distracting topics and discussions upon abstract questions, chiefly, to the neglect of the great vital and material interests of every section of the Union." The new party stood in stark contrast to the others, which sought power and used sectionalism to their own advantage, but also "to the dis-

Fig. 23. Bell Campaign Banner, 1860. (Library of Congress)

paragement of the country, to the withdrawal of vigilance and watchfulness from the conduct of public affairs." Although he denied that his new organization was the Whig Party, it clearly stood for the Whig principles to which Bell and men such as Clay and Crittenden had so long adhered.[27]

Although their opponents derided the Constitutional Unionists as "old men," the party actually attracted a wide age range of supporters and leaders, including many vigorous operatives in the prime of life.[28] And the older men who did join the party were often elder statesmen who brought a wealth of experience to the campaign. They knew how to organize a party and a campaign and knew what it took to win. Speeches, pamphlets, parades, and campaign banners all required organization. Campaigns relied on political clubs and the endorsement of important leaders to rally voters to their cause. Whole families turned out to hear speeches. The ladies participated as well, attending rallies and sometimes forming political clubs for women, especially in the North. Although limited to the traditional activities allowed to them, they pitched in by making banners, cheering for speakers, and baking pies for the political barbecues. Women had to be careful not to cheer too loudly; that would make them appear masculine and detract from the campaign. They were allowed to participate—but only

Fig. 24. Bell and
Everett, Grand
National Union
Banner for
1860. (Library
of Congress)

if they remained within the proper roles that society prescribed for them. Still, in the mid-nineteenth century, politics was a family affair, and non-voting women and children joined the men who cast the ballots in supporting their favorite candidate.

Some activities remained exclusively male, especially Election Day, which often became physical, with violent brawls disrupting the voting. The 1860 campaign featured marching clubs that supported their candidates by marching and chanting at rallies and intimidating opponents. Their tendency to fight each other and resort to violence to break up their opponents'

Fig. 25. The Union, the Constitution and the Enforcement of the Laws. Bell and Everett Banner. (Library of Congress)

rallies led some to consider them paramilitary organizations. Northern Democrats in the "Little Giants" and the "Chloroformers" rivaled the famous Lincoln "Wide Awakes " and the "Rail Splitters." In the South, Breckinridge's "National Democratic Volunteers" marched for their candidate. To match their opponents, the Constitutional Unionists fielded the "Bell Ringers," the "Bell-Everetters," the "Union Sentinels," and the "Minute Men."[29]

The compromisers kept to tradition by publishing a campaign biography of Bell that included a sketch of Everett's life as well. Usually dismissed by scholars as too short and too biased, the book actually provides a clear view of what motivated John Bell in 1860. To be sure, it was one sided and biased in his favor, but it conveyed his Whig ideology of compromise. Entitled *The Life, Speeches, and Public Services of Hon. John Bell,* the book began by noting that "the emergency in which the country is now placed is one that requires skillful pilotage at the helm of State" and that "Strife and partisanship are rife; politics is but another word for discord; at the North and at the South passion rages." Indeed, the campaign argued that, "European senators comment openly . . . on the lamentable state of affairs that prevails here, and warn the reformers of the results to which republicanism has already led; English journals . . . openly proclaim that the democratic States of America are a failure." After several pages spent decrying the situation and warning that the ship of state was sinking, the book noted that at this moment of crisis that "a number of men, honest, upright, known for their long public services, their unblemished integrity, and their unquestioned patriotism, have nominated for the Presidency John Bell of Tennessee." The campaign claimed that Bell had been nominated by "many from the North and the South, old Democrats, and old Whigs, and former members of the American party" and by those who were "impelled by the desperate state of the country [to] make now a strong effort to save it from disunion." Bell was the fitting candidate because, as a native of Tennessee, "he was neither from the extreme south nor the extreme north; his birth-place is neutral ground."[30]

The biography went on to describe Bell's early life and career, praising him for keeping "his head clear from prejudices either towards one side or the other." He also possessed "a peculiar trait of" character, "a freedom from undue partiality; a really unbiased judgment: always moderate, calm, and conservative, amid the wild strife of party, he was conscientious, and unmoved by any considerations save those of patriotism and honor." In other words, Bell was a moderate, the perfect compromise candidate. Against those who charged him with "fluctuations" on the issues, the biographer shot back that Bell was "proof against such attacks" and that he "calmly but determinately persisted in his course." Far from waffling or shifting with the political winds, Bell had remained consistent. For that reason, "he is to-day the candidate of the party whose rallying word is conservatism; which is eminently the moderate one, which goes all lengths with neither side, and is content to bear the reproaches . . . from the more violent adherents both of the South and the North." In such passages, the Bell campaign expressed the Whig ideology of compromise.[31]

Throughout, this short biography repeatedly emphasized the candidate's moderate stands and politics of compromise. The book portrayed Bell as consistent, independent, honorable, intelligent, calm, reasonable, practical, and always moderate and ready to compromise in order to achieve the greater good of uniting the country. Throughout his career, his campaign maintained, he had fought to "stem the current of violence and disunion." Whatever his stance on the sectional issues surrounding the extension of slavery, he "endeavored incessantly to allay the troubled waves, to pour oil on the waters of strife." During the crisis in 1850, he "brought in a compromise bill, but, without any vanity or pique, laid it aside when he discovered that it did not prove acceptable; for with him personal honor or success was always subordinate to patriotism." When his own plan failed, he "favored the great compromise measures of 1850." In 1854, Bell opposed Douglas's "famous Nebraska bill and the repeal of the Missouri compromise." He denounced the Kansas-Nebraska Act "as a violation of a compact fairly sealed . . . as an imperiling of the peace and safety of the Union." He "had endeavored successfully to recommend the compromises effected by Clay and Webster," but he now feared that the Douglas plan would result in bloodshed.[32]

Despite his devotion to compromise, Bell "never swerved in his fealty to the South or her institutions." Far from being an opponent of slavery, in his many speeches he maintained "the peculiar institution to be, in many of its peculiarities, excellent, and expresses an opinion that abstract notions must not be allowed to conflict with the practicalities" of the system. Accused of being "too much inclined to yield, too willing to accede for the sake of peace," Bell remained a supporter of slavery. But "he has indeed always been willing to yield somewhat; he has openly avowed this as a principle." John Bell stood proudly on the politics of compromise and "he boasts that he is not impracticable." Instead, he promoted the Whig ideology: "Rather than that the fabric of our union should be destroyed, he has been ready to sacrifice several minor things; emulous in this of the character of Clay and Webster and other worthies of that high sort." Bell hoped "to obey the parting mandate of Washington and know no north and no south; he is, and has always been, emphatically a Union man, a Union lover, a Union preserver." Appendices containing some of Bell's speeches and explanations of his views on various issues throughout his career followed the brief biography. In every instance, the campaign portrayed him as a moderate promoter of compromise dedicated to the preservation of the Union.[33]

Other campaign literature published by the party followed the same line of argument, presenting Bell's Whig ideology of compromise and his moderate stand on the issues as a virtue and the means of saving the Union from impending disaster. Opponents at the time and later historians argued that Bell avoided slavery, the major issue of the day. But he did not avoid it by remaining silent. His campaign answered the charges of avoiding slavery head on in July 1860, when the chairman of the party's national committee, Alexander R. Boteler, published a pamphlet entitled

John Bell's Record. Dedicated to "a full exposition of Mr. Bell's course on the Slavery question," the publication aimed "to silence any man who may charge Mr. Bell with every having enunciated a principle or advocated a doctrine in regard to Slavery, which should render him unworthy of the confidence and support of his fellow-citizens, in any section of our country." What followed was a moderate position on the issue of slavery that promoted compromise in order to save the Union.[34]

Noting the importance of slavery as an issue, the pamphlet began by arguing that in his public life, Bell "has shown firmness, forbearance, consideration, foresight, far reaching thought, and in a high degree the spirit of conciliation and compromise. He has ever shown himself a man of the Union." Drawing on Bell's speeches over the course of his long career, the pamphlet trumpeted the politics of compromise. In an 1829 congressional speech, the young Tennessee politician argued for "the principle of compromise" and stated that he would "adhere to it as the only principle by which the States were able to agree upon any compact." He urged his fellow congressmen to "renounce the extremes of both these great parties, as dangerous to order and union." And Bell thought that the man who "shall succeed in placing himself at the head of a great constitutional party, and shall become the advocate of the administration of the Government upon the principle of compromise, as it was understood to have operated in the formation of the Constitution" would "deserve the highest gratitude of his country." There, in the pages of the congressional debates from more than thirty years before, were the same principles that motivated John Bell in 1860. Boteler noted the irony of the fact that "more than thirty years after the utterance of these opinions, "a great Constitutional party" should rise up" and nominate Bell himself "to lead them in a contest for "the administration of the Government upon the principle of compromise, as it was understood to have operated in the formation of the Constitution!"

Three years after stating his principle of compromise on the floor of the House of Representatives, Bell again sought to save the Union during the nullification crisis. Lamenting the fact that "in the intensity of the conflict between the extremes," those who were vanquished "cry out, and departing from the spirit of the Constitution, proclaim their determination to accept no compromise," Bell noted that, "the victors, the majority . . . announce their determination to yield nothing." Such positions spelled the doom of the republic. Only "a moderate party of sufficient strength and influence to turn the balance between the extremes" could save the Union by using "some portion of that spirit of moderation and compromise which are characteristics of the constitution itself." Over the course of his long career in politics, Bell had stood on the same ground, taking moderate positions and urging compromise, denouncing the abolitionists on the one hand and the Southern fire-eaters on the other. Throughout the 1830s and 1840s, he held fast to his republicanism and his Whig ideology of compromise. In 1850, he again called for "compromise and conciliation" in long speeches that dealt with the issue of slavery and its territorial expansion. In 1854, he opposed the Kansas-Nebraska bill and argued against repealing the Missouri Compromise, which he saw as a political answer to the issue forged by Northern men who hated slavery but who "respect and revere the Constitution and its compromises." Far from being silent on the issue of slavery, Bell had engaged it repeatedly and forcefully over three decades in politics.[35]

His surrogates also made the case for Bell as a moderate proponent of compromise in their speeches, arguing that a vote for Lincoln or for Breckinridge was a vote for disunion. In the South, the Constitutional Unionists appealed to Southern honor, arguing that Breckinridge's campaign aimed at subverting democracy and destroying the Union. In the North, the compromisers pointed to Bell's moderate record on slavery and his strong commitment to Whig principles. Everywhere, his campaigners trumpeted that he was Union man, dedicated to the true spirit of the Constitution, to the politics of compromise. None was more effective than John J. Crittenden, whose widespread popularity brought out large crowds to hear him speak on Bell's behalf. The Kentuckian received invitations to speak from across the country, with the Constitutional Unionists hoping to capitalize on his reputation. He chose to concentrate his efforts in the border states and Upper South, especially Kentucky and Tennessee, where Bell was strongest. Crittenden and other Bell surrogates faced the criticisms of the Southern Democrats who supported John C. Breckinridge and the Republicans working for Abraham Lincoln. The Breckinridge camp excoriated Bell as a traitor to the South, publishing a pamphlet that charged the Constitutional Unionist with complicity in the abolitionist cause and denouncing him as a politician without principles. The Republicans published their own attacks, accusing Bell of being a proslavery advocate who always "stood by" and allowed the extension of the peculiar institution. In an ironic twist, even his opponents agreed that Bell had been consistent throughout his career, although they each interpreted his moderate politics of compromise as antithetical to their own positions.[36]

As the campaign wore on, it became clear that Bell would not be able to pull enough support away from the Democrats and Republicans to win on his own. The Constitutional Unionists began to realize that despite their best efforts, the election was splitting along sectional lines, with Northerners choosing between Douglas and Lincoln and Southerners voting for either Breckinridge or Bell. Without support in the North, Bell had no chance of defeating Lincoln, which would lead to disunion. As early as July, Bell feared that the Republican nominee would win. Writing to Boteler, he worried that Pennsylvania would go for Lincoln. Although he argued that the state's iron and coal industries needed Southern markets, it seemed likely that Keystone State was "infatuated with some cause" and leaned toward the Republican. Bell thought that voters in Pennsylvania, like other Northerners, simply wanted change. They were tired of the corruption of the Buchanan administration and weary of Democratic rule. Thus, they were motivated by "the passion for novelty in part—for seeing a new power at Washington.—A new dynasty on the throne, & the gratification of seeing the hated Democracy—pretty nearly synonymous with *Southern Oligarchy* (in their vocabulary) overthrown." The Constitutional Union candidate feared that the "opposition to [a Lincoln] administration *will be the whole South*—yes the whole South, in 30 days after the election." Southerners "would feel his election to be an insult to them," and their sense of honor would require them to resist. At best, Lincoln might be able to hold the country together, but there would be no hope of improvement. Southern opposition would prevent the Republican president from carrying out his agenda or any real legislation of any kind. At worst, Lincoln's election would drive the sectional wedge deeper, and secession would dissolve the Union.[37]

Ever ready to compromise for the good of the Union, Bell remained open to plans for a fusion with one or more of the other candidates. If the Northern states such as Pennsylvania "cannot be made to see their true policy, & will still incline" to Lincoln, "as I greatly fear . . . then there is no other way in which his election can be defeated but by a fusion of several branches of the opposition in N. Jersey, New York, Connecticut, R. Island, Pennsylvania, Ohio, Indiana." By "running but one ticket in these states, against Lincoln" the opposition might defeat the Republican outright or at least deny him an Electoral College majority. That would throw the election into the House of Representatives, where Bell himself stood a good chance of winning the presidency. Fusion schemes and scenarios had been part of the Constitutional Unionist thinking from the new party's inception. Crittenden and other leaders initially hoped to revive the Whig Party by fusing with the old Whigs in the Republican fold. Although Seward and a few other former Whigs turned Republicans seemed open to that suggestion as late as the summer of 1860, they abandoned the idea when a Lincoln victory became quite likely. The compromisers then turned to Northern Democrats, particularly Stephen A. Douglas, hoping to fuse the two campaigns. Although Bell's chief rival in the South was Breckinridge, his campaign also considered fusion with the Southern Democratic candidate. In fact, one possible scheme involved bringing together all three of the major opponents to Lincoln in order to deny the Republican a victory.[38]

All of these fusion scenarios rested on numerical calculations. For Lincoln to achieve victory, he needed to add 35 votes in the Electoral College to the 114 taken by the Republican John C. Frémont, who had won eleven Northern states in 1856. Frémont had lost only five Northern states: Pennsylvania, Indiana, Illinois, New Jersey, and California. New free states such as Minnesota and Oregon made Lincoln's task a bit easier, because both seemed likely to vote Republican. If he carried Minnesota, as expected, the Rail Splitter needed 34 more electoral votes. Pennsylvania was the key prize with 27 votes, so taking it would require only one of the others, with Indiana (13) and Illinois (11) the most likely to go for Lincoln. Fusion centered on denying the Republican the Electoral College majority by defeating him in Pennsylvania and/or New York (35), both big states that made a Lincoln victory possible. Taking as many other Northern states as possible would make the job easier. Stephen A. Douglas rivaled Lincoln in the North; thus, he had to be on board for any fusion plan to work. Bell's strength lay in the Upper South and the border states. He also enjoyed pockets of strength in the Deep South, where Breckinridge held the advantage. For fusion to work out, the campaigns had to agree to cooperate and to have their electors cast their ballots for the candidate most likely to defeat Lincoln in a given state. They also had to be sure to deny one another a victory, throwing the election into the House of Representatives. There, with each state casting only one vote, Bell stood a good chance of winning, because conservative and moderate elements of all parties would see that fusion was working and support the possibility of a compromise to save the Union. If not, and no candidate was elected, then the election would move to the Senate, which would elect a vice president who would then become the new president. In that body, it seemed likely that the Democratic majority would elect Joseph Lane of Oregon, Breckinridge's running mate. Although not ideal for the Constitutional Unionists, Lane seemed preferable to either Lincoln or Breckinridge. The Oregon politician held proslavery views, but at least he was a Northerner and that could be enough to save the Union.[39]

Fusion efforts continued throughout the campaign, usually on the state level, especially in New York and New Jersey. Of course, the campaigns were most open to the idea in states where their candidate's chances were slim. Where their man seemed likely to do well, they did not want to entertain the possibility of fusion. This made things difficult. Douglas did not want to combine unless it helped him. Breckinridge did not want to cooperate unless it pushed him closer to victory. The Republicans had rejected the plan already because they thought that Lincoln could win on his own. Even the compromisers found it difficult to compromise from a position of strength, because the Constitutional Unionists refused to consider such plans seriously in states such as Virginia, Tennessee, and Kentucky, where Bell was strongest. In critical Pennsylvania, the ever more unpopular Buchanan still carried enough weight to make fusion possible in some parts of the state. In New York, which might render all of the other numbers irrelevant if Lincoln could be defeated there, the campaigns achieved fusion among all three of the major opponents to the Republican nominee. After several rounds of negotiations, the agreement called for dividing the fusion-ticket electors in proportion to each candidate's strength in the Empire State, with 18 for Douglas, 10 for Bell, and 7 for Breckinridge. Promises made privately assured both Douglas and Bell that the other's electors would cast their votes for him if it looked like it would be enough to give him an outright victory. With Democrats controlling New York City and a large portion of the state's economy tied to the South, it seemed quite possible that New York would reject Lincoln in favor of the fusion ticket, opening the door to victory for any one of the three candidates cooperating in it.[40]

In the end, of course, fusion failed. The anti-Republican ticket in New York lost to Lincoln, who carried the other Northern states as well. With 1,865,908 popular votes (39.8 percent), the Republican also won 180 electoral ballots, far more than the 152 needed to win the election. In the popular vote, Douglas finished second, with 1,380,201 (29.4 percent). However, so much of his vote came in the Northern states where he lost to Lincoln that he managed to get only 12 electoral votes—nine from Missouri, where he won, and three from New Jersey, thanks to a partial fusion plan. Breckinridge finished third in the popular vote with 848,019 (18.1 percent), and taking 72 in the Electoral College. Bell finished last in the popular election, with only 590,901 votes (12.6 percent), but carrying Tennessee, Kentucky, and Virginia gave him 39 electoral votes. When the popular vote totals are broken down to include fusion, the fusion ticket took 595,846 votes, with Douglas getting 979,425, Breckinridge 669,472, and Bell 576,414.[41]

As expected, Bell's greatest strength was in the Upper South and the border states Those areas had the most to lose in a war between the North and South. He did not fare so well in the lower Midwest, in states like Indiana, Ohio, and Illinois, although cultural attachments to the South in areas of those Northern states served to divide them internally along sectional lines. The Constitutional Unionist won three states outright: Virginia, Kentucky, and his home state of Tennessee. As historians have noted, he did very well in Missouri, where he lost to Douglas by a mere 429 votes. Only the combined votes for Lincoln and Douglas denied him a victory in Maryland, where he narrowly lost to Breckinridge by 722 ballots. North Carolina was also close, where the Southern Democrat beat Bell by about 3,700 votes. That would have added 27 electoral votes to his total, giving him 66 and moving him into second place ahead of Breckinridge and reducing Douglas to a mere three votes in the Electoral College. But none of that mattered. It would have been relevant only if fusion had worked. It did not.[42]

Various attempts at gauging the results have noted that Bell ran well in the South. A number of scholars have expressed surprise that the Constitutional Unionist did best in Southern counties where slaveholding was most concentrated and that he had an edge in urban areas, where Unionist sentiment remained strongest across the country. Breckinridge enjoyed his greatest support in areas of fewer slaveholders and in rural parts of the South. Those historians who take an economic view argue that "old wealth" supported Bell, whereas "new wealth" voted for Breckinridge. But other scholars dismiss such notions in favor of the ideology of republicanism, arguing that the defense of white liberty and equality mattered more than class and wealth. Party identity deserves more consideration, because Bell ran better in Whig areas, whereas Breckinridge did best in Democratic strongholds, although there were exceptions to this general rule. On the surface, it would seem that those in the areas that would be the battleground in a sectional conflict of arms favored the candidate running to avoid a civil war. Honor also mattered, with Breckinridge and Bell vying for respect and making their campaigns out to be a defense of

Southern honor against those who slighted it. Breckinridge claimed to defend honor against the North and the Republicans; Bell's camp defended it against those who would drive the South to secession. Such analysis of voter behavior breaks down general applications of interpretations about class or age or slave ownership. Instead, we need to point to that for which the Bell campaign stood. In 1860, those who wanted compromise voted for the Constitutional Unionist. Ultimately, however, Bell's hopes for victory declined into a slim chance at defeating Lincoln. And on Election Day, the majority of voters rejected compromise.[43]

To understand why Americans refused compromise requires turning to the context of the election itself. Many Northern voters simply wanted change. They were tired of Democratic dominance, disgusted by the corruption of the Buchanan administration, and sick of the Slave Power's efforts to expand slavery. Many Southerners believed that they must defend their honor against abolitionism and "Black Republicans." In both sections, new ideologies replaced the politics of compromise, with free-labor and proslavery ideas spreading rapidly among voters looking to explain the situation and their views of it. Compromise no longer appealed to voters seeking victory. The idea that everyone must sacrifice something for the greater good did not enjoy the support of Americans now seeing politics in moral terms. Compromising on ideology meant selling out on basic principles, on core beliefs. To do so was unthinkable and indicated immorality, corruption, and dishonor. No doubt a minority of voters in both the North and South did hope for disunion, believing that the time had come to settle the issue of slavery at last. Despite the fact that a majority of Americans still held fast to the Union and believed in the Constitution, they no longer interpreted those terms in the way that the Whig Party had defined them. Instead of compromise, they wanted the Union on their own terms and desired that the Constitution benefit their interests. To many Southerners, John Bell was dangerous, a threat to their institutions and way of life. He called for selling out on the issues that mattered most. For most Northerners, the Constitutional Unionist represented more of the same old corruption, more acquiescence to the Slave Power. Instead of seeing the compromiser as the moderate candidate, voters argued that their own favorite—Breckinridge, Douglas, or Lincoln—was the true conservative, the true moderate, the true Union man, the true defender of the Constitution. In such a context, it was not surprising that Bell lost. Rather, it was more surprising that he did so well.[44]

Having lost the election, Bell at first attempted to stay the course with compromise and moderation. Like other Constitutional Unionists, he hoped that Crittenden might somehow pull out a compromise to prevent disunion. But the Kentuckian's efforts at compromise in the U.S. Senate's Committee of Thirteen fell short. At the same time that those last-minute efforts were underway, South Carolina seceded; soon, the other Deep South states followed. In April s1861, the Civil War began. He denounced secession but also criticized Lincoln and the Republicans. In a December letter he wrote in response to a request that he visit Mississippi to provide his views while that state considered secession, he argued that about a third of those who voted for Lincoln did so because they hated the Democrats. Another third voted for the Republican as a means of expressing their views about Kansas and the repeal of the Missouri Compromise in Douglas's legislation. The final third of Lincoln voters were the real danger, Bell thought, because they were the radicals who hated both slavery and the South. Lincoln posed a very real threat, but the compromiser thought that the South could still find relief within the Union. He argued that secession was "but another name for . . . *revolution.*" He urged caution and advised that Mississippi stay in the Union. Lincoln's election had been constitutional. Constitutional remedies remained for the South.[45]

By April, when the war began at Fort Sumter and Tennessee left the Union, Bell had changed his mind. Lincoln's mobilization of troops to smash the rebellion convinced the compromiser to become a rebel. Although he still insisted that secession was a "heresy" and opposed joining the Confederacy, he came out publicly in favor of Tennessee's action and urged preparation for war. Here, again, he stood on the old Whig principles, interpreting the Constitution as a compact, with the concept of dual sovereignty allowing the state to do what it did. But few understood such fine points of federalism. Instead, they saw his views changing with the winds. Many of his old friends denounced him as a hypocrite, arguing that he had stood for the Union and the Constitution only as long as he had a chance of winning the election. Once that chance was gone, he turned coat against the very principles that he supposedly held so dear. Many of his old enemies criticized him from the other side, disgusted that the man they considered a traitor to the Southern cause now tried to speak out in partial favor of it. The longtime defender of compromise waffled so much that no one liked him, it seemed.[46]

And so he retired. His health had been declining for years and his political activities had worn him out. He put his mines in Kentucky up for sale
and returned home to Nashville. His sons and other male relatives joined
the Confederate service, and he followed the war as a father. Forced to flee
the city when the Union forces approached, he took his family to safety in
a rural area. Still hoping for compromise, in 1862 he considered going to
Washington, D.C., with a peace plan, but he eventually canceled the trip.
The fortunes of war forced the family to move multiple times, which did
not help Bell's health. When the war ended, he tried to revive his business interests and lived out his days in a modest home in Stewart County,
Tennessee. He died in 1869. Among the eulogies offered were memorials
by former friends and foes alike, all praising Bell as a man of honor, remembered for being courteous, fair, impartial, and moderate. Those closest to him insisted that he remained a true Union man and supported
the rebellion only because he yielded to intense pressure. However, neglect of him had already begun. Few talked about his legacy, unsure about
how to interpret him and his actions. By then, talk of rebuilding the Whig
Party had moved to the very margins of the political arena. His party, the
party of Clay and Webster, was long dead. Unfortunately for John Bell, his
time had passed, and he outlived the age in which the Whig Party forged
its chief principle. In 1860, he hoped to revive that party under a new
name and stood strong for the politics of compromise. But Americans had
moved on and did not vote for the man who was the last true Whig candidate for president.[47]

1. The author would like to thank John Scott Parkinson for his help in the formulation of this essay, especially through the narrative he composed in his symposium
paper, "Truly a Dark Horse: John Bell and the Presidential Election of 1860," delivered
at the Civil War Study Group Symposium hosted by the Institute for the Study of War
and Diplomacy at the University of Indianapolis, September 17, 2010. One sign of
the scholarly neglect of the Bell campaign is the fact that there is only one full-length
biography of this Tennessee politician, published in 1950: Joseph H. Parks, *John Bell
of Tennessee* (Baton Rouge: Louisiana State Univ. Press, 1950). For some of the few
studies of the Constitutional Union Party, see John Burgess Stabler, "A History of the
Constitutional Union Party: A Tragic Failure" (PhD diss., Columbia Univ., 1954); John
V. Mering, "The Slave-State Constitutional Unionists and the Politics of Consensus,"
Journal of Southern History 43, no. 3 (August 1977): 395–410; James L. Huston,
"Southerners Against Secession: The Arguments of the Constitutional Unionists in

1850–51," *Civil War History* 46, no. 4 (December 2000): 281–99. The quotation from the party platform is from Stabler, "History of the Constitutional Union Party," 335. An excellent and sophisticated work that traces the roots of the Constitutional Union Party and places it in the broader ideological context of republicanism is Peter B. Knupfer, *The Union as It Is: Constitutional Unionism and Sectional Compromise, 1787–1861* (Chapel Hill: Univ. of North Carolina Press, 1991). For examples of the scholarly tendency to dismiss Bell respectfully, see Emerson David Fite, *The Presidential Campaign of 1860* (1911; repr., Port Washington, N.Y.: Kennikat Press, 1967), esp. 186–87; Douglas R. Egerton, *Year of Meteors: Stephen Douglas, Abraham Lincoln, and the Election that Brought on the Civil War* (New York: Bloomsbury Press, 2010), 83–101. A thorough, but still dismissive treatment is found in Ollinger Crenshaw, *The Slave States in the Presidential Election of 1860* (Baltimore: Johns Hopkins Univ. Press, 1945), 29–34; 40–41; 63; passim. Darcy G. Richardson argues that Bell was the "original peace candidate" and that his performance was "heroic"; see Richardson, "Rising from the Ashes: John Bell and the Constitutional Unionists of 1860," in *Others: Third-Party Politics from the Nation's Founding to the Rise and Fall of the Greenback-Labor Party,* (New York: iUniverse, Inc., 2004), 323. A serious but all too brief treatment of the Constitutional Union effort in 1860 can be found in Carl N. Degler, *The Other South: Southern Dissenters in the Nineteenth Century* (New York: Harper & Row, 1974), 158–63, in which the author argued that Bell's campaign "provides one of the most useful measures of the extent of Unionism in the South on the eve of the Civil War" and that "the Bell candidacy testified to the persistence of a strong Southern resistance to secession." Another important, but cursory exception to the tendency to dismiss Bell in the 1860 election is Roy F. Nichols, *The Stakes of Power, 1845–1877* (New York: Hill and Wang, 1961), 82–83. Nichols gave the Bell ticket little attention in his long and detailed treatment of the election in an earlier work (see Nichols, *The Disruption of American Democracy* [New York: Macmillan, 1948], 259–60, 340), but argued in his shorter study of the Civil War era that "[t]he Constitutional Union . . . improved the chances of the Republicans, not only by creating a third party, but also by driving a deeper wedge into the Democratic ranks." Nichols, *Stakes of Power,* 82. Degler and Nichols gave Bell's campaign fewer than seven pages between them. It was scant analysis, to be sure, but at least the Bell campaign mattered.

2. Egerton, *Year of Meteors,* 101. Lincoln was a Whig until the party's demise and gave a eulogy for Clay in 1852. For an important recent analysis of this oration, in which Lincoln ignored Clay's record of compromise and instead argued that he was a champion of liberty, see Eric Foner, *The Fiery Trial: Abraham Lincoln and American Slavery* (New York: Norton, 2010), 60–62. Foner's interpretation agrees with that of Michael S. Green, *Lincoln and the Election of 1860* (Carbondale: Southern Illinois Univ. Press, 2011). Ronald C. White Jr. discusses Clay's influence on Lincoln in *A. Lincoln: A Biography* (New York: Random House, 2009), 140–42. For Breckinridge's association with Clay, see my essay in chap. 3 of this book. Stephen A. Douglas tried to claim the mantle of Clay before 1860, including an attempt during his famous 1858 campaign against Lincoln for the Senate. For Douglas's effort, see Foner, *Fiery Trial,* 105. For the Whig formulation of the Union and the Constitution and compromise, see Peter B. Knupfer, *The Union as It Is,* esp. 119–57. In his essay on the election, Elting Morison noted that all of the candidates "were inheritors of the vision of Henry Clay"; see Morison, "Election of 1860," *History of American Presidential Elections, 1789–1968,* ed. Arthur M. Schlesinger Jr., vol. 2, *1848–1896* (New York: Chelsea House, 1971), 1101.

3. Parks, *John Bell of Tennessee*, 6–8.

4. Parks, *John Bell*, 9–23. There is an extensive literature on republicanism and the ways in which it decried corruption and called for virtue. For one example that explores republicanism's concern with corruption and its relationship to Southern honor, see Kenneth S. Greensberg, *Masters and Statesmen: The Political Culture of American Slavery* (Baltimore: Johns Hopkins Univ. Press, 1985). For more on republicanism and its application in the election of 1860, see the essay by Thomas E. Rodgers in chap. 6 of this book.

5. Parks, *John Bell of Tennessee*, 37–83. Also useful on Bell's congressional career is Norman L. Parks, *The Career of John Bell as Congressman from Tennessee, 1827–1841* (Nashville: Vanderbilt Univ. Libraries, 1942). The classic introduction to the literature on republicanism remains the now very dated Robert E. Shalhope, "Toward a Republican Synthesis: The Emergence of an Understanding of Republicanism in American Historiography," *William and Mary Quarterly* 29, no. 1 (January 1972): 49–80. See also Robert E. Shalhope, *The Roots of Democracy: American Thought and Culture, 1760–1800* (Boston: Twayne, 1990). Joel H. Silbey explored the ideology's significance in the nineteenth century in *The American Political Nation, 1838–1893* (Stanford: Stanford Univ. Press, 1991), esp. 10–22. A concise and useful synthesis of republicanism is in Harry L. Watson, *Liberty and Power: The Politics of Jacksonian America* (New York: Hill and Wang, 1990), 42–72. For examples of how Southerners applied republican ideology and used the fear of losing freedom and power to political advantage, see William J. Cooper Jr., *Liberty and Slavery: Southern Politics to 1860* (New York: Alfred A. Knopf, 1983); J. Mills Thornton III, *Politics and Power in a Slave Society: Alabama, 1800–1860* (Baton Rouge: Louisiana State Univ. Press, 1978); and Kenneth S. Greensberg, *Masters and Statesmen: The Political Culture of American Slavery* (Baltimore: Johns Hopkins Univ. Press, 1985). For an example of how critics have attacked the republicanism synthesis with profound insights, see Joyce Appleby, *Capitalism and the New Social Order: The Republican Vision of the 1790s* (New York: New York Univ. Press, 1984).

6. For the contest for the speakership, see Michael F. Holt, *The Rise and Fall of the American Whig Party: Jacksonian Politics and the Onset of the Civil War* (New York: Oxford Univ. Press, 1999), 42. Robert V. Remini discusses the speakership and Jackson's hatred of defectors in both *Andrew Jackson*, vol. 3, *The Course of American Democracy* (1984; repr., New York: History Book Club, 1998), 173–74 and in *Henry Clay: Statesman for the Union* (New York: Norton, 1991), 468–69. For Jackson's view of friendship, see Andrew Burstein, *The Passions of Andrew Jackson* (New York: Alfred A. Knopf, 2003).

7. Parks, *John Bell of Tennessee*, 131–93. Michael Holt argues that the Tennessee Whigs, led by Bell and White, cost Henry Clay the nomination in 1840 because they opposed party conventions. Thus, the state's delegation refused to attend, denying the Kentuckian crucial votes; see Holt, *Rise and Fall of the American Whig Party*, 103–4. For the death of Bell's first wife and his remarriage, see Parks, *John Bell of Tennessee*, 56, 114–17. For his work in 1844 and his subsequent election to the Senate, see Parks, *John Bell*, 203–7, 212–16.

8. For the principles of the Whig Party, see Holt, *Rise and Fall of the American Whig Party*, 49, 105, 952, passim. For Bell's views on the issues, see Parks, *John Bell of Tennessee*, 84–131. Parks repeatedly notes Bell's opposition to the patronage of the spoils system and his defense of the Constitution but does not interpret this as a philosophical consistency. Instead, he argues that Bell changed his views or was slow to develop his ideas; see *John Bell*, 7, 118–62, passim.

9. For Bell's opposition to the gag rule, see Parks, *John Bell*, 171–73. The quotation by Bell is in the *Congressional Debates* and is quoted in Parks, *John Bell*, 172.

10. Bell's opposition to the war with Mexico can be found in Park, *John Bell*, 217–39. The quotes are taken from Parks, *John Bell*, 225.

11. For Bell's support for the Compromise of 1850, see Parks, *John Bell*, 240–62. In this section of his biography, Parks shows how Bell truly embodied moderate politics in the Compromise of 1850, voting for some measures, not voting on others, supporting the extension of slavery in some aspects, opposing it in others.

12. Parks, *John Bell*, 289–92. For the politics of the 1850s and the destruction of the Second American Party System from an ethnocultural perspective that deemphasizes slavery, see Michael F. Holt, *The Political Crisis of the 1850s* (New York: Norton, 1978). For a more recent synthesis that restores the expansion of slavery as the key issue, see Michael S. Green, *Politics and America in Crisis: The Coming of the Civil War* (Santa Barbara: Praeger, 2010).

13. Parks, *John Bell of Tennessee*, 292, 314–18. The Douglas quote is from Green, *Politics and America in Crisis*, 74. A thorough account of the collapse of the Whigs is found in the final two chapters of Holt, *Rise and Fall of the American Whig Party*, 909–85.

14. For this view of Clay, see Knupfer, *The Constitution as It Is*, esp. 119–57, 158–200. The Democrat Stephen Douglas struggled to hold a very different view of the Union and the Constitution in forging a vision of egalitarian democracy; see James L. Huston, *Stephen A. Douglas and the Dilemmas of Democratic Equality* (New York: Rowman and Littlefield, 2007).

15. The best biography of Crittenden is Albert Dennis Kirwan, *John J. Crittenden: The Struggle for Union* (Lexington: Univ. of Kentucky Press, 1962), but see also Mrs. Chapman Coleman, *The Life of John J. Crittenden with Selections from His Correspondence and Speeches* (Philadelphia: J. B. Lippincott, 1873). Crittenden's sons took different sides in the Civil War, with one fighting for the Union and the other for the Confederacy. The family's division is the subject of Damon R. Eubank, *In the Shadow of the Patriarch: The John J. Crittenden Family in War and Peace* (Macon, Ga.: Mercer Univ. Press, 2009).

16. For more on the Know Nothings, see Tyler G. Anbinder, *Nativism and Slavery: The Northern Know Nothings and the Politics of the 1850s* (New York: Oxford Univ. Press, 1994); William E. Gienapp, *The Origins of the Republican Party, 1852–1856* (New York: Oxford Univ. Press, 1987), 69–102.

17. For Bell and the American Party, see Parks, *John Bell of Tennessee*, 303–7. Tyler Anbinder argues that "[t]he Constitutional Union party in the North was run almost exclusively by former Know Nothings," Anbinder, *Nativism and Slavery*, 269.

18. The fight for the speakership is covered in high drama and great detail in Nichols, *Disruption of American Democracy*, 270–75.

19. Kirwan, *John J. Crittenden*, 336–54.

20. Kirwan, *John J. Crittenden*, 336–56. For the Tennessee state convention in February 1860, see Egerton, *Year of Meteors*, 88.

21. For the various candidates for the nomination, see Kirwan, *John J. Crittenden*, 353; Egerton, *Year of Meteors*, 90–91; Parks, *John Bell of Tennessee*, 349–51.

22. For the balloting at the convention and Bell's nomination, see William B. Hesseltine, ed., *Three Against Lincoln: Murat Halstead Reports the Caucuses of 1860* (Baton Rouge: Louisiana State Univ. Press, 1960), 131–37.

23. Parks, *John Bell of Tennessee*, 356–57.

24. For women's role in the 1860 campaigns, see Erika Rozinek, "Trembling for the Nation: Illinois Women and the Election of 1860," *Constructing the Past* 2, vol. 1 (2001), art. 4. Rozinek discusses beautiful women as a point of pride for campaigns on p. 12. For Jane Bell being considered ugly and ambitious, see Egerton, *Year of Meteors,* 91. For Bell's appearance, see Bruce Chadwick, *Lincoln for President: An Unlikely Candidate, An Audacious Strategy, and the Victory No One Saw Coming* (Naperville, Ill.: Sourcebooks, 2009), 41. Just what role Jane Bell played in her husband's campaigns and career begs further investigation in light of her reputation as an ambitious woman and hints of her influence over him. Although the lack of papers makes it difficult to judge, the Bell marriage seems to have paralleled the complexities of the relationships explored in Carol K. Bleser and Lesley J. Gordon, eds., *Intimate Strategies of the Civil War: Military Commanders and Their Wives* (New York: Oxford Univ. Press, 2001).

25. Chadwick, *Lincoln for President,* 208–9.

26. "Presidential Speech of Hon. John Bell at Philadelphia," *New York Times,* May 14, 1860.

27. "Presidential Speech of Hon. John Bell."

28. Peter Knupfer, "Aging Statesmen and the Statesmanship of an Earlier Age: The Generational Roots of the Constitutional Union Party," in *Union and Emancipation: Essays on Politics and Race in the Civil War Era,* ed. David W. Blight and Brooks D. Simpson (Kent, Ohio: Kent State Univ. Press, 1997), 57; Richardson, "Rising from the Ashes," 273.

29. Rozinek, "Trembling for the Nation," discusses the role of women in the campaign. Elizabeth Varon has argued that the Bell campaign encouraged white women to influence the men around them to vote for the Constitutional Union candidate. See Elizabeth R. Varon, *We Mean to Be Counted: White Women and Politics in Antebellum Virginia* (Chapel Hill: Univ. of North Carolina Press, 1998), 144–46; A brief description of the marching clubs and their tendency to fight can be found in Reinhard H. Luthin, *The First Lincoln Campaign* (1944; repr., Gloucester, Mass.: Peter Smith, 1964), 173–74.

30. N.a., *Bell and Everett. The Regular Campaign Edition, known as "The Union Edition" of The Life, Speeches, and Public Services of Hon. John Bell, together with a life of Hon. Edward Everett, Union Candidates for the Offices of President and Vice-President of the United States* (New York: Rudd & Carleton, 1860), 5–7.

31. *Bell and Everett,* 13–14.

32. *Bell and Everett,* 29–30.

33. *Bell and Everett,* 30–31, 33–96.

34. For an example of historians who claim that Bell avoided the issue of slavery, see Elting Morison, who argued that "John Bell sought no solution at all" on "the central issue"; Morison, "Election of 1860," 1099; Alexander R. Boteler, *John Bell's Record* (Washington, D.C.: W. H. Moore, 1860), 1.

35. Boteler, *John Bell's Record,* 2–26. For the sake of clarity, I have eliminated the italics that Boteler added for emphasis.

36. For Crittenden's campaigning on Bell's behalf, see Kirwan, *John J. Crittenden,* 360–63. The Southern Democratic attack was published by the National Democratic Executive Committee: n.a., *The Public Record and Past History of John Bell and Edward Everett* (Washington, D.C.: McGill and Witherow, 1860). The Republican attack was launched in Henry Wilson, *The Position of John Bell and His Supporters.*

Speech of Hon. Henry Wilson, at Myrick's, September 18, 1860 (Boston: Bee Printing Co., 1860).

37. John Bell to Alexander R. Boteler, July 2–30, 1860, quoted in Parks, *John Bell of Tennessee,* 364–67, Alexander R. Boteler Papers at Duke University Library, Durham, N.C.

38. Bell to Boteler, July 2–30, 1860.

39. For these fusion calculations, see David M. Potter, *The Impending Crisis, 1848–1861* (New York: Harper & Row, 1976), 436–37.

40. Parks, *John Bell of Tennessee,* 370–79.

41. Many sources include the results of the election, often with considerable variations caused by disagreements between totals at the time and the calculation of fusion votes. The usual popular vote total given for Bell ranges between about 588,000 and about 598,000. I take the totals in this paragraph from Egerton, *Year of Meteors,* 209–13. The consideration of fusion totals is from Potter, *The Impending Crisis,* 442–43n58.

42. Egerton, *Year of Meteors,* 212–13.

43. Stabler, "History of the Constitutional Union Party," 532; William L. Barney makes the economic argument in *The Secessionist Impulse: Alabama and Mississippi in 1860* (Princeton, N.J.: Princeton Univ. Press, 1974). A classic statement of the republicanism interpretation of the election is Thornton, *Politics and Power in a Slave Society,* 343–46. A useful examination of some of these issues is found in Michael F. Holt, *Political Parties and American Political Development from the Age of Jackson to the Age of Lincoln* (Baton Rouge: Louisiana State Univ. Press, 1992), 303–12. Noting that Breckinridge had less support than Bell in counties where slaveholding dominated, William C. Davis has argued that Breckinridge actually represented moderation and compromise, whereas Bell was the candidate of those who wanted disunion. Davis, *Breckinridge: Statesman, Soldier, Symbol* (Baton Rouge: Louisiana State Univ. Press, 1974), 246. Obviously, I find this argument unpersuasive. For the utility of honor in interpreting the election of 1860, see my essay on Breckinridge in chap. 3 of this book.

44. In the last two sentences of this paragraph, I am building on a point made by Michael Holt in refuting an economic interpretation of secession, arguing that if Southerners had really believed that they faced an economic crisis, it is surprising that Southern Democrats "faced any opposition at all." See Holt, *Political Parties and American Political Development,* 305–8.

45. Parks, *John Bell of Tennessee,* 389–98.

46. Parks, *John Bell,* 399–404.

47. Parks, *John Bell,* 405–7; Holt, *Rise and Fall of the American Whig Party,* 984–85; Knupfer, *The Union As It Is,* 208–11. C Vann Woodward saw the Compromise of 1876–77 that ended Reconstruction and put Rutherford B. Hayes in the White House was a revival of Whiggery; see *Reunion and Reaction: The Compromise of 1877 and the End of Reconstruction* (Boston: Little, Brown, & Co., 1951).

5

Frederick Douglass and the Abolitionist
Response to the Election of 1860

John R. McKivigan

Secessionists vehemently branded Abraham Lincoln an abolitionist in rationalizing their departure from the Union after his election to the presidency in November 1860. This view was arguably more the product of the growth of Southern nationalism and corresponding paranoia over the preceding thirty years than of any rational analysis of the position that Lincoln or his Republican Party had adopted toward slavery. This appraisal of the president-elect also was significantly out of line with that made by many of the nation's leading abolitionists, including the prominent black editor and orator Frederick Douglass, who found that Lincoln and his party fell quite below their militant antislavery standards. Douglass's response to Lincoln's presidential candidacy ironically reveals the ambivalence that many veteran abolitionists maintained toward their more moderate antislavery political counterparts.

To use Frederick Douglass as a vehicle to explore the abolitionist response to the election of 1860, it is necessary to first explore his political activities in the years leading up to that critical election. Doing so is very fortuitous because in his twenty years as an abolitionist before 1860, Douglass had been a member for a time of each major antislavery camp: first the Garrisonians, then the Liberty Party, and finally the militant abolitionist conspiracy led by John Brown. At the same time Douglass had observed and sometimes supported more moderate antislavery political efforts by the Free Soilers in 1848 and 1852 and then the newly formed Republican Party in 1856. Briefly tracing Douglass's early political career

Fig. 26. Frederick Douglass, 1860. (Library of Congress)

yields significant insights about the political goals of various abolitionist groups that will help explain their response to Lincoln's candidacy in 1860.

Although abolitionists worked together in groups, they also made political decisions as individuals based on unique personal factors. Douglass's unusual personal history, first as a runaway slave and then a leading voice of Northern free blacks, shaped his politics. Changes in his personal circumstances between the early 1840s and 1860 definitely affected his political behavior. Throughout these years, it appears that three goals that guided Douglass's response to antebellum political events. First, as an abolitionist, Douglass sought the immediate and complete emancipation of his slave brethren. Second as a black man, Douglass fought to overturn discriminatory practices he saw his people encounter in every phase of their lives in the "free" states. Finally, as a sensitive and ambitious individual, Douglass used the political stage as a means to win the respect of members of both the free blacks and white abolitionist communities. In the 1860 election, all three of these factors would play a large role in guiding Douglass's behavior.

The abolitionists' ambivalence toward moderate antislavery political activity had its roots in the origins of the immediatist movement in the early 1830s, well before Douglass had escaped from his youthful enslavement in Maryland. Abolition emerged as a by-product of the upsurge of religious revivalism popularly known as the Second Great Awakening. The original abolitionist principles and objectives revealed the deep influence of evangelical tenets. Revivalist assumptions led may churchmen to regard slavery as a product of personal sin and to demand emancipation as the cost of repentance. Early abolitionists therefore focused on a campaign of "moral suasion" to use religious institutions to reach and convert the consciences of slaveholders rather than pursuing political or governmental means to achieve emancipation.[1]

The rejection of this emancipation program by nearly every major American religious body in the 1830s forced abolitionists to reconsider their church-oriented strategy. Many followed the lead of the Boston abolitionist editor William Lloyd Garrison and abandoned the churches as hopelessly corrupted by slavery. Many of these Garrisonians also adopted pacifistic or "nonresistant" political practices and counseled Northerners to withhold their sanction from the proslavery Constitution by refusing to vote. The Garrisonians hired Douglass as a traveling lecturer only two years after he escaped from slavery in Maryland, resettled in New Bedford, Massachusetts, and espoused their basic political ideology.[2]

After the 1840 schism in the antislavery ranks, some non-Garrisonian abolitionists focused on reforming the churches. Many of these abolitionists joined the newly formed American and Foreign Anti-Slavery Society, the most prominent leader of which was the New York City merchant Lewis Tappan. Throughout the 1840s, this abolitionist faction concentrated on lobbying denominations and other religious institutions to adopt stronger sanctions against slaveholders. Tappan and many who worked with him shared the view that the business of politics was morally corrupt and maintained a wary distance from that sphere.[3]

Not all the abolitionists who broke with Garrison opposed political activism. Beginning in the mid-1830s, abolitionists had petitioned legislatures and interrogated political candidates on slavery-related issues. When no candidate expressed antislavery sentiments, abolitionists often

Fig. 27. William Lloyd Garrison.
(Library of Congress)

protested by "scattering" their ballots among write-in candidates. When the federal government failed to respond to petitioning or lobbying, politically minded abolitionists held a series of conventions that led to the formation of an independent antislavery party in 1840.[4]

Abolitionists launched the new Liberty Party to pursue emancipation through partisan politics. Although some political abolitionists wanted to introduce economic considerations into arguments against slavery, the Liberty Party platforms in the 1840 and 1844 presidential elections differed little from those of the old antislavery societies. They condemned not only slaveholding but also the nation's pervasive racial prejudice as an affront to God's law. They called for an immediate abolition of slavery wherever constitutionally possible and for the repeal of all racial discriminatory legislation as a religious as well as a political duty.[5]

The fledgling Liberty Party deeply divided the abolitionists. Most Garrisonians condemned any political activity, including that of the Liberty

Party, as an implied endorsement of the legality of slavery by working under a constitution they branded "a covenant with death and an agreement with Hell."[6] By the mid-1840s, most Garrisonians endorsed a "disunionist" ideology that called on Northerners to cease all participation in the proslavery government, including voting in elections. In time, Douglass would come to view this position as an abrogation by Northerners of their moral duty to help end slavery, but he later recalled that in the mid-1840s "he thought as a child."[7]

Though not so philosophically opposed to political institutions as the Garrisonians, some non-Garrisonian abolitionists such as Lewis Tappan persisted in their mistrust of all politics as sordid and compromising. Another reason for their reluctance to support the Liberty Party was the strong allegiance of most abolitionists and many other reform-minded Northerners to the Whig Party. Compared with the laissez-faire ideology of their antebellum rivals in the Democratic Party, the Whigs' moralistic rhetoric and occasional support of Sabbatarian practices and prohibition were highly attractive to the same evangelical voters who were most inclined to abolitionism. Even on issues of slavery and racial discrimination, Northern Whig politicians often took positions that won the sympathy of proabolition evangelicals.[8]

By bringing a new ethically defined issue into politics, the Liberty Party challenged the Whig hold on evangelical voters. However, the scant support attracted by the Liberty Party's presidential candidate, James G. Birney—7,000 votes (0.29 percent) in 1840 and 62,000 (2.31 percent) in 1844—showed that the single issue of slavery was not yet strong enough to turn a significant number of voters, evangelical or not, away from the Whigs.[9]

Events in the 1840s fostered the growth of Northern political antislavery sentiment. Public controversy over such issues as the congressional "gag rule" against antislavery petitions, the annexation of Texas as a new slaveholding state, and the disposition of territory won in the Mexican-American War made opposition to the Slave Power more respectable in Northern circles. In 1848, a Liberty Party faction led by Salmon P. Chase, Gamaliel Bailey, and Henry B. Stanton advocated cooperation with political groups that opposed extension of slavery into the Western states.[10] In a complicated series of intraparty battles, the Liberty Party merged with antiextensionist Whigs and Democrats to create the Free Soil Party. The new party dropped the Liberty Party's support for immediate abolition and for black civil rights. With this more moderate stance, it attracted far more voters than the Liberty Party.[11]

Not all Liberty men could accept the compromised antislavery position of the new party. As early as 1845, Birney, William Goodell, and Gerrit Smith had proposed broadening the Liberty Party platform into a program of universal reform. Calling themselves the Liberty League, the members of this faction advanced the theory that the Constitution did not sanction slavery and that Congress therefore had the power to abolish slavery everywhere in the Union. Although the Liberty League failed to capture control of the Liberty Party or to block the Free Soil merger, its members continued to work for an undiluted abolitionist program.[12]

As the abolitionist political world evolved in the late 1840s, the antislavery career of Frederick Douglass changed, too. A highly successful lecturer for the American Anti-Slavery Society, Douglass had traveled throughout the North on speaking tours where his sophistication in expressing Garrisonian ideology had grown significantly. In 1845, he published his remarkable autobiographical *Narrative,* revealing specific details about his youth in slavery. Fearful for his safety, the Garrisonians had sent Douglass on a speaking tour of the British Isles. This nearly two-year sojourn further increased Douglass's self-confidence and heightened his sensitivity toward hints of condescension that he felt he had experienced from many white Garrisonians. On his return to the United States, Douglass set himself up as a newspaper editor in Rochester, New York, in late 1847, with financial assistance from new British admirers.[13]

As he established his weekly, the *North Star,* Douglass began to interact more with other leaders of the Northern free black community. As the most successful black-run periodical, the *North Star* became the forum for many discussions and debates among free blacks about their status. In an 1848 editorial, Douglass provided readers with a list summarizing the types of discrimination that he and all free blacks faced:

> Slaves as individuals at the South, we are but little better than slaves to community at the North. The community sport with our rights with as much impunity, as if we formed no part of the family of man. They tax us, deny us the right to suffrage, take our money to build schoolhouses, and spurn our children from their doors. Prejudice pursues us in every lane of life. Even our courts of law are against us. We are tried by our enemies.

The judge, jury, and counsellors [*sic*] are all under the influence of a bitter prejudice against us. In such a state, justice is but a name.[14]

As a new resident of New York State, Douglass found conditions for himself and his growing family even worse than they had been in Massachusetts. He rallied against segregation in the Rochester public school system and ultimately educated his children privately. He protested Jim Crow practices on trains, in hotels, and in many public facilities, both in Rochester and all across the North, as he traveled on antislavery lecture tours.[15] As a New York black male, Douglass faced the unique requirement of needing to possess $250 in personal property in order to be eligible to vote, a requirement that had been rescinded for white men when the state's constitution was rewritten in 1821.[16] As a nonvoting Garrisonian abolitionist, Douglass personally would not be affected by that particular barrier, but the rapidly changing political environment soon led those circumstances to change.

Although now relocated far from the East Coast strongholds of the Garrisonians, Douglass initially viewed the upcoming 1848 presidential election with his mentors' vehement disdain of all the competing political parties. He attended the June 1848 Buffalo convention, where the Liberty League renamed itself the National Liberty Party and nominated Gerrit Smith for president. Called on by the delegates to address them, Douglass had disappointed them when he declared his loyalty to the Garrisonian view that the Constitution supported slavery and his refusal to vote under it.[17]

Two months later, Douglass attended the Buffalo convention organizing the new Free Soil Party as an observer and again was called on to address that gathering. Although he spoke only briefly, Douglass voiced sympathy for the gathering's "noble undertaking."[18] Soon after, he editorially praised the Free Soil Party as "springing legitimately out of the principles which the American Anti-Slavery Society and Liberty Party have long been proclaiming."[19] Douglass advised voting abolitionists to support the Free Soil ticket rather than the rump Liberty Party because of the former's more advantageous "circumstances."[20] Acknowledging shortcomings in the Free Soilers' positions, Douglass observed aptly that "what is morally right is not always politically possible."[21] Douglass's attitude differed little in 1848 from that of his mentor Garrison, who applauded the Free Soil Party as "the beginning of the end of slavery" even as he rejected the party's compromised principles.[22] Although Douglass, Garrison, and most in

Fig. 28. Hon. Gerrit Smith of New York, between 1855 and 1865. (Library of Congress)

their abolitionist camp still refrained from voting, they encouraged those with looser scruples to cast their ballots for the Free Soilers.

Although Douglass adopted a favorable attitude toward the Free Soilers, die-hards in the Liberty Party camp continued to criticize the lowered antislavery standard of the new party. Although the Liberty League failed to block the Free Soil merger, its members vowed to continue to work for an undiluted abolitionist program. Picking up the abandoned Liberty Party name, they ran Gerrit Smith for president in opposition to the Free Soil and major party candidates in 1848. The reborn Liberty Party presented a host of philosophical, legal, and historical arguments to support its cardinal tenet that slavery was unconstitutional. Defining slaveholding as both sinful and illegal, Smith's followers charged the Free Soilers with sanctioning slavery on the grounds that the antiextension platform recognized slavery's right to remain undisturbed in the South.[23]

It was significant that many free blacks complained that the free-soilers had displayed little concern for matters of civil rights in their platform or in their final choice of the ticket of Martin Van Buren for president and Charles Francis Adams for vice president. The New York African American minister Samuel Ringgold War denounced Van Buren's Democratic followers as "ready to rob black men of their rights now as they ever were."[24] In August, Douglass briefly advised voting blacks to support Smith's candidacy on account of his endorsement of black rights but shifted back to the free-soilers the following month.[25] A nationwide gathering of black leaders in Cleveland in September elected Douglass their chair and, like him, gave the Free Soiler candidates a very qualified endorsement.[26]

Despite such failings, the new party received 290,000 votes from among pragmatic political abolitionists and more moderate antiextensionist Northern voters.[27] Douglass supplied an overall optimistic assessment of the election outcome:

> What good has the free soil movement done? Much in many ways but not every way. It has for once rallied a large number of the people of the North in apparent hostility to the whole system of American slavery; it has subjected this vile abomination to wide-spread exposure; it has rebuked and humbled quite a number of corrupt and cringing politicians, by drawing them to change their positions on this subject, and driven them from office. It has awakened the whole south to a sense of danger, and perhaps has checked the proud and arrogant pretensions of the slaveholder with respect to the extension of slavery. So far so good.[28]

The 1848 campaign displayed Douglass's characteristic pragmatism toward electoral politics, which guided him through a series of shifting allegiances down through the election of 1860.

After this first taste of political activism, Douglass began strengthening his ties with upstate New York's largely political abolitionist leaders. The most important of these men was the wealthy real estate owner Gerrit Smith of Peterboro, near Syracuse. Smith became an avid reader of Douglass's *North Star,* a friend, and an occasional financial supporter.[29] The two men frequently corresponded about the precise relationship of slavery under the U.S. Constitution. By this time, Smith had adopted a position in complete opposition to that of the Garrisonians and argued that slavery was not legal anywhere in the nation under the principles of the Constitution. In 1851, after two years of study on the subject, Douglass finally announced his conversion to Smith's position. His former Garrisonian friends denounced Douglass's apostasy and accused him of being bought out by the wealthy Smith. These accusations became even louder after Douglass merged his newspaper with the Syracuse *Liberty Party Paper,* which Smith had financially underwritten. The new Rochester-based *Frederick Douglass' Paper* also became dependent on Smith's subsidies to remain solvent.[30]

During these same years, Douglass also began to play a more prominent role as a leader in black campaigns to secure equal treatment in Northern states. Operating an independent antislavery newspaper, Douglass had turned to the Northern free black community to support its survival. Douglass attended black conventions in New York and throughout the North, working to forge a united voice against the region's pervasive racial discrimination. Douglass also discovered that Gerrit Smith, unlike most of the white Garrisonians, treated blacks without condescension and contributed generously to their campaigns for civil rights.[31]

Douglass attended the 1852 national convention of the Free Soil Party, renamed the Free Democrats, in the company of Gerrit Smith. The two labored unsuccessfully to persuade that party to take a stronger stance against slavery and on behalf of black rights. They urged Free Democrats to destroy slavery everywhere, not just in the territories.[32] Through the late summer and early fall, Douglass remained publicly hopeful that the Free Democratic ticket of John P. Hale and George W. Julian would take the higher ground held by the Liberty Party remnant. When that was not forthcoming, Douglass withdrew his tentative endorsement of the Free Democrats.[33]

The Liberty Party remnant led by Gerrit Smith pressured Hale and Julian to adopt more outright abolitionist positions and to endorse equal rights for blacks. When rebuffed by the Free Democrats, they nominated William Goodell for president. Emphasizing the Liberty Party's unqualified endorsement of racial equality, Douglass shifted his editorial endorsement from Hale to Goodell.[34] This move further separated Douglass from his old Garrisonian colleagues, who still refrained from voting, regarded continued Liberty Party efforts as futile, and applauded the Free Democrats, as they had the free-soilers four years earlier, as evidence of growing Northern antislavery sentiment.[35] Douglass devoted most of his campaign effort on the stump in 1852 to helping Gerrit Smith achieve a surprising victory as an antislavery independent in a central New York congressional race.[36] In the country as a whole, the passage of the Compromise of 1850 appears temporarily to have depressed Northern antislavery sentiment, and the Free Democratic Party received only 156,000 votes in 1852, half of their showing of four years earlier.[37]

This trend was reversed in 1854, with passage of the controversial Kansas-Nebraska Act, which repealed the Missouri Compromise's bar on slavery in western territories north of 36° 30´ latitude. The simultaneous rise of nativism weakened traditional party allegiances, and the Whig party could no longer satisfy either Northern or Southern militants. That party had performed poorly in the 1852 election and disintegrated amid the turmoil accompanying the Kansas-Nebraska Act.[38] At the same time, free-soilers and antiextensionsists from the Whigs and Democrats merged to form the Republican Party. The new party attracted a wide range of voters, including many who were more concerned with economic development and freedom from competition with black labor than with ending slavery.[39] At the same time, opposition to events in Kansas, coupled with resistance to the Fugitive Slave Act of 1850, helped produce a new, more militant strain of abolitionism. Free blacks joined many younger white abolitionists in blocking the rendition of fugitive slaves from the Northern states. A well-organized "emigration" effort recruited hundreds of antislavery settlers for Kansas and armed them to resist the proslavery statehood movement there.[40]

Founded in a three-day convention in Syracuse in June 1855, the new Radical Abolition Party, led by Smith, Douglass, Goodell, and a few veteran abolitionists, sought to urge the young Republican Party to take stronger positions against slavery and racism.[41] Douglass gave praise to the antislavery zeal of such leading Republicans as Charles Sumner, George Julian, and Joshua Giddings, but complained that that party did "not give a full recognition to the humanity of the Negro."[42] It was significant that in attendance in Syracuse was the Kansas free-state guerrilla leader John Brown. The new Radical Abolitionist Party not only adopted the position that the Constitution did not protect slavery but even affirmed that violence was an acceptable tactic to end that system of oppression.[43]

Douglass shocked his Radical Abolitionist friends when he announced in August his decision to endorse the young Republican Party's first presidential nominee, John C. Frémont. Douglass acknowledged that his critics would cry "inconsistency," but he claimed that the "difference between our paper this week and last week is a difference of Policy, not of Principle." [44] In answer to criticism from both Radical Abolitionists and Garrisonians,

Douglass editorialized that he adopted a pragmatic philosophy: "Generally speaking, this rule of political action will be found to be a wise and right one: VOTE FOR THE BEST MEN YOU CAN REASONABLY EXPECT TO ELECT."[45] Douglass explained to Smith, "I support Fremont as the best thing I can do now, but without losing sight of the great doctrines and measures, inseparable from your great name and character."[46] Douglass expected no censure from Smith, because the latter, though maintaining his own symbolic presidential campaign in 1856, also contributed five hundred dollars to Frémont's organization.[47]

The prospects of the new Republican Party excited even Garrison, who editorialized in his *Liberator:* "It seems to us that the sympathies and best wishes of every enlightened friend of freedom must be on the side of Fremont."[48] Other Garrisonians, such as Samuel May of Syracuse, endorsed Frémont because they believed it would be better to have a Republican than a Democrat in the White House when the inevitable clash between the South and North occurred.[49] Garrison and most of his followers, nevertheless, stopped short of actually abandoning their disunionist principles to vote for Frémont. In his correspondence and editorials, Douglass gave no indication of his actions on Election Day but probably voted for Frémont. In that election, the Radical Abolitionist candidate Smith carried at most a few hundred votes, mainly in upstate New York, whereas the Republican Frémont received over 1.3 million votes and carried all but five Northern states, including New York.[50]

The defeat of Frémont to the Democrat James Buchanan in a three-way election produced considerable despair in the antislavery community. Nowhere was this felt more strongly than among the small Radical Abolition band that had welcomed Douglass back into its ranks after the presidential election.[51] When he plotted an invasion of the South to destabilize slavery, John Brown quickly recruited many of the Radical Abolitionists, who already supported the use of violence by free-state militiamen in Kansas. In 1857 and 1858, Brown assembled a small, racially integrated company that aimed to set up a base in the southern Appalachians to aid escaping slaves. Smith, Douglass, and many other Radical Abolitionists were aware of and supported of Brown's goals. Smith was a prominent member of the "Secret Six," a small group of wealthy white abolitionists who supplied Brown with the funds to recruit and arm members of his small army.[52]

Douglass hosted Brown in his Rochester home for several weeks in 1858 while the militant abolitionist wrote a constitution for the "provisional government" that would guide his invasion. Brown attempted to persuade Douglass to play a more active role in the conspiracy. By this time, Douglass's disappointment with the lack of success of the moral suasion tactics of the Garrisonians, the largely symbolic crusade of the Liberty Party, or even the compromised antiextensionist campaigns of first the free-soilers and then the Republicans led him to flirt with taking up Brown's revolutionary political tactics. Douglass already had come to sanction violence by free blacks and abolitionists to resist attempts to recapture runaways under terms of the 1850 Fugitive Slave Law.[53] He applauded the guerrilla-style warfare that Brown and other members of the free-state militia had conducted in Kansas to resist efforts to force that territory to become a slave state against the will of a large majority of its residents.[54]

Ultimately, personal considerations as a father of five young children led Douglass to balk at actually joining Brown's invasion. Brown's plot had slowly evolved into an attack on the federal arsenal at Harpers Ferry, (West) Virginia. Douglass traveled to Chambersburg, Pennsylvania, shortly before the attack to confer with Brown for a final time. Once again, Douglass declined to join the raiding party; nevertheless he brought along a young free black recruit, Shields Green, from Rochester to enlist under Brown's banner. A few days later, in mid-October 1859, Brown's small army captured the Harpers Ferry arsenal. When this action failed to spark the hoped-for mass slave insurrection, Brown seemed confused on how to proceed. His delay in retreating into the nearby mountains allowed local militia and, eventually, federal forces to surround and capture most of his band.[55] The collapse of Brown's conspiracy caused Gerrit Smith to suffer a mental breakdown. He had to be hospitalized for months at the Utica Insane Asylum. Douglass barely escaped the authorities and sought refuge in Great Britain.[56]

In exile, Douglass made public his support for Brown's violent antislavery tactics. Before English audiences, Douglass defended Brown's violent mission into the South as justified: "Slavery is a system of brute force. It shields itself behind might, rather than right. It must be met with its own weapons. Capt. Brown has initiated a new mode of carrying on the crusade of freedom, and his blow has sent dread and terror throughout the entire ranks of the piratical army of slavery."[57] The Harpers Ferry incident revealed just how disenchanted Douglass and many abolitionists had become with the failure of conventional antislavery tactics, including politics, to make any significant gains in ending slavery. The upcoming presidential election, just one brief year after Harpers Ferry, would put all of those attitudes to the test once again.

The initial public furor over Harpers Ferry subsided in the spring of 1860, and Douglass was able to return to the United States without fear of arrest. As the nation entered another presidential election year, Douglass watched the developments with the eye of a skilled political analyst. In a pragmatic assessment in May, he decided that a Republican victory would "humble the slave power and defeat all plans for giving slavery any further guarantees of permanence."[58] After the Republicans selected Abraham Lincoln of Illinois as their presidential candidate, Douglass had a positive appraisal of his character, calling him "a man of unblemished private character; a lawyer, standing near the front rank at the bar of his own State, has a cool well balanced head; great firmness of will; is perseveringly industrious; and one of the most frank, honest men in political life. . . . His political life is thus far to his credit, but it is a political life of fair promise rather than one of rich heritage."[59] Douglass praised Lincoln's performance two years earlier against Stephen A. Douglas in the Illinois senatorial contest: "In his debates with Douglas, he came fully up to the highest mark of Republicanism, and he is a man of will and nerve, and will not back down from his own assertions."[60]

The Republicans' platform, however, worried Douglass. In an editorial, Douglass complained that Lincoln's party still campaigned for "No more Slave States" rather than "Death to Slavery." Nevertheless, Douglass conceded the great superiority of Republican principles over anything held by the Democrats and implied that "incomplete as its platform of principles" was, he preferred the former. Douglass concluded, "While we should be glad to co-operate with a party fully committed to the doctrine of 'All rights, to all men,' in the absence of all hope of rearing up the standard of such a party for the coming campaign, we can but desire the success of the Republican candidates."[61]

In private letters to his benefactor Gerrit Smith, however, Douglass soon voiced misgivings about the best political course in 1860. To Smith he declared, "I cannot support Lincoln, but whether there is life enough in the Abolitionists to name a candidate, I cannot say. I shall look to your letter for light on the pathway of duty."[62] When Smith and other Radical Abolitionists revived their organization in a convention at Syracuse in August, Douglass attended. He served on the convention's business committee and helped write a series of resolutions that not only condemned the Democratic Party but also criticized the Republicans for their "almost infinitesimal amount of anti-slavery professions," which were "inadequate . . . to 'quiet the agitation' upon the subject of the slave's right to liberty."[63] The Radical Abolitionists likewise judged Lincoln harshly in another resolution: "For the Abolitionists to vote for a candidate like Abraham Lincoln, who stands ready to execute the accursed Fugitive Slave Law, to suppress insurrections among slaves, to admit new slave States, and to support the ostracism, socially and politically of the black man of the North is to give the lie to their professions; to expose their hypocrisy to the world; and to do what they can, to put far off, the day of the slave's deliverance."[64]

The Radical Abolitionists nominated Gerrit Smith for president, with the veteran Pennsylvania abolitionist Samuel McFarland as his running mate. The party also selected Douglass as one of its two at-large electors in New York State, the first time a black had ever been selected for such a position.[65]

Smith's candidacy initially showed signs of rallying abolitionist ranks. In mid-September, Stephen S. Foster, a dissident in the Garrisonian camp, organized the Political Anti-Slavery Convention in Worcester, Massachusetts, "to consider the propriety of organizing a Political party upon an Anti-Slavery interpretation of the U.S. Constitution, with the avowed purpose of abolishing slavery in the states, as well as the Territories of the Union."[66] Douglass suspected that most Garrisonians continued to regard the Constitution as proslavery and opposed voting. Nevertheless, he decided to attend the Worcester gathering to help Foster's effort "to reunite the scattered anti-slavery elements of the country, and produce one solid abolitionist organization, who will use all of the powers of the Federal as well as State Governments of the country for the abolition of slavery."[67] Douglass served on the Worcester convention's business committee and authored a resolution wishing "earnest sympathy and Godspeed" to Smith's presidential candidacy.[68]

As in the past, Garrison and a dwindling band of abolitionist followers clung to their disunionist position and refused to vote. Garrison dismissed Gerrit Smith's candidacy as "extremely farcical" and denounced the Republicans as a "time-serving, temporizing, and cowardly party." Nevertheless, Garrison observed that the "pending election witnessed a marked division between the political forces of the North and South" and predicted "decisive action" on the slavery question if the Republican triumphed.[69] A small, breakaway Garrisonian group led by Stephen S. Foster and Parker Pillsbury condemned their leader for this equivocation and predicted that a Lincoln victory would pose no threat to slavery.[70]

In early August Douglass addressed an abolitionist rally in Geneva, New York, and sarcastically assessed the confused situation in the major parties contending in the upcoming election: "The Presidential track is crowded with aspirants. A frightful number of patriots are modestly consenting to assume the burden of Presidential honors. Instead of the five loaves and two fishes—the usual number of political principles—we have five parties and no principles in the present canvass."[71] Douglass dismissed the alternatives offered by the rival Democrats Stephen A. Douglas of Illinois and John C. Breckinridge of Kentucky, the Constitutional Unionist John Bell of Tennessee, and the independent candidacy briefly conducted by Sam Houston of Texas as all defenders of the institution of slavery. Even the Republican Party measured up poorly in Douglass's estimation. Douglass traced the course of the moderate stream of antislavery political efforts since they had begun with the Free Soilers in 1848: "The National Conventions, held successively in Pittsburgh, Philadelphia, and Chicago, have formed a regular gradation of descent from the better utterances of '48 at Buffalo, till at last good readers have been puzzled to find *even a fibre,* to say nothing of a plank of abolition in the platform adopted at Chicago."[72]

Instead of then endorsing the Radical Abolitionist Party, however, Douglass surprised his audience with the following pragmatic political assessment:

> While I see with others, and our noble friends GERRIT SMITH and WILLIAM GOODELL among them, the Republican party is far from an abolition party, I cannot fail to see also that the Republican party carries with it the anti-slavery sentiment of the North, and that a victory gained by it in the present canvass will be a victory gained by that sentiment over the wickedly aggressive pro-slavery sentiment of the country. I would gladly have a party openly combined to put down slavery at the South. In the absence of such a party, I am glad to see a party in the field against which all that is slaveholding, malignant and negro-hating, both at the North and the South, is combined. . . . The slaveholders know that the day of their power is over when a Republican President is elected. . . . [T]he threats

of a dissolution of the Union in case of the election of LINCOLN, are tolerable endorsements of the anti-slavery tendencies of the Republic[an] party; and for one, Abolitionist though I am, and resolved to cast my vote for an Abolitionist, I sincerely hope for the triumph of that party over all odds and ends of slavery combined against it.[73]

In an editorial the same month Douglass responded to abolitionist critics of the Republicans: "Great sins are laid at the door of the Republican party and its candidates, and they are such as make that party unworthy the support of all genuine Abolitionists. Yet we cannot refuse the admission that that party is now the great embodiment of whatever political opposition to the pretensions and demands of slavery now in the field. It is so recognized by the slave power of the country, and a victory by it in the coming contest must and will be hailed as an anti-slavery triumph."[74]

Although Douglass had once again opted for the pragmatic position in his quasi endorsement, he still felt a keen disappointment in the weak position of the Republicans on the matters of immediate emancipation and racial equality. Criticism of Gerrit Smith's candidacy by the Republican press provoked Douglass in October to castigate that party in an editorial: "It is simply opposed to allowing slavery to go where it is not at all likely to go. . . . It promises to be about as good a Southern party as either wing of the old Democratic Party."[75] He concluded that ten thousand votes for Smith would do more for abolition than 2 million for Lincoln.

Douglass's equivocation caused subsequent historians to disagree about which candidate he supported in 1860.[76] Waldo Martin, Leslie Friedman Goldstein, and Peter Myers interpret Douglass as pragmatically backing Lincoln. James McPherson concludes that Douglass supported Smith. David Blight contends that "Douglass resolved to vote for Gerrit Smith but to work and hope for a Republican victory." Of Douglass's biographers, William McFeely largely echoes Blight; Phillip Foner regards surviving evidence as contradictory; Benjamin Quarles simply ignores Douglass's role in this crucial election; and in two books, including a dual biography of Douglass and Lincoln, John Stauffer sidesteps the question of whom Douglass supported in 1860. Douglass himself, in his final autobiography, *Life and Times of Frederick Douglass* (published in 1881), recalled: "Against both [Stephen A.] Douglass and Breckinridge, Abraham Lincoln proposed his grand historic doctrine of the power and duty of the

National Government to prevent the spread and perpetuity of slavery. Into this contest I threw myself, with firmer faith and more ardent hope than ever before, and what I could do by pen or voice was done with a will."[77]

To be charitable, Douglass probably "mis-remembered" his actions in the last weeks of the 1860 election. Douglass's abolitionist principles and his financial self-interest pulled him toward supporting his Radical Abolitionist friends, especially his wealthy patron Gerrit Smith. His hope that a Lincoln victory would be a significant setback to the Slave Power, however, drew him toward the Republicans. Douglass seems to have resolved this dissonance by concentrating the bulk of his efforts on working to advance black rights rather than a presidential candidate in the 1860 election.

After years of lobbying to repeal racially discriminatory suffrage requirements in the state constitution, New York blacks had finally gotten the Republican-controlled legislature to place a referendum on that issue on the fall 1860 ballot.[78] Douglass complained through his editorial columns that white Republicans and even some abolitionists were ignoring the equal-suffrage question while only blacks were campaigning actively for it. New York blacks set up local clubs and even a state central committee that hired six traveling lecturers to campaign for passage of the referendum. One of Douglass's former assistant editors, William C. Nell, published a pamphlet extolling African American contributions to the health and prosperity of the state.[79] Eager to assist the friends he had made in the state's black community, such as James McCune Smith, Henry Highland Garnet, William J. Wilson, Nell, and others, Douglass himself devoted most of October 1860 to a speaking tour of western New York in support of the equal-suffrage referendum. On Election Day, November 6, 1860, Douglass worked all day in front of polling places in Rochester, buttonholing neighbors to vote for black rights.[80]

Although most political commentators focused on the significance of Lincoln's victory in the crowded presidential field both in New York State and nationwide, the postelection issue of Douglass's *Monthly* devoted most of its attention to the fate of the equal-suffrage referendum. Douglass and other New York state black leaders had tried desperately to rally support for that measure, but it had gone down to defeat by a margin of 337,984 to 197,503 votes. Although the New York electorate cast 53.7 percent of its ballots to elect Lincoln, only 36.7 percent had supported equal suffrage for African Americans.[81] In his *Monthly,* Douglass complained: "The victory over us is simply one of blind ignorance and prejudice."[82]

He blamed New York Republicans for abandoning his race: "While the Democrats at the polls never failed to accompany their State and national tickets with one against the proposed amendment, Republicans—many of them—refused to touch a ticket in favor of the amendment."[83] Despite his personal efforts, support for black suffrage had dropped in Rochester and across much of western New York from the levels in the 1846 referendum, in part due to the increase in immigrant residents in the region. Although he berated Republicans, Douglass was perceptive enough to blame "drunken Irishmen, and ignorant Dutchmen, controlled by sham Democrats" for standing almost unanimously against the referendum.[84] For the record, in 1869 New York voters also rejected another referendum to repeal the discriminatory suffrage requirements. Only the ratification of the Fifteenth Amendment to the United States Constitution the following year gave equal rights to the state's black voters.[85]

The outcome of the New York State referendum on equal suffrage was a telling reminder to Douglass that the Republican Party was not yet a party that supported black rights.[86] This ambivalence toward the Republicans as well as toward Abraham Lincoln continued into the secession crisis that followed the election. Douglass predicted that the secession movement would be short lived once slaveholders realized that slavery would be "as safe, and safer, in the Union under such a President [Lincoln] than it can be under any President of a Southern Confederacy."[87] In an ironic twist, Douglass's pessimism during the secession crisis contrasted with the confidence of his former Garrisonian colleagues that the commencement of "disunion" forecast the ultimate doom of slavery.[88]

Even once sectional fighting commenced after the Confederate firing on Fort Sumter, Douglass and many other abolitionists openly criticized Lincoln for failing to make the war into a crusade to end slavery. Only after the issuance of the Emancipation Proclamation in 1863 and the recruitment of black soldiers into the Union army did Douglass and the bulk of the abolitionists warmly embrace Lincoln and the Republicans.[89]

The concerns that Douglass and many abolitionists expressed during the 1860 election about the strength of the Republicans' commitment to the full citizenship rights for African Americans reemerged after the Civil War. Although Douglass and the aging cadre of former abolitionists found allies among the Radical wing of the Republican Party, resulting in passage of the landmark Fourteenth and Fifteenth Amendments, they found themselves disappointed by other Republicans. They unfortunately encountered a growing caution on pushing for black rights among Republicans during the years of Reconstruction. Despite the achievements of the Radical Republicans, most of the party did not want to move beyond the limits imposed by the prejudices of white voters in the North as well as the South. Ultimately, in order to retain their political ascendancy, their Republican friends would sacrifice many of the gains made by African Americans.[90] Whether they actually voted for him or not, abolitionists had deep doubts about Abraham Lincoln and his party in 1860. Their doubts regarding the Republican Party's principles about race proved sadly warranted.

1. James Brewer Stewart, *Holy Warriors: The Abolitionists and American Slavery* (New York: Hill and Wang, 1976), 35–40, 45–46, 51; Merton L. Dillon, *The Abolitionists: The Growth of a Dissenting Minority* (DeKalb: Northern Illinois Univ. Press, 1974), 56–57; Lawrence J. Friedman, *Gregarious Saints: Self and Community in the American Abolitionism, 1830–1870* (Cambridge: Cambridge Univ. Press, 1982), 16–21; John R. McKivigan, *War against Proslavery Religion: Abolitionism and the Northern Churches, 1830–1865* (Ithaca, N.Y.: Cornell Univ. Press, 1984), 18–35.

2. William McFeely, *Frederick Douglass* (New York: Norton, 1991), 74–90; John Stauffer, *Giants: The Parallel Lives of Frederick Douglass and Abraham Lincoln* (New York: Twelve, 2008), 80–85; Peter C. Myers, *Frederick Douglass: Race and the Rebirth of American Liberalism* (Lawrence: Univ. of Kansas Press, 2008), 50. 68, 84–89.

3. Friedman, *Gregarious Saints,* 93; McKivigan, *War against Proslavery Religion,* 56–73.

4. Jonathan H. Earle, *Jacksonian Antislavery and the Politics of Free Soil, 1824–1854* (Chapel Hill: Univ. of North Carolina Press, 2004), 149–51.

5. Stewart, *Holy Warriors,* 97–99; Dillon, *Abolitionists,* 144–45; Friedman, *Gregarious Saints,* 90–91.

6. As quoted in Dillon, *Abolitionists,* 190.

7. Douglass, *My Bondage and My Freedom,* ed. John W. Blassingame et al. (New Haven: Yale Univ. Press, 2003), 228–29; John R. McKivigan, "The Frederick Douglass–Gerrit Smith Friendship and Political Abolitionism in the 1850s," in *Frederick Douglass: New Literary and Historical Essays,* ed. Eric J. Sundquist (Cambridge: Cambridge Univ. Press, 1990), 206–7, Myers, *Frederick Douglass,* 84–85, 89–90.

8. Ronald G. Walters, *The Antislavery Appeal: American Abolitionism after 1830* (New York: Norton, 1984), 11–13; Richard H. Sewell, *Ballots for Freedom: Antislavery Politics in the United States, 1837–1860* (New York: Oxford Univ. Press, 1976), 75; Stewart, *Holy Warriors,* 88–96; Earle, *Jacksonian Antislavery,* 238n.

9. Fredrick J. Blue, *The Free Soilers: Third Party Politics, 1848–1854* (Urbana: Univ. of Illinois Press, 1973), 6; Earle, *Jacksonian Antislavery,* 151.

10. Blue, *Free Soilers,* 7–12.

11. Friedman, *Gregarious Saints,* 180.

12. Sewell, *Ballots for Freedom,* 117–21; Blue, *Free Soilers,* 9, 14, 107; Earle, *Jacksonian Antislavery,* 158; Friedman, *Gregarious Saints,* 117–19.

13. McFeely, *Frederick Douglass,* 119–53; Stauffer, *Giants,* 91–94; Friedman, *Gregarious Saints,* 187–92.

14. Phillip S. Foner, ed., *The Life and Writings of Frederick Douglass* (New York: International Publishers, 1950–55), 1:302.

15. Douglass, *My Bondage and My Freedom,* 230–33; Leonard P. Curry, *The Free Black in Urban America, 1800–1850* (Chicago: Univ. of Chicago Press, 1981), 81–95, 148, 162–64.

16. Phyllis F. Field, *The Politics of Race in New York: The Struggle for Black Suffrage in the Civil War Era* (Ithaca, N.Y.: Cornell Univ. Press, 1982), 35–37.

17. *North Star,* June 23, 1848; Quarles, *Douglass,* 143–44; Stauffer, *Giants,* 142–46.

18. As quoted in Charles H. Wesley, "The Participation of Negroes in Antislavery Political Parties," *Journal of Negro History* 29 (January 1944): 53.

19. *North Star,* August 11, 1848.

20. Quoted in David W. Blight, *Frederick Douglass's Civil War: Keeping Faith in Jubilee* (Baton Rouge: Louisiana State Univ. Press, 1989), 29–30. In August 1848, Douglass briefly advised voting blacks to support Smith's candidacy on account of his endorsement of black rights, but shifted back to the Free Soilers the following month. See Blue, *Free Soilers,* 119.

21. Quoted in Stewart, *Holy Warriors,* 149. See also Friedman, *Gregarious Saints,* 181.

22. As quoted in Dillon, *Abolitionists,* 167. Garrison described the Free Soil party in 1848 as "attempting to make brick without straw—to live without food." James Brewer Stewart, *William Lloyd Garrison and the Challenge of Emancipation* (New York: Harlan Davidson, 1992), 155.

23. McKivigan, *War against Proslavery Religion,* 149–50; Friedman, *Gregarious Saints,* 120–26; Stewart, *Holy Warriors,* 119–20.

24. As quoted in Earle, *Jacksonian Antislavery,* 168.

25. Blue, *Free Soilers,* 119.

26. Blue, *Free Soilers,* 120–21.

27. Blue, *Free Soilers,* 141–51.

28. "What Good Has the Free Soil Movement Done?" *North Star,* March 25, 1849.

29. I have described the Douglass-Smith relationship in my essay "Frederick Douglass-Gerrit Smith Friendship" (see note 7), 195–232.

30. Quarles, *Frederick Douglass,* 146–47; Stauffer, *Giants,* 146–47; Myers, *Frederick Douglass,* 88–89.

31. McKivigan, "Frederick Douglass–Gerrit Smith Friendship," 211–24; John Stauffer, *The Black Hearts of Men: Radical Abolitionists and the Transformation of Race* (Cambridge, Mass.: Harvard Univ. Press, 2004), 160–63; Friedman, *Gregarious Saints,* 188–94.

32. Douglass had told the gathering: "I am, of course, for circumscribing and damaging slavery in every way. But my motto is extermination." Quoted in Quarles, *Douglass,* 148. See also Earle, *Jacksonian Antislavery,* 191.

33. Douglass had encouraged the National Liberty Party to second the Free Soilers' ticket, but a faction of the group had persisted in nominating the abolitionist minister William Goodell for president. Quarles, *Douglass,* 149–50; Blue, *Free Soilers,* 248–49.

34. *Frederick Douglass' Paper,* October 15, 1848; Quarles, *Frederick Douglass,* 147–50; Blue, *Free Soilers,* 248–59.

35. *Anti-Slavery Bugle,* January 1, 1853; James Brewer Stewart, *Wendell Phillips: Liberty's Hero* (Baton Rouge: Louisiana State Univ. Press, 1986), 163.

36. Blight, *Frederick Douglass' Civil War,* 34–37; Quarles, *Frederick Douglass,* 151–52; Blue, *Free Soilers,* 261.

37. Blue, *Free Soilers,* 255–56; Earle, *Jacksonian Antislavery,* 191–92. Smith's small National Liberty Party organization had remained in nominal existence and even ran Douglass for New York's secretary of state in 1854. Stauffer, *Black Hearts,* 24.

38. Michael Holt, *The Political Crisis of the 1850s* (New York: Wiley, 1978), 101–38; Blue, *Free Soilers,* 256–57.

39. Eric Foner, *Free Soil, Free Men, Free Labor: The Ideology of the Republican Party before the Civil War* (New York: Oxford Univ. Press, 1970), 19–23, 168–76, 261–71; Holt, *Political Crisis of the 1850s,* 183–216; Blue, *Free Soilers,* 269–87; Friedman, *Gregarious Saints,* 229–30.

40. Dillon, *Abolitionists,* 175–98, 219–24; Stewart, *Holy Warriors,* 157–64; Friedman, *Gregarious Saints,* 206–8.

41. "How Do the Radical Abolitionist Propose to Abolish Slavery?" *Frederick Douglass' Paper,* June 20, 1856; Stauffer, *Black Hearts,* 8–9; Stauffer, *Giants,* 151–52.

42. *Radical Abolitionist,* July 1856, as quoted in Quarles, *Douglass,* 160–61. During the same visit to Syracuse, Douglass was invited to address a Republican Party meeting and confronted his audience on the race question: "You are called Black Republicans. What right have you to that name? Among all the Candidates you have selected, or talked of, I have not seen or heard of a single black one. Nor have I seen one mentioned with any prospect of success, who is friendly to the black man in his sympathies, or an advocate for the restoration of his rights." New York Radical Abolitionists, July 1856, quoted in Frederick Douglass Papers, Library of Congress, ser. 1, vol. 3: 141.

43. Stauffer, *Black Hearts,* 8–9; Stauffer, *Giants,* 152–53.

44. In June, Douglass had endorsed the Radical Abolitionist Party ticket of Gerrit Smith and Samuel McFarland. "Our Candidates," *Frederick Douglass' Paper,* June 20, 1856. He announced his changed position in *Frederick Douglass' Paper,* August 15 and September 12, 1856; James M. McPherson, *The Struggle for Equality: Abolitionists and the Negro in the Civil War and Reconstruction* (Princeton, N.J.: Princeton Univ. Press, 1964), 16; Blight, *Frederick Douglass' Civil War,* 50.

45. "Can An Abolitionist Vote for Fremont?" *Frederick Douglass' Paper,* September 12, 1856.

46. Douglass to Smith, August 31, 1856, Gerrit Smith Papers, Special Collections Research Center, Syracuse University Library, Syracuse, N.Y. The following year, Douglass encouraged Smith by predicting, "[W]e have turned Whigs and Democrats into Republicans; and we can turn Republicans into Abolitionists." Quoted in Quarles, *Frederick Douglass,* 163.

47. Foner, *Free Soil,* 303.

48. As quoted in Stewart, *William Lloyd Garrison,* 166. See also Foner, *Free Soil,* 302–3.

49. Dillon, *Abolitionists,* 194.

50. McKivigan, *War against Proslavery Religion,* 159–60; Stewart, *Holy Warriors,* 171–72.

51. Douglass attended the Radical Abolitionist Party conventions in 1857 and 1858 and campaigned for the party's gubernatorial candidate, Gerrit Smith, in the latter year. Philip S. Foner, *Frederick Douglass: A Biography* (New York: Citadel Press, 1964), 173.

52. Jeffery Rossbach, *Ambivalent Conspirators: John Brown, the Secret Six, and a Theory of Slave Violence* (Philadelphia: Univ. of Pennsylvania Press, 1982), 139–45, 188, 206–7; Stauffer, *Black Hearts*, 61–64, 198–200, 240–48; Friedman, *Gregarious Saints*, 208–9.

53. Leslie Friedman Goldstein, "Violence as an Instrument for Social Change: The Views of Frederick Douglass (1817–1895)," *Journal of Negro History* 61 (January 1976): 62–66; Myers, *Frederick Douglass*, 68.

54. Stauffer, *Black Hearts*, 171–73, 197–200.

55. For the history of the Harpers Ferry raid, see Steven B. Oates, *To Purge This Land with Blood: A Biography of John Brown* (Amherst: Univ. of Massachusetts Press, 1970); David S. Reynolds, *John Brown, Abolitionist: The Man Who Killed Slavery, Sparked the Civil War, and Seeded Civil Rights* (New York: Vintage, 2005); Robert E. McGlone, *John Brown's War against Slavery* (Cambridge: Cambridge Univ. Press, 2009).

56. John R. McKivigan and Madeleine Leveille, "The 'Black Dream' of Gerrit Smith, New York Abolitionist," *Syracuse University Library Associates Courier* 20 (Fall 2005): 56; McFeely, *Frederick Douglass*, 195–204; Stauffer, *Black Hearts*, 244–45; Rossbach, *Ambivalent Conspirators*, 128–29, 139–45.

57. *Douglass' Monthly* (November 1859); Foner, *Frederick Douglass*, 180–81; Myers, *Frederick Douglass*, 225–26n.

58. *Douglass' Monthly*, June 1860, quoted in Blight, *Frederick Douglass' Civil War*, 53.

59. *Douglass' Monthly*, June 1860.

60. *Douglass' Monthly*, June 1860.

61. *Douglass' Monthly*, June 1860.

62. Quoted in Blight, *Frederick Douglass' Civil War*, 53.

63. New York *Principia*, September 15, 1860, quoted in Foner, *Frederick Douglass*, 184–85.

64. New York *Principia*, September 15, 1860; *Douglass' Monthly*, October 1860.

65. Foner, *Frederick Douglass*, 185; Quarles, *Douglass*, 165.

66. *Douglass' Monthly*, September 1860; McPherson, *Struggle for Equality*, 9–10.

67. Douglass to Elizabeth Cady Stanton, 25 Aug 1860, Elizabeth Cady Stanton Papers, Library of Congress.

68. *Douglass' Monthly*, October 1860.

69. As quoted in McPherson, *Struggle for Equality*, 9, 18, and in Stewart, *William Lloyd Garrison*, 170–71.

70. Wendell Phillips branded Lincoln the "Slavehound of Illinois" but maintained close ties to Garrison. Stewart, *Wendell Phillips*, 210.

71. Speech in Geneva, N.Y., on August 1, 1860, Frederick Douglass Papers, ser. 1, 3:369–70.

72. Ibid.

73. Ibid.

74. "Hon. Gerrit Smith," *Douglass' Monthly*, August 1860.

75. *Douglass' Monthly*, October 1860, as quoted in McPherson, *Struggle for Equality*, 18–19.

76. Leslie Friedman Goldstein, "Morality and Prudence in the Statesmanship of Frederick Douglass: Radical as Reformer," *Polity* 16, no. 4 (Summer 1984): 620; Waldo Martin, *The Mind of Frederick Douglass* (Chapel Hill: Univ. of North Carolina Press,

1982), 35; Myers, *Frederick Douglass,* 96, 101; McPherson, *Struggle for Equality,* 19; Blight, *Frederick Douglass' Civil War,* 57–58; McFeely, *Frederick Douglass,* 208; Foner, *Frederick Douglass,* 185–86; Stauffer, *Black Hearts,* 278.

77. *Life and Times,* 265.

78. Field, *Politics of Race,* 99, 108–10.

79. *Douglass' Monthly,* November 1860; Field, *Politics of Race,* 124–25.

80. Frederick Douglass Papers, ser. 1, 3: xxxii; Blight, *Frederick Douglass' Civil War,* 60.

81. Field, *Politics of Race,* 126–27.

82. *Douglass' Monthly,* December 1860.

83. *Douglass' Monthly,* December 1860. See also "Republican Opposition to the Right of Suffrage," *Douglass' Monthly,* October 1860; Field, *Politics of Race,* 131–32.

84. As quoted in Foner, *Life and Writings of Douglass,* 2:532; Field, *Politics of Race,* 134–35.

85. Field, *Politics of Race,* 198–206.

86. Blight, *Frederick Douglass' Civil War,* 60; Field, *Politics of Race,* 114–46.

87. "The Late Election," *Douglass' Monthly,* December 1860. See also Foner, *Frederick Douglass,* 190–91.

88. Blight, *Frederick Douglass' Civil War,* 63–70.

89. Foner, *Frederick Douglass,* 191–97; Quarles, *Frederick Douglass,* 191–98; McFeely, *Frederick Douglass,* 212–16; Stauffer, *Giants,* 246; Blight, *Frederick Douglass' Civil War,* 106–8.

90. Eric Foner, *Reconstruction: America's Unfinished Revolution, 1863–1877* (New York: Harper & Row, 1988), 228–80; David Montgomery, *Beyond Equality: Labor and the Radical Republicans, 1862–1872* (New York: Knopf, 1969), 335–85; Blight, *Frederick Douglass's Civil War,* 189–239.

6

Saving the Republic

Turnout, Ideology, and Republicanism in the Election of 1860

Thomas E. Rodgers

In the voter turnout estimates published by Walter Dean Burnham in 1975, the election of 1860 had the second highest turnout of any presidential election in American history. Subsequent estimates have suggested a lower turnout but still rank the 1860 contest as having one of the highest turnouts in the three decades between the mid-1840s and the mid-1870s. This article explores the factors that led to the high voter turnout in 1860. Although some of these factors, such as level of competition, will be familiar, one will be new to the literature. This new element, here labeled the *republicanism factor,* was the single most important cause of high political turnout in mid-nineteenth-century elections.

Before exploring turnout for the nation, regions, states, and counties, some background is necessary to explain how scholars estimate turnouts and why the results vary so widely. Among the major estimates for 1860 are Burnham's 81.2 percent, John P. McIver's 72.1 percent, and Gerald Ginsburg's 68.2 percent. These estimates vary primarily because they are based on different assumptions. A percentage estimate of voter turnout is derived from a numerator divided by a denominator. Numerators consist of vote totals. These are generally fairly consistent, but there can be variations in the numerators used in making turnout estimates for elections in the mid-nineteenth century. Sometimes it is difficult to find complete tallies, and sometimes those available vary because one compilation might accept or reject disputed local vote totals. Before 1892, popular votes were cast for individual presidential electors rather than for the electors as a group or for a presidential candidate, who on the modern presidential short ballot represents his or her electors as a group. Voters sometimes gave slightly varying numbers of votes for the different presidential electors representing a given candidate in a state. In some reports of election results, the highest total for any elector is used for a presidential candidate's total, whereas in other reports an average of the various elector vote totals is given. Another possible complication is the inflation of vote totals by fraud. Although numerator disparities might cause some of the variation in turnout figures, the estimates of the denominator create most of the differences in the numbers.[1]

The denominator represents the total number of potential voters. Voter registration was rare in 1860 and thus of little help in providing a precise number of eligible voters. The main source of information for voter numbers in the nineteenth century is the United States census. State census numbers supplement the federal census statistics in some cases. Populations for noncensus years are estimated using linear interpolations. In 1860, only males 21 years of age and over were allowed to vote in the U.S. In most states, voting was further restricted only to white male citizens. The New England states, except for Connecticut, allowed black adult males to vote, and the state of New York allowed black males who satisfied a property requirement (fewer than 10 percent did) to vote. Some states, such as Indiana and Wisconsin, allowed immigrants who had started the naturalization process to participate in elections. A major problem with the federal numbers is that before 1870, the census compilations reported neither the number of males over 21 nor the number of male immigrants over 21. To estimate the number of white men over 21, the figures for white males aged 20 to 29 are usually reduced by 10 percent and then added to the numbers for white men aged 30 and over. Total male immigrant numbers for each state are given without ages in the 1860 census. White foreign males are lumped together with all white males in the age category tables. Estimates of how many of these native and foreign males of voting age were citizens have to be extrapolated from census reports from later years that provide information on citizenship. Next, estimates of the number of aliens who had started the naturalization process have to be calculated for those states that allowed such individuals to vote. Significant anecdotal evidence also indicates that some aliens voted in other states despite the fact that it was against the law. Some scholars ignore the anecdotal evidence and assume aliens banned by law from voting did not vote, whereas others include up to half of the aliens as potential voters.[2]

Still other complications are those concerning the accuracy of the census and of interpolations. In recent censuses the issue of undercounting has been raised, and many think an undercounting problem existed in the nineteenth century as well. Obviously, no count of the uncounted can exist. Therefore, once again estimates and assumptions come into play. Some scholars think that undercounting in the nineteenth century is a minimal problem because they believe those most likely to be uncounted were immigrants who were ineligible to vote. Other scholars, by cross-comparing census counts with other available sources, suspect that undercounting was substantial. Some believe that the real population was 10 percent higher than that given in the census and include this assumption in calculating the denominator number. Linear interpolations are the only reasonable way to estimate population in noncensus years. Such estimates, however, can be skewed in frontier areas that might experience highly inconsistent growth with a huge percentage growth increase in some years, but not others.[3]

Given the numerous assumptions and estimates involved in calculating mid-nineteenth-century turnouts, it is no wonder that there is a potential for so many estimates to exist for the election of 1860. The motivation for so many estimates being made has to do with the fact that turnout numbers are tied to efforts to periodize American political history, and this larger concern drives the varying estimates. The purpose of this paper is not to engage in the periodization debate, but instead to explain the turnout in 1860. Whatever the variations among the estimates of different scholars, certain patterns appear within the numbers created by various researchers. One is that presidential election years tended to have higher turnouts than off-year elections. Another is that whatever the actual number a given scholar assigns to turnout in 1860, it is one that is unusually high for the time period. These patterns provide two questions to be pursued in explaining the turnout in 1860: Why, in general, do presidential elections have larger turnouts? And why did 1860 have a turnout higher than normal for presidential elections in the mid-nineteenth century?[4]

The first thing to note in pursuing these two tasks is how the process of voting differed in 1860 from today. Ease or difficulty of voter registration was not a major factor in turnout because only a few places, such as Massachusetts, had registration requirements. In addition, where it did exist it did not always hamper turnout. According to William Gienapp, New York, which implemented registration in 1859, had a higher turnout in

1860 than ever before in its history. Residency requirements were based on the time one had been in state in some places and residency in the state and a particular county, township, or voting precinct in others. Lack of literacy would seem to have had no real effect, because there were no government-printed ballots to read and decipher. State laws might set requirements for the size and color of ballots, but each party printed its own ballots, which listed only the candidates of the party that printed them. In many states, separate ballots for candidates for office at the local, state, and national levels were required, even if these contests took place on the same day. An 1845 federal law required that presidential electors be chosen on the first Tuesday after the first Monday of November, but states were free to hold elections for state and local offices and the U.S. House of Representatives at other times. A voter might also need an additional ballot for noncandidate contests, such as a referendum on an amendment to the state constitution. The absence of government-printed ballots meant that minor parties had no problem with gaining ballot access: all they had to do was to print their own ballots listing the nominees they had chosen or a slate of electors they had selected for their presidential candidate. In 1860, supporters of none of the four major candidates for president were frustrated because their candidate was left off a government-printed ballot. In addition, it was possible, as happened in New York and Pennsylvania, to create fusion tickets as the campaigns progressed, because there were no filing deadlines as well as no official government ballots.[5]

In 1860, more than eight out of ten Americans lived outside cities. Typically a rural township had one voting place. As Richard Bensel has described it, the act of voting generally consisted of handing one's ballot, or ballots, through a window to an official. What enforcement there was of the few rules—on age, citizenship, residency—appears to have been provided by the members of the various parties present at the voting place as much as by any official. Urban voting procedures were similar. Although government regulations placed few obstacles in the way of voting, it appears as though travel did in rural areas. In his study of an Ohio township, Kenneth Winkle found that an important factor in whether or not a person voted in the elections of 1858 and 1860 was the distance of his home from the voting site: the farther away one lived, the less likely one was to vote. Thus, whatever the stimulus might be to vote, it had to be sufficiently powerful to motivate those not living close to the voting place to undertake the sometimes arduous task of simply getting to the voting window.[6]

In trying to explain voter turnout in 1860, we cannot automatically assume that current explanations of voter participation were also operative in the mid-nineteenth century. For instance, level of education, income, and age are all major determinants in today's election turnouts: the better educated, the wealthier, and the older are the most likely to vote. Paul Kleppner has found these factors to have been of little importance in most regions of America during the nineteenth century. In *Who Voted,* he presents statistical analysis to demonstrate this point, but he also makes a few commonsensical observations as well. Given that the much larger part of the electorate was made up of young people in the nineteenth century, the high turnouts of the period could not have been possible if the young were not voting in large numbers. New England, which had the most educated population and the highest per capita income level, had relatively low turnout rates. In addition, Burnham has shown that another common twentieth-century determinant that does not apply to the nineteenth century is the tendency of rural areas to have lower turnouts than urban areas.[7]

Some current factors, however, do seem to have been of significance during the nineteenth century as well. One of these is the level of competition. Usually the more competitive the races are in a given state, the higher the turnout. Although the overall turnout in 1860 was high, in one region it was not. In all six of the New England states, the turnout rate for 1860 was lower than in the previous presidential election in 1856. In fact, the popular presidential vote in five of six of these states was lower in 1860 than in the previous presidential election. Why did this region behave so differently from most of the rest of the nation? The political realignment of the 1850s resulted in the utter dominance of the Republican Party in New England. The Republicans were ascendant at both the state and local level. This dominance was never greater than in 1860. Abraham Lincoln won every county in New England. No other presidential candidate carried every county in an entire region in any other contest from the time party politics developed in the mid-1830s down to 1892.[8]

Both similarities and contrasts with New England can be found in other areas of the nation. Not surprisingly, Michigan and Wisconsin, which were demographic outposts of New England, followed the New England pattern. Republicans won 44 of 51 counties in Michigan and 46 of 56 in Wisconsin. Both states had fairly high turnouts for 1860 but, as in New England, their turnouts were lower than in 1856. Illinois, Indiana, and Ohio had diverse populations, and both parties carried a number of counties. In Illinois, Lincoln carried the state despite the fact that Stephen A. Douglas (58) carried more counties than the Rail Splitter (44). In these highly competitive states of the lower Midwest, turnout ran very high.

Turnout in the South (73.7 percent), according to McIver's estimates, was higher than in the non-South (71.7 percent) and in the nation as a whole (72.1 percent). Southern state percentages demonstrated no real relationship between competition and turnout. According to Rusk's state estimates, some noncompetitive states, such as Kentucky and Texas, had below average turnouts, whereas other noncompetitive states, such as Alabama and Mississippi, had quite high turnouts. As for competitive states, such as North Carolina and Tennessee, the former had a low turnout, but the latter had a high one. In the Far West, both California and Oregon had very competitive three-way races. According to Rusk's estimates, this stiff competition produced only an average turnout in California, whereas Oregon had the second highest turnout in the nation. A study of average turnout between 1856 and 1864 in competitive and noncompetitive counties in Indiana found, as in the state-level contests, a tendency toward higher turnouts in competitive counties, but that this effect was not consistent. Overall, then, the influence of the competition-level factor seems to be evident in New England but is not reliable in other regions. And, of course, it does not explain what motivations led to the development of competition in the first place.[9]

Party organization is another factor that is often mentioned as being important to turnout levels. In fact, high voter turnout is one of the defining characteristics of what Joel Silbey has called the "partisan-factional era," running from 1838 to 1893. Silbey dates this period from 1838 because this was when candidates of the same party running for various offices received roughly similar vote totals. In other words, people tended to vote for the party rather than the man. This consistency, which political scientists would call a low roll-off, joined with high turnout to define the period. Some scholars disagree with the work of Silbey, Kleppner, and Burnham, who have posited with varying end dates a special period of high turnout and party loyalty in the nineteenth century. As noted earlier, these disagreements have fueled the ongoing debates over turnout estimates.[10]

Whatever the arguments over long-term periodization, it seems undeniable that party organization and activity must have had some impact on turnout. To understand party influence on turnout, we need first to look at how parties were organized. Party organization began at the ward and township level. In rural areas, where the vast majority of Americans lived, prominent men of a township assumed leadership roles in parties. Such men did not normally seek major offices or patronage jobs but instead took on political activities out of a sense of civic duty. Each county normally had a political committee that ran the party at that level. County-level politicians usually lived in the county seat and were typically interested in elective and appointive offices and judgeships. Committees also might be established at the congressional and judicial-district levels. Each party would also have a state committee. Outside of the largest cities, almost all newspapers sided with one party or another. Editors often served on party committees. Conventions were held at the county, congressional-district, and state levels, and sometimes even at the ward or township levels. Conventions were institutions within which the voters or, at the higher levels, their delegates and their leaders worked out policy positions and candidate choices. The national parties were coalitions of state parties. The national committees exercised little control over the state parties. Despite the pyramidal structure of the state parties, state committee power was limited by its need to be responsive to lower-echelon leaders and voters. The four presidential candidates in 1860 might get some votes here and there, but they had no real chance of getting the electoral votes of most states unless they stood atop a party pyramid that put forth a slate of electors for the candidate and worked for the slate's election.[11]

The key to victory was motivating the party base, and this was done through a remarkable array of public activities starting with pole raisings and ending with voting. Party members came in large numbers to township and county conventions, in which not only delegates and candidates were chosen but resolutions were also passed expressing the views of the participants on issues of the day. Congressional-district conventions and rallies at various levels could draw large crowds with special speakers of regional or national reputation, special railroad-ticket rates to ease travel, and even special attractions such as hot-air balloons or fireworks. In cities, the parties often held parades. All the parties had marching clubs, such as the famous Republican Wide Awakes of the 1860 contest, but many others among the party faithful could be counted on to march as well. Torchlight parades in which marching throngs of the party faithful lit up otherwise mostly dark towns were a favorite method of invigorating party spirit and giving the rank and file a sense of the numbers and strength of the party. In rural areas, party barbecues attracted voters and their wives and children from miles around for speeches, parades, and food.

Debates were also a major attraction. The number of debates between two candidates could be astonishing. For instance, Daniel W. Voorhees and Thomas Nelson, candidates for Congress in Indiana in 1860, held five debates in five different places in five days in just one county of their district. The audiences at debates were not simply passive listeners. It would not be unusual for the audience to divide by party and march behind each candidate to the site of the debate. Given the party-line voting of the time, the level of success or failure of a presidential candidate in a given county, district, or state was tied to these months-long efforts to inspire and motivate his party's base.[12]

It is hard to believe that the extensive efforts of party leaders to motivate the party faithful to vote did not have a substantial impact on turnout. However, if this was an overriding factor, all elections turnouts would be similar. Presidential elections would all have about the same turnout, and there would be very little drop-off in off-year elections. In sum, the party's mobilizing effort was probably a significant cause of why turnouts were generally higher in the partisan-factional period, but it cannot help much in explaining variations from one election to another in the mid-nineteenth century.

For those scholars who contend that the mid- and late nineteenth century had unusually high voter turnout, the political party was more than an efficient mobilizing institution. The political party became a kind of symbol of important beliefs of the voter. This symbolic role was most important for what is called the core voter. For the core, voting was a way of promoting their most treasured values, and the party was a vehicle for projecting those values into the political arena. Over time, core voters identified closely with the party that symbolized their values. Consequently, core voter tended to vote in almost all elections regardless of whether or not there were exciting issues or candidates. Fluctuations in turnout were caused by marginal voters who needed more stimuli—such as an exciting race, issue, or candidate—to turn out in substantial numbers. The nonvoter, as the name implies, normally did not vote under any circumstances. The bottom line is that the larger the proportion of core voters in the electorate, the larger the average turnout and the smaller the drop-off in nonpresidential election years. According to Kleppner, the nineteenth-century voting universe was characterized by high proportions of core voters motivated by ethnocultural values they associated with a party.[13]

Critics of the core voter and turnout concept take two positions. One of these outlined above is to question the assumptions on which nineteenth-century turnout levels are calculated. The other is to question the relationship of ethnocultural concerns to many of the issues of a given election. If, say, temperance is a major issue in an election, then the relationship of ethnocultural concerns to the election and the parties is obvious, but in many elections issues seem to have little direct connection to ethnocultural values. In addition, how parties symbolized voter values is left somewhat vague. Also, is it cogent to argue that party identification and loyalty are enough to motivate the core to go to the polls when there were no major ethnocultural issues in an election contest? There is much to be learned in examining and addressing the problem of the relationship of ethnocultural values to voter loyalty and motivation. In fact, the resolution of this problem is the key to understanding why turnout was so high in 1860.[14]

In the mid-nineteenth century, most voters consistently supported one party or the other. It was not uncommon for multiple generations of a family to vote for the same party. Such long-term loyalty points to the fact that parties were more than organizations created by politicians to win office. They were, in fact, vehicles for the projection of the values of their constituents into the political arena and the governing process.

Why was such a projection of values important? To answer this question, the analysis needs to be done in two parts: one for the North and one for the South. As Burnham pointed out long ago, the presidential election of 1860 was really two elections. Although there were four candidates, in most states only two candidates had any chance of winning. Lincoln received no popular votes at all in nine Southern states and only 26,388 in the other slave states in which a presidential vote was held and the Republicans had some organization and a slate of electors for whom voters could cast ballots. South Carolina had no popular vote for president because its presidential electors were chosen by the state legislature. Douglas won the slave state of Missouri with a plurality but otherwise contested strongly only in free states. John Bell and John C. Breckinridge received some votes in the North, but outside the two states of the Far West where Breckinridge did well, they seriously contended as individual candidates for electoral votes only in slave states.[15]

Indiana politics in the 1850s and 1860s provide important insights for understanding the presidential contest in the North in 1860. In the

Hoosier state, party loyalty revolved around culture and ideology. Various cultural groups associated with the party whose ideology was most consonant with their cultural values. The more fully a group's cultural values coincided with the party ideology, the more strongly that group supported the party. Ideology was a kind of common denominator of the cultural values of a party's constituent cultural groups. Most groups had a fairly strong association with one party or another, but there were a few exceptions. One such exception was German Protestants, who consequently became a rare swing-vote group that shifted from one party to the other depending on which issues were emphasized.

Culture consists of values and attitudes as well as specific beliefs, and connections to ideology can be made from values and attitudes as well as from specific beliefs. Some of the most important connections between culture and ideology had to do with liberty, equality, the role of government, and the Union. Those groups associated with the Republican Party had a generally optimistic view of life rooted for most in a Finney-style evangelicalism that caused them to believe in the ability of men and society to change for the better. For a Republican, liberty did not mean simply doing whatever one wanted. Instead, true freedom came through self-control developed over time by conforming oneself to a set of absolute values rooted in Protestant Christianity. Equality meant equality of opportunity. Men started out as equals, but they did not finish as equals. Those who exercised self-control to improve themselves were better than those who did not. Thus, the ladder of success created an open hierarchy of merit in society. Lincoln as the rail splitter who became a successful lawyer was made a symbol of this viewpoint in 1860. Reforms, such as temperance, that enhanced the self-control of individuals should be supported by government. Similarly, the market economy should be promoted, because it rewarded good character and a work ethic rooted in self-control and proper values. Every man deserved the fruits of his own labor, because those rewards reinforced proper behavior, led to self-improvement, and created social harmony between classes in a democratic society. Slavery should be ended because it undermined the work ethic and the imperative of self-improvement that was vital to organizing society properly and obtaining true liberty. It robbed the slave of the fruits of his own labor and rewarded laziness in those who reaped the fruit of the slave's labor. Government should therefore be of a positive state variety that promoted reforms, market development, and the end of slavery. The Union, Republicans believed, predated the states, and it should be economically, socially, and ideologically homogeneous, because there was one right way to live one's life and only through that one right way could one be truly free. The Republican Party was thus culturally and ideologically imperialistic; it was determined to make all Americans truly free by hegemonically imposing its values on the entire nation.[16]

Democratic ideology was rooted in the quite different cultural views of its constituent groups. Democrats tended to be quite pessimistic, believing that neither man nor society could be greatly improved or changed. To Democrats, Republican ideas of changing people and society through temperance, abolition, and other reforms were absurd and unrealistic. They not infrequently used terms such as "fanatical" or "insane" to describe Republican policies they saw as going completely against reality as they understood it. Democrats defined a free man as one who was not dependent on others and who possessed the will to fight for his freedom. They thought that only white men possessed such attributes and rigidly excluded other groups, such as blacks and women, from the political universe. All white men began as equals and ended as equals because substantive improvement and change were not possible. All men were self-interested; ultimately, they put the pursuit of their own interests before all else. Nothing could change this fact. The Democratic type of liberty was threatened, not enhanced, by reforms imposed by law, such as temperance. The market economy aroused the opposition or, at least, the suspicions of many Democrats, because one could lose one's independent status when one was caught up in a web of debt spun by the market spider. Government should be of the negative type because promoting reforms was inane and endangered true liberty, and because politicians, like all men, pursued their personal self-interests. The more the government did, the more opportunities leaders had to enrich themselves or to impose their values on others through the power of government. The Union was and should be a loose coalition of states. Local control was a major ingredient in liberty as Democrats defined it. The Union was, for Northern Democrats, indissoluble, but it was also so loose and heterogeneous with so much local control of public affairs that the way of life of no white male should be sufficiently threatened to justify secession. The cultural imperialism of Republicans was seen as a dire threat to liberty as defined by the ideology of Democrats.[17]

In some instances the relationship of ideological values to issues that arose in a given election was obvious enough that voters could understand them on their own. In other cases, the relationship was not so clear. Writers, ministers, and reformers, including those, such as women, who were excluded from voting, might help explain the ideological implications of current events and issues. Most often, however, connections that were not readily apparent between a given political problem and a party's ideology were made by politicians and party newspaper editors. The politician and constituent voter were in a kind of symbiotic relationship. The ideological and cultural values of the constituents limited the effective positions a politician could take. Politicians had to explain to voters what a person with their values should believe about a given issue. Politicians could not lead in whatever direction they chose. Only positions that ideologically resonated with voters would motivate the base and lead to success. Voters wanted their party to project their values cogently into the political arena. High voter turnouts are a good indicator of the success politicians had in explaining the ideological importance of an issue to their followers. Low turnouts often meant that politicians had failed to make the proper connections between voter ideological concerns and the issues of the day.[18]

Devising proper ideological positions was not an exact science, and politicians often might not have understood fully the process in which they were involved. A good example of how the search for ideologically cogent positions took place was the experience of Democratic leaders in Indiana's 7th Congressional District in 1860. The potential Democratic candidates for Congress were lawyers who rode the judicial circuit. As they traveled through the district, they made political speeches. Local leaders studied the reaction of constituents to both each candidate and the positions he took, then communicated their impressions to other leaders in the district. By the time a district convention was held, those running the Democratic meeting knew which candidate the people most wanted and the positions on issues of the day that resonated best with voters. There was, of course, no guarantee that this hit-or-miss process would always turn up powerful positions. In the previous election of 1858, Republicans in this same district thought it would be clever politics to nominate the incumbent anti-Lecompton Democrat. Their gambit created voter confusion, relatively poor turnout, and remarkably anomalous voting patterns that resulted in a Republican victory. Republicans, however, soon regretted their electoral success, because the man they sent to Congress opposed virtually everything in the Republican agenda and later became an outspoken leader of the Peace Democrats.[19]

Ideological motivation was enhanced by being mediated through republicanism. Republicanism is a much contested concept. By the early 1970s it seemed to be the key to understanding politics from the Revolutionary era to that of the Civil War. Michael Holt's 1978 work *The Political Crisis of the 1850s* is a good expression of the exciting potential interpretative power republicanism seemed to possess. Then difficulties arose in tracing republicanism as a cohesive ideology over time. Another problem was that the self-sacrifice of republicanism seemed quite at odds with the acquisitive liberalism many saw as dominant in the United States by the antebellum period. For many historians specializing in the new-nation and antebellum periods, republicanism was at most an empty rhetorical form long before the Civil War. Nevertheless, many Civil War historians have continued to use republicanism, in part because Civil War Americans used it. As James McPherson has stated, "Both sides believed they were fighting to preserve the heritage of republican liberty."[20]

What, then, was republicanism? It was a term used by Americans in the mid-nineteenth century to define the experiment in democratic-republican government established by the founding fathers and handed down for safekeeping from one generation to the next. Republicanism was also a set of shared goals and assumptions: America was an experiment in democratic-republican government; the goal of the experiment was to preserve the greatest amount of personal liberty possible and still maintain public order; the experiment could be destroyed by internal subversion as well as foreign attack; to be a true American was to be committed to the experiment; and putting the preservation of the experiment above one's personal desires epitomized republican virtue and manhood. These shared goals were attached to and mediated through varying political ideologies that defined these shared goals in different ways. Liberty, for instance, as outlined above, meant different things to Republicans and Democrats. Because each group thought that its combination of the goals of republicanism and ideological definitions of those goals was the true republicanism, it was logical to see the republicanism of other groups as dangerously subversive. Other parties were tolerated because true republicanism had to be accepted voluntarily, not imposed by coercion. Each election thus became a contest in which each party tried to make its version of true republicanism dominant while trying to win over erring, subversive brothers to the true views of the founders.[21]

The emotive power of a given version of republicanism was rooted in the intertwining of the general goals of republicanism, political ideology, and the cultural values of those who adhered to that ideology. The fight for true republicanism was thus a fight for the values—cultural, religious, ideological—that one held most dear and by which one defined the world. In defending republicanism, one was at the same time defending the values of one's community and America, which one tried to define by projecting one's values, via party ideology, into the national political arena. Thus, localism and nationalism were intertwined. The values one defended in the political arena were those by which one defined oneself and guided one's life. Thus, one's sense of self-definition and self-worth was tied into politics.

The patriarchal society of the mid-nineteenth century not only gave privileges to men but also imposed special duties and responsibilities. To be a man was to accept and carry out these duties and responsibilities. Exercised in one's daily life among family and community, they became intertwined with republican, defined duties to the nation. Thus definitions of one's manhood were interwoven into duties to family, community, and nation. This republicanism factor—the interconnection of sense of self and manhood, culture, ideology, and republicanism—which propelled men to the polls to try to save the Republic with ballots, also propelled many of them into military service at the beginning of the Civil War to try to save the Republic with bullets.[22]

Scholars often suggest that exciting issues boosted turnout, but what made an issue exciting in the mid-nineteenth century? It was the republicanism factor. An issue became exciting when one's position on it seemed vital to preserving republicanism as one defined it. An issue such as the policy on slavery in the territories was so exciting and powerful because it provided an opportunity for competing forms of republicanism to assert themselves: whoever imposed their views on the territories was ascendant in the nation's politics. Similarly, in presidential elections there could be only one winner. Only one representative of one form of republicanism could occupy the White House. The winner would symbolize the dominance of one form of republicanism over the others. Hence, presidential contests motivated the party faithful to turn out in larger percentages than other elections that lacked the symbolic importance of winning the presidency and with it the republicanism and ideological ascendancy that would rule the nation. If this explains why presidential elections generally had a higher turnout, how can we explain variations in turnout between presidential elections in the mid-nineteenth century?

The literature on turnout often seems to focus on elections as a whole and on factors that affected the election as a whole such as party organization, exciting issues, or dynamic candidates. An analysis of elections in Indiana in the 1850s and 1860s suggests that motivation was party specific. In other words, each party had its own motivational source. One party could be motivated and the other one not motivated in the same election. Even without exciting issues, most party members—the core—could be counted on to vote in order to assert their values and protect true republicanism as they saw it. With the exception of swing voters, such as the Protestant Germans, most marginal voters appear to have been divided by party. The increase in turnout for each party in presidential elections was drawn from the party's own pool of marginal voters who were oriented toward the republicanism and ideology of the party and might act on those beliefs by voting if sufficiently motivated.

The voting numbers for presidential years normally tends to mask the party-specific nature of turnout. Both parties usually increased their turnout because of the symbolism of republicanism and ideology associated with the presidency. Variation in party motivation is more evident in off-year elections. For instance, in 1862 Republicans had a typical off-year drop-off in participation in Indiana, whereas Democrats had an unusually high turnout. Why was there such a difference in the turnout of the two parties? Democratic leaders, such as Daniel Voorhees, were able to make strong connections between the issues of the day and the Democratic version of republicanism. Democrats assumed Republicans were a threat to republicanism as they understood it. They expected tyranny. Logic indicated that if they were the true believers in democracy and republican government, then their subversive opponents must necessarily be potential monarchists, oligarchists, or some other form of antidemocratic tyrants. Republican policies such as the draft and the suspension of the writ of habeas corpus were easily tied to this expectation. In addition, most Hoosier Democrats believed the war could be ended only by negotiations. The key to reconciliation was to knock the Republicans out of power to show the South that there were many nonfanatics in the North with whom they could negotiate. Democrats thus flocked to the polls to save the Republic and their liberty. Similarly, in 1854, in the wake of the Kansas-Nebraska

Act, anti-Democratic groups in Indiana formed a Fusion Party, which won sweeping victories across the state by achieving a large turnout, whereas the Democrats had a normal, off-year decline. As a temporary party, the Fusionists did not have the level of organization or time-tested loyalty of the established parties but still were able to generate high turnout on the basis of a republican-ideological appeal to non-Democrats and to those Democrats likely to leave their party during the realignment of the mid-1850s to save the Republic. Despite potentially exciting issues such as the Lecompton Constitution and the Dred Scott decision, both parties had a normal drop-off in 1858 because the party leaders failed to make cogent ideological connections to these issues. In 1866, both parties made such strong republican-ideological appeals concerning the future course of the nation that overall turnout in Indiana exceeded 90 percent.[23]

In 1860, turnout in the North was unusually large, even for a presidential year, because both parties were able to persuade their constituents that their version of republicanism, and thus the Republic itself, was in dire jeopardy. For Lincoln, slavery was not merely against his own values but also against those of the founders, who had intended for slavery to end. The planters of the South perversely refused to carry out the founders' wishes. This political sin led the South to abandon all of the founders' beliefs as summarized in Republican republicanism and ideology. Thus, they presented a threat—a Slave Power conspiracy—against the true republicanism of the founders, championed by the Republican Party. For Lincoln and the Republicans, winning the election of 1860 was tantamount to saving the Republic.

Similarly, Douglas and the Northern Democrats believed that their version of republicanism embodied the experiment of the founders. In his 1859 *Harper's Magazine* article, Douglas explained how the Revolution was fought to preserve the kind of local autonomy that was at the heart of Democratic republicanism and ideology and of his concept of popular sovereignty. The Northern Democratic version of republicanism was threatened by the South's demand for a federal slave code that violated local control (hence, the party's schism in 1860), but it was even more endangered by the ideological imperialism of the Republicans. To Northern Democrats, Lincoln and his party, not the Slave Power, were the main threat to the Republic. Convinced that republicanism as they defined it was in great peril, the supporters of Lincoln and Douglas flocked to the polls in 1860 in unusually high numbers to save their version of the Republic. Thus, the republicanism factor provides the primary explanation for the high voter turnout in the North in 1860.[24]

In the South, where Bell and Breckinridge contended for electoral votes, turnout was slightly higher than in the North. What motivated Southern voters to turn out in such high numbers? The South underwent a remarkable array of shifting political alliances in the roughly six-month period from the election of 1860 to the final state secessions. One set of alliances resulted in a two-party presidential political contest in most Southern states in which both sides fought zealously. This was followed by another set of coalitions that contested the secession issue. With the creation of the Confederacy, yet another alliance resulted in a nation with a one-party political system.

How could a situation arise in which both major parties could command the fervent loyalty necessary for the high turnout in both North and South in the election of 1860? How could that loyalty suddenly give way as alliances shifted, and then an end come to the two-party competition to which just months before Southern voters had seemed so wedded? In addition, Republican victories in the October state elections in the key states of Ohio, Indiana, and Pennsylvania made it all but certain Lincoln would win regardless of the Southern vote. Indeed, early state elections in Kentucky and Missouri made it clear that Breckinridge, who dominated in the Deep South, would not even carry all of the slave states. How or whether Southerners voted was irrelevant to the outcome of the presidential election of 1860. To make things even more curious, some of the largest turnouts in the South took place in noncompetitive states.[25]

Given all these circumstances, the overall high turnout of the South presents a perplexing and complex problem. The republicanism factor does, however, suggest a way of understanding the complicated situation in the South. The South did not experience the competition of two major forms of republicanism as the North did. Instead, Southern politics operated within the context of one form of republicanism that will here be labeled "planter republicanism." The Northern division into two forms of republicanism ultimately was rooted in the diverse cultures of the North. Most immigrants settled in the North, and because most Catholics were immigrants, this religious group settled mainly in this section as well. Among the native population, large numbers of Southern and Northern migrants interacted in the lower Midwest and Far West. Even more important, the Second Great Awakening left the predominant, Protestant portion of the Northern population divided into two groups. Daniel W. Howe labeled them evangelicals and confessionals; together they formed the underpinning of the major Northern political division. In contrast, the South was largely homogeneous. It had few immigrants or Catholics, and most of these were on the edges of the South in places such as Missouri, Maryland, and Louisiana. Its Protestantism did not have the great division present in the North. The relative cultural uniformity of the South undergirded a single set of ideological values that blended with republicanism to give definition to the planter republicanism that dominated this region.[26]

As with all forms of American republicanism, the central goal and concept of the South's version was liberty. As William Cooper has noted, the concepts of liberty and honor were closely related in the South. Liberty meant independence, being in control of one's life. Only a person with this form of liberty could be said to have honor. Honor was socially defined: it had to be recognized by one's peers, or one did not have it. Thus, men in the South were aggressive in defending their honor, which in turn was a symbol of their liberty. The presence of a large, dependent, unfree slave population embodied an ever-present antithesis of liberty that intensified the devotion of both elite planters and common men with no slaves to their mutual conception of freedom and honor.

The democratization of the early Republic ended an earlier, deferential society. In the North, elites used the concept of equality of opportunity and evangelical-based reforms to attempt to make the common man a safe citizen and, thereby, to make a reconciliation with democratization. In the South, planters responded to the challenge of democratization by expanding the long-standing situation in the South that Edmund Morgan has labeled the paradox of freedom and slavery. They struck a kind of unofficial deal whereby nonslaveholders left slavery (the workforce of the planters) alone, the planters controlled many important offices, and the nonslaveholders were granted extensive control of their local affairs and assessed low taxes. The resulting relationship between the planters with their elitist pretensions and the yeomen with their vigorous adherence to democracy and liberty was potentially volatile.[27]

Until the early 1830s, one party at a time dominated in the South. In the wake of the nullification crisis and the rise of abolitionism early in that decade, a new party, the Whigs, arose to defend the South and planter republicanism. Much more than earlier antislavery movements, abolitionism not only opposed slavery but also attacked the South and its white population, denigrating Southern whites as bad Americans and bad Christians. Southerners felt compelled to refute vigorously this frontal assault on Southern honor. Over time, Southern Whigs made an alliance with Northern Whigs. At the same time, both Southern Whigs and Southern Democrats worked through the national parties to protect Southern values and interests. By the 1840s, Southern Whigs and Democrats had developed different views on the economy and government. The Whigs generally wanted government support for economic development and participation in a national market economy. They thought slavery best could be defended by compromises worked out by statesmen in Congress. In contrast, the Democrats thought slavery was protected best by limiting federal power and by keeping yeomen happy with limits on state government interference in their lives and the Southern economy. These divisions strengthened planter republicanism because it gave voters choices, providing a sense of empowerment within the confines of a common form of republicanism. As this intramural contest developed in the 1840s, turnout increased dramatically in Southern elections.

In certain nonplantation areas of the South, some Democrats adhered to the Northern Democratic form of ideology and republicanism. This small portion of the population was the only significant white group that stood outside planter republicanism. This group usually allied with the Democratic faction of planter republicanism to oppose Southern Whig expansion of government, interference in local control, and promotion of a market economy. By the late 1850s, the Whigs had collapsed in the Deep South, but the Bell candidacy revived the old Whigs and thus created a stimulus for a substantial Democratic turnout. The Upper South, where the Whigs were stronger, had maintained vigorous electoral competition throughout the 1850s and into the 1860 contest. Thus, it was the longstanding internal conflict within planter republicanism that stimulated the high turnout in 1860. Southerners were not deterred from voting by the early signs of a Lincoln victory because their focus was on the battle within the South over state government activism. They debated whether it was better to respond to a Lincoln victory by working within the national political system as the Whigs preferred or by the Democratic approach of limiting federal power over the Southern states, limits that might now involve secession. The dominance of Breckinridge and the Democrats in the Deep South meant that Southerners there had reached a consensus on aggressive action to block federal interference with slavery. The strength of the Whigs in the Upper South meant that support there for protecting slavery by working within the political system was still widespread.[28]

The Democrats in the South who shared the republicanism of the Northern Democrats were strongly Unionist. They supported the planter-ideology Democrats in the 1860 election to stop the Whig economic agenda within Southern states. However, when the crucial issue shifted to whether or not to leave the Union in subsequent votes concerning possible secession, they shifted sides to join whatever Whigs were opposing immediate secession. For the Southern Democrats who adhered to planter republicanism, the failure of Douglas and the Northern Democrats to respect them by supporting the federal slave code meant they could no longer be trusted as allies. This disrespect for the South and what it saw as its equal rights in the territories violated the sense of honor of those Southern men who were part of planter republicanism. Without reliable allies in the North, the Democratic planter republicans had no chance effectively to project their vision of republicanism onto the nation. What they saw as true republicanism could never be dominant in the United States again. This meant that they had lost control over their own destiny within the political system. In essence, they were reduced to the powerlessness characteristic of slaves. When the founding fathers had found themselves similarly powerless, they had seceded from the British empire to preserve true republicanism. Now the Democratic planter republicans of the South had to show they were the worthy sons of the founders by seceding from the United States to preserve their liberty and the true version of the founders' experiment in democratic-republican government. Thus, the Deep South, dominated by the Southern Democrats, who believed political solutions were at an end, seceded before Lincoln took office.

In the Upper South, the Whigs and Democrats who subscribed to the Northern Democratic form of republicanism held off secession in Virginia, Tennessee, Arkansas, and North Carolina. Most of the Whigs in this region held planter-republican views, but they also believed they could still work through the political system to project and defend their true republicanism. These Whigs made many statements expressing their love of the Union and denouncing secession during and after the election of 1860. However, within weeks of making such statements in the early spring of 1861, many of these Whigs were assuming leadership positions in the Confederacy. How can this be explained, aside from mendacity? Like their Northern counterparts, when these Whigs used the term *Union,* they meant the Union as defined by their version of republicanism. When Lincoln called for troops to coerce the South, any hope of defending planter republicanism through the political system was ended. The Whigs quickly joined their fellow planter republicans in creating a one-party political system reflecting this ideology in the new Confederate States of America. The Southern Democrats who shared the Northern Democratic form of republicanism continued to oppose secession. Since they had no viable political means of opposing the Confederacy, their opposition took such forms as joining the Union Army or fighting a guerrilla war in the South.[29]

A number of factors were involved in the turnout of the presidential election of 1860. A low level of competition tended to depress turnout in New England and possibly in a few other states in the North and the South. Party organization and mobilization efforts also played a role. Only those candidates standing at the apex of a party pyramid had a chance of winning electoral votes in a state, and the mobilization efforts of the parties and their publications surely stimulated party constituents to get out and vote. The republicanism factor, however, was by far the most important determinant of the level of voter turnout. A male voter in 1860 saw and understood the world through his particular cultural beliefs. Those beliefs oriented him toward the ideological values of one party. Ideologies defined the commonly held political values of each of the three major forms of republicanism that existed in 1860. Republicanism defined the goals of the political contest for all four major candidates and their followers. All of the issues of the day—slavery in the South, slavery in the territories, ethnocultural concerns, promotion of or opposition to an active state, and all the rest—were mediated through this system of culture, ideology, and republicanism. This mediation blended together a man's most strongly held beliefs and sense of manhood with his nationalism. Voting was a means of defending all that the male voter held dear and an expression of the duties of American manhood. Only by understanding the interplay of culture, ideology, and republicanism, can we fully understand the behavior of the voters of 1860.

1. For Burnham's figure see U.S. Bureau of the Census, *Historical Statistics of the United States: Colonial Times to 1970* (Washington, D.C.: U.S. Bureau of the Census, 1975), Part 2, 1072; for John P. McIver numbers, see U.S. Bureau of the Census, *Historical Statistics of the United States: Earliest Times to the Present* (Cambridge: Cambridge Univ. Press, 2006), 5:169; and Gerald Ginsburg, "Computing Antebellum Turnout:

Methods and Models," *Journal of Interdisciplinary History* (Spring 1986): 579–611. Jerrold G. Rusk gives the same figure as McIver—72.1 percent—for 1860. This turnout for 1860 is the eleventh highest among his calculations for the various presidential elections from1788 to 1996; see Rusk, *A Statistical History of the American Electorate* (Washington, D.C.: Congressional Quarterly Press, 2001), 52. In 1892, Massachusetts became the first state to require one vote for the electors of a given presidential candidate as a group; see Spencer D. Albright, "The Presidential Short Ballot," *American Political Science Review* 31 (October 1940): 955–59. Although all scholars agree that fraud did happen in the nineteenth century, it does not seem to have been common and thus is a limited problem in calculating turnout. William E. Gienapp, "'Politics Seem to Enter into Everything': Political Culture in the North, 1840–1860," in *Essays on American Antebellum Politics, 1840–1860*, ed. Stephen E. Maizlish and John J. Kushma (College Station: Texas A & M Univ. Press, 1982), 23–31. Burnham's description of his approach in *Historical Statistics*, 2:1067–70, Ginsburg's critique of Burnham in "Computing Antebellum Turnout," 579–611, and Burnham's response to Ginsburg in "Those High Nineteenth-Century American Voting Turnouts: Fact or Fiction?" *Journal of Interdisciplinary History* 16 (Spring 1986): 613–44, together provide a primer on the complexities of computing turnout figures for the mid-nineteenth century.

2. Some additional limits were imposed on white male voting. Twelve states excluded paupers, who seem to have been defined as men on welfare of some kind. Men who had committed serious crimes might also be excluded. Some states had a tax requirement to vote. Residency requirements are discussed below. In 1860, only five states—Wisconsin, Indiana, Michigan, Minnesota, and Oregon—allowed immigrants who had begun the naturalization process to vote. In 1849, Wisconsin passed an amendment to the state constitution, allowing blacks to vote, but a vote in 1857 rejected black voting. Despite this amendment, it appears no blacks voted in Wisconsin until after the Civil War. See Ginsburg, "Computing Antebellum Turnout," 5, 85–611; Burnham, "American Voting Turnouts," 616–20, 625–43; Burnham , *Historical Statistics*, 2:1067–70; Kenneth J. Winkle, "A Social Analysis of Voter Turnout in Ohio, 1850–1860," *Journal of Interdisciplinary History* 13 (Winter 1983): 421–22; Alexander Keyssar, *The Right to Vote: The Contested History of Democracy in the United States* (New York: Basic Books, 2000), 54–67, 83, 342–61, 363–73; Leon F. Litwack, *North of Slavery: The Negro in the Free States, 1790–1860* (Chicago: Univ. of Chicago Press, 1961), 91–93.

3. Burnham thinks the census undercount was no more than 5 percent, whereas Ginsburg thinks it was at least 10 percent. Ginsburg, "Computing Antebellum Turnout," 597–601; Burnham, "American Voting Turnouts," 637–40. The comment on frontier areas is based on recently settled areas of Indiana in the 1850s in which linear interpolation yielded anomalous turnouts of over 100 percent. Some of these figures are listed in Thomas E. Rodgers, "Northern Political Ideologies in the Civil War Era: West-Central Indiana, 1860–1866" (PhD diss., Indiana Univ., 1991), 658–62.

4. The seminal work that began the debate over turnout and periodization was Walter Dean Burnham, "The Changing Shape of the American Political Universe," *American Political Science Quarterly* 54 (March 1965): 7–28. For background on the debate over realignments and periodizations, see Ginsburg, "Computing Antebellum Turnout," 579–84; Richard L. McCormick, *The Party Period and Public Policy: American Politics from the Age of Jackson to the Progressive Era* (New York: Oxford Univ. Press, 1986), 64–88; David R. Mayhew, *Electoral Realignments: A Critique of*

an American Genre (New Haven, Conn.: Yale Univ. Press, 2002); James E. Campbell, "Party Systems and Realignment in the United States, 1868–2004," *Social Science History* 30 (Fall 2006): 359–86.

5. The Constitution required that presidential electors not be persons holding a federal office or trust, but other than this stipulation and the day of election, states were free to determine other rules for presidential elections. Ballots were sometimes called tickets because they resembled tickets used by railroads. On registration, residency, election days, presidential electors, and ballots, see Keyssar, *Right to Vote*, 28, 65–67, 142–43, 363–67; Richard Franklin Bensel, *The American Ballot Box in the Mid-Nineteenth Century* (Cambridge: Cambridge Univ. Press, 2004), 14–17, 30–40, 86–186 passim; Gienapp, "'Politics Seem to Enter into Everything,'" 25; Spencer D. Albright, *The American Ballot* (Washington, D.C.: American Council on Public Affairs, 1942), 19–22, 24–29, 33–34, 99–101. On fusion tickets in 1860, see Douglas R. Egerton, *Year of Meteors: Stephen Douglas, Abraham Lincoln, and the Election that Brought on the Civil War* (New York: Bloomsbury Press, 2010), 192; Robert W. Johannsen, *Stephen A. Douglas* (New York: Oxford Univ. Press, 1973), 788–97.

6. Bensel, *American Ballot Box*, 26–85; Jean H. Baker, *Affairs of Party: The Political Culture of Northern Democrats in the Mid-Nineteenth Century* (Ithaca, N.Y.: Cornell Univ. Press, 1983), 305–11; Winkle, "Turnout in Ohio," 431–32.

7. Paul Kleppner, *Who Voted? The Dynamics of Electoral Turnout, 1870–1980* (New York: Praeger Publishers, 1982), 33–39; Burnham, "Changing Shape," 16–17. Winkle's Ohio township study found some age and wealth influence on voting, but it is difficult from his description to disentangle these factors from that of persistence. In addition, he focuses on voting in one place. Younger voters who moved from that one place presumably could have been voting in other places. Aside from the turnout issue, a number of studies indicate that persisters (i.e., people remaining in a given place over a number of years) had a disproportionately high influence on the politics of their locality. On persistence and politics see Winkle, "Turnout in Ohio," 420–30; Winkle, *The Politics of Community: Migration and Politics in Antebellum Ohio* (Cambridge: Cambridge Univ. Press, 1988), 109–31; Richard S. Alcorn, "Leadership and Stability in Mid-Nineteenth-Century America: A Case Study of an Illinois Town," *Journal of American History* 61 (December 1974): 685–702.

8. The estimates of both Rusk and Burnham show a decline in turnout in all six New England states. The only New England state with a higher actual vote in 1860 was Rhode Island, whose 19,951 vote total was only 129 more than its 1856 vote. In Rusk's estimate, Rhode Island had the worst turnout in the nation at 43.5 percent; Burnham has it with the second worst (59.4 percent), just behind Louisiana (58.6 percent). Overall, Lincoln won 62.3 percent of the New England vote, with his highest percentage, 75.7 percent, in Vermont. Burnham, *Historical Statistics*, 2:1072; Rusk, *Statistical History*, 71–72; *Presidential Elections, 1789–2004* (Washington, D.C.: Congressional Quarterly Press, 2005), 126–27 (actual vote totals). On New England counties, see Walter Dean Burnham, *Presidential Ballots, 1836–1892* (Baltimore: Johns Hopkins Univ. Press, 1955), 77, 79. For discussions of competition as a factor in turnout, see Kleppner, *Who Voted*, 25–27; William N. Chambers and Philip C. Davis, "Party, Competition, and Mass Participation: The Case of the Democratizing Party System, 1824–1852," in *The History of American Electoral Behavior*, ed. Joel H. Silbey, Allan G. Bogue, and William H. Flanigan (Princeton, N.J.: Princeton Univ. Press, 1978), 174–97.

9. Studies of more recent voting have also found that level of competition had a mixed impact on turnout. One study suggests that the extra mobilizing efforts parties put into close races, rather than simply the closeness of the race, increases turnout in competitive contests. John G. Matsusaka, "Election Closeness and Voter Turnout: Evidence from California Ballot Propositions," *Public Choice* 76, no. 4 (1993): 313–34. Burnham provides a thorough statistical overview of state and county results for the presidential race of 1860 in his *Presidential Ballots,* 71–87. County numbers for Illinois, Michigan, and Wisconsin are computations based on the county election results listed in Burnham, *Presidential Ballots,* 368–90, 514–33, 864–81. Other data are from *Presidential Elections,* 127; McIver, *Historical Statistics,* 5:169; Rusk, *Statistical History,* 72; and Rodgers, "Northern Political Ideologies," 172–78. Obviously, some states in 1860 were still on the frontier. Did this influence turnout? It did not, according to Ray M. Shortridge, "An Assessment of the Frontier's Influence on Voter Turnout," *Agricultural History* 50 (July 1976): 445–59.

10. Joel H. Silbey, *The American Political Nation, 1838–1893* (Stanford: Stanford Univ. Press, 1991; Burnham, "Changing Shape"; Paul Kleppner, *The Third Electoral System, 1853–1892: Parties, Voters, and Political Culture* (Chapel Hill: Univ. of North Carolina Press, 1979); Kleppner, *Who Voted;* Ginsburg, "Computing Antebellum Turnout."

11. Rodgers, "Northern Political Ideologies," 125–72; Silbey, *American Political Nation,* 46–71, 125–75; Gienapp, "'Politics Seem to Enter into Everything,'" 14–69.

12. Baker, *Affairs of Party,* 281–304; Rodgers, "Northern Political Ideologies," 152–70; Alan D. Watson, "The Public Meeting in Antebellum North Carolina: The Example of Edgecombe County," *North Carolina Historical Review* 64 (January 1987): 19–42; Silbey, *American Political Nation,* 46–71; Egerton, *Year of Meteors,* 182–83; William J. Cooper, Jr., *The South and the Politics of Slavery, 1828–1856* (Baton Rouge: Louisiana State Univ. Press, 1978), 29–42.

13. Kleppner, *Who Voted,* 20–54.

14. Allan G. Bogue, "The New Political History in the 1970s," in *The Past before Us,* ed. Michael Kammen (Ithaca, N.Y.: Cornell Univ. Press, 1980), 231–51; Ronald P. Formisano, "The Invention of the Ethnocultural Interpretation," *American Historical Review* 99 (April 1994): 453–77; Robert P. Swierenga, "Ethnoreligious Political Behavior in the Mid-Nineteenth Century: Voting, Values, Cultures," in *Religion and American Politics: From the Colonial Period to the 1980s,* ed. Mark A. Noll (New York: Oxford Univ. Press, 1990), 146–71; McCormick, *Party Period,* 29–63; Kleppner, *Third Electoral System,* 3–15.

15. Breckinridge carried the most counties of the four candidates with 660 out of 1,921, but outside of Californian and Oregon, where he won 27, he won only one county in a free state without a fusion ticket and 12 more with one. Lincoln won only 2 slave state counties; both were in Missouri. Bell won no counties in the free states. Douglas won just 68 (43 of these were in Missouri) of his 275 county victories and 11.8 percent of his popular votes in the slave states. See Burnham, *Presidential Ballots,* 76–87; Burnham, *Historical Statistics,* 2:1072; Thomas B. Alexander, "The Dimensions of Voter Partisan Constancy in Presidential Elections from 1840 to 1860," in *Essays on American Antebellum Politics, 1840–1860,* ed. Stephen E. Maizlish and John J. Kushma (College Station: Texas A & M Univ. Press, 1982), 70–121; Silbey, *American Political Nation,* 125–40, 151–58; Kleppner, *Who Voted,* 43–49; Egerton, *Year of Meteors,* 209–13. A misleading statement made about Lincoln's vote in the South that

is seemingly ubiquitous is that Lincoln was left off of the ballot in the Southern states in which he received no votes. There was no popular election for president in South Carolina and in the other nine states in which Lincoln received no votes. He was not left off of the ballot, because there were no official ballots off which to be left. For a few examples among many of the Lincoln-left-off-the-ballot comment, see Terry L. Jones, *The American Civil War* (New York: McGraw-Hill, 2010), 46; David Herbert Donald, Jean H. Baker, and Michael F. Holt, *The Civil War and Reconstruction* (New York: Norton, 2001), 123; George B. Tindall and David E. Shi, *America: A Narrative History,* 8th ed. (New York: Norton, 2010), 1: 641.

16. Although my views on republicanism have changed since I finished my dissertation, the relationship between culture and ideology described in it and this article are basically the same. I also found substantial ideological continuity between the Whigs and the Republicans in Indiana. Rodgers, "Northern Political Ideologies," x–xviii, 171–98, 233–60, 269–377, 597–624. For more on culture, politics, and the German vote see Kleppner, *Third Electoral System,* 59–76; William E. Gienapp, "Who Voted for Lincoln?" in *Abraham Lincoln and the American Political Tradition,* ed. John L. Thomas (Amherst, Mass.: Univ. of Massachusetts Press, 1986), 50–97. The views presented here on evangelical-based optimism are similar to those in Daniel Walker Howe, "The Evangelical Movement and Political Culture in the North during the Second Party System," *Journal of American History* 77 (March 1991): 1216–39. Silbey has also portrayed Republicans as hegemonic. The optimistic, evangelical-based imperialism suggested here does, however, differ significantly from Silbey's Puritan, Yankee cultural imperialism. See Joel H. Silbey, "The Surge in Republican Power: Partisan Antipathy, American Social Conflict, and the Coming of the Civil War," in *Essays on American Antebellum Politics, 1840–1860,* ed. Stephen E. Maizlish and John J. Kushma (College Station: Texas A & M Univ. Press, 1982), 199–229.

17. Thomas E. Rodgers, "Liberty, Will, and Violence: Democratic Political Ideology in West-Central Indiana during the Civil War," *Indiana Magazine of History* 92 (June 1996): 133–59; Rodgers, "Northern Political Ideologies," 378–487.

18. Kleppner, *Who Voted,* 43–48; Silbey, *American Political Nation,* 72–77, 90–124; Rodgers, "Northern Political Ideologies," 125–30; Rodgers, "Liberty, Will, and Violence," 138–41; Rodgers, "Hoosier Women and the Civil War Home Front," *Indiana Magazine of History* 97 (June 2001): 114–28; Nina Silber, *Daughters of the Union: Northern Women Fight the Civil War* (Cambridge, Mass: Harvard Univ. Press, 2005), 123–61.

19. Rodgers, "Northern Political Ideologies," 155–56, 183–90.

20. James M. McPherson, *Battle Cry of Freedom: The Civil War Era* (New York: Oxford Univ. Press, 1988), 310. For background on republicanism and works on Civil War works that apply this concept, see Robert E. Shalhope, "Toward a Republican Synthesis: The Emergence of an Understanding of Republicanism in American Historiography," *William and Mary Quarterly,* 3rd ser., 29 (January 1972): 49–80; Shalhope, "Republicanism and Early American Historiography," *William and Mary Quarterly,* 3rd ser., 39 (April 1982): 334–56; Daniel T. Rodgers, "Republicanism: The Career of a Concept," *Journal of American History* 79 (June 1992): 11–38; Steven J. Ross, "The Transformation of Republican Ideology," *Journal of the Early Republic* 10 (Fall 1990): 323–30; Richard B. Latner, "Preserving 'the National Equality of Rank and Influence': Liberalism, Republicanism, and Equality of Condition in Jacksonian Politics," in *The Culture of the Market: Historical Essays,* ed. Thomas L. Haskell and

Richard F. Teichgraeber III (Cambridge: Cambridge Univ. Press, 1993), 189–230; Michael F. Holt, *The Political Crisis of the 1850s* (New York: Norton, 1978); Baker, *Affairs of Party;* George C. Rable, *The Confederate Republic: A Revolution against Politics* (Chapel Hill: Univ. of North Carolina Press, 1994).

21. Classical republicanism was strongly opposed to parties. Thus, it may seem odd that classical republicanism gave birth to parties. Wilson has demonstrated how even Martin Van Buren, the epitome of the party mechanic, saw his party as the embodiment of the people and not a faction-type party. He did not accept the legitimacy of the opposing party. Kruman has basically extended the idea in Wilson's article to show how republicanism and parties intertwined in the Second Party System. Kruman, however, thinks this intertwining led to a modern party system by the 1850s, when Whigs accepted equality of white males and Democrats accepted the market economy. A brief reversal to republicanism was brought on by war in the North and the absence of parties in the Confederacy. What is suggested here is that Kruman's position on parties in the 1850s and 1860s is not persuasive and that the blending of republicanism and three different ideologies came about in the 1830s and continued at least through the end of the Civil War. See Major Wilson, "Republicanism and the Idea of Party in the Jacksonian Period," *Journal of the Early Republic* 8 (Winter 1988): 419–42; Marc W. Kruman, "The Second American Party System and the Transformation of Revolutionary Republicanism," *Journal of the Early Republic* 12 (Winter 1992): 509–37; Thomas E. Rodgers, "Liberty, Order, and Republican Manhood: The Ideological Origins of the Civil War," paper presented at the Missouri Valley History Conference, Omaha, March 2005.

22. For more on these points see Thomas E. Rodgers, "Billy Yank and G.I. Joe: An Exploratory Essay on the Sociopolitical Dimensions of Soldier Motivation," *Journal of Military History* 69 (January 2005): 93–121. I do not refer to the republicanism factor as a political culture for two reasons. First, as Formisano has shown, *political culture* is a highly contested term that might obscure more than it clarifies. Second, the emphasis here is on the differences among the forms of republicanism. They shared republican goals but defined these goals in different ways and did not accept the validity of the republicanism of other groups. Ronald P. Formisano, "The Concept of Political Culture," *Journal of Interdisciplinary History* 31 (Winter 2001): 393–426.

23. The overall turnout for the secretary of state race in Indiana in 1862 was 8.5 percentage points lower than the turnout for the governor's race in 1860 (the best gauge of party strength with the presidential vote divided four ways). However, the Democratic drop was just 1.2 percentage points. In 36 of Indiana's 92 counties the Democratic turnout was higher than in 1860, and in an additional 13 counties the drop-off was one percentage point or less. Those Democrats who shifted in the realignment of the mid-1850s were primarily Yankees. Cultural changes among this group undermined its interconnections with Democratic ideology and the Democratic version of republicanism. The appeals of the Fusion Party in Indiana in 1854 overcame the inertia of longtime political connections to shift some Democrats into what would eventually become the Republican party. Rodgers, "Northern Political Ideologies," 178–98, 298–306, 454–81, 654–55, 662–66.

24. On Lincoln's views, see his 1858 speeches in Springfield and Alton and his 1859 speech in Columbus, Ohio. On Douglas's views, see his 1858 speech in Chicago; his 1859 speeches in Columbus and Cincinnati, Ohio; and his *Harper's Magazine* article. These can be found in Robert W. Johannsen, ed., *The Lincoln-Douglas Debates*

of 1858, 150th Anniversary Ed. (New York: Oxford Univ. Press, 2008); and Harold V. Jaffa and Robert W. Johannsen, eds., *In the Name of the People: Speeches and Writings of Lincoln and Douglas in the Ohio Campaign of 1859* (Columbus: Ohio Historical Society/Ohio State Univ. Press, 1959).

25. See the works on Southern politics in footnote 26. On the state races see Johannsen, *Douglas,* 787, 797.

26. The interpretation here is rooted in the republicanism factor, but what has been written in this and the paragraphs that follow has been especially influenced by Holt, *Political Crisis;* William J. Cooper Jr., *Liberty and Slavery: Southern Politics to 1860* (New York: Alfred A. Knopf, 1983), esp. 170–285; J. Mills Thornton III, *Politics and Power in a Slave Society: Alabama, 1800–1860* (Baton Rouge: Louisiana State Univ. Press, 1978), esp. 267–461; Daniel W. Crofts, *Reluctant Confederates: Upper South Unionists in the Secession Crisis* (Chapel Hill: Univ. of North Carolina Press, 1989); Edmund S. Morgan, *American Slavery, American Freedom: The Ordeal of Colonial Virginia* (New York: Norton, 1975); Forrest McDonald, *Novus Ordo Seclorum: The Intellectual Origins of the Constitution* (Lawrence: Univ. Press of Kansas, 1985); Harry L. Watson, "Conflict and Collaboration: Yeomen, Slaveholders, and Politics in the Antebellum South," *Social History* 10 (October 1985): 273–98; Bertram Wyatt-Brown, *Southern Honor: Ethics and Behavior in the Old South* (New York: Oxford Univ. Press, 1982); Thomas Brown, *Politics and Statesmanship: Essays on the American Whig Party* (New York: Columbia Univ. Press, 1985), esp. 117–230. On religion in North and South, see Dickson D. Bruce, Jr., *And They All Sang Hallelujah: Plain-Folk Camp-Meeting Religion, 1800–1845* (Knoxville: Univ. of Tennessee Press, 1974); Donald G. Matthews, *Religion in the Old South* (Chicago: Univ. of Chicago Press, 1977); Kleppner, *Third Electoral System,* 180–97; Howe, "Evangelical Movement"; John L. Hammond, "Revival Religion and Antislavery Politics," *American Sociological Review* 39 (April 1974): 175–86.

27. Hammond, "Revival Religion and Antislavery Politics," 175–86. For a view that emphasizes the role of honor, see A. James Fuller's interpretation of the Breckinridge campaign in chap. 3. Lacy Ford has proposed a Southern formulation of republicanism that played a role in antebellum politics. His formulation is similar in content in some ways to the one presented here, but it differs in the timing and nature of how this formulation came about. Ford's Southern republicanism is rooted in the internal contradictions of slavery in a free society, was developed in the 1820s and 1830s primarily in the Lower South in response to Northern attacks on slavery, and was resisted by many in the Upper South until the Civil War. The formulation in this article is focused on an accommodation in the both the Upper and Lower South to democratization in the early Republic that drew on the colonial slavery-freedom paradox and Forrest MacDonald's agrarian republicanism, which characterized the South in the Revolutionary period. Ford's views are summarized in "Reconfiguring the Old South: 'Solving' the Problem of Slavery, 1787–1838," *Journal of American History* 95 (June 2008): 95–122, and elaborated in his *Deliver Us from Evil: The Slavery Question in the Old South* (New York: Oxford Univ. Press, 2009). On agrarian republicanism see MacDonald, *Novus Ordo Seclorum,* 66–87.

28. Cooper, *Liberty and Slavery,* 170–285; Holt, *Political Crisis;* John Ashworth, *Slavery, Capitalism, and Politics in the Antebellum Republic,* vol. 1, *Commerce and Compromise, 1820–1850* (Cambridge: Cambridge Univ. Press, 1995), 125–91; Thornton, *Politics and Power,* 343–461.

29. Crofts, *Reluctant Confederates;* Cooper, *Liberty and Power,* 248–85; Holt, *Political Crisis,* 219–59; William W. Freehling, *The South vs. the South: How Anti-Confederate Southerners Shaped the Course of the Civil War* (New York: Oxford Univ. Press, 2001); Rodgers, "Liberty."

7

The Election of 1860 and Political Realigment Theory

Indiana as a Case Study

A. James Fuller

The election of 1860 was the most critical political contest in all of American history. It has been at the heart of the electoral-realignment genre, which includes the work of such political scientists as Walter Dean Burnham, V. O. Key Jr., E. E. Schattschneider, and James L. Sundquist. Popular among the historians of the "new political history" in the 1960s and 1970s who emphasized ethnocultural matters such as religion, immigration, and social or moral reform movements, realignment theory offered scholars a useful framework of periods of stability followed by crisis and critical elections. In realignment analysis, the political struggles of the 1850s culminated in 1860 with a party realignment that brought Republican dominance for a generation. With the election of Lincoln, the coming of the Civil War, the dramatic shift in government policy, and the long string of Republican victories in the decades that followed, even critics of realignment admit that it works for 1860.

Or does it? In his devastating critique of realignment theory, the political scientist David R. Mayhew outlined the major claims of the genre and set out to refute them all. Among his targets was the assertion that realignments feature contests, especially congressional races, that become nationalized. On the surface, the 1860 election in Indiana fits the classic realignment model in nearly every particular, including the nationalization of the contest. Certainly, the election as a whole was nationalized, with the issues of race and slavery dominating the campaigns of candidates for both state and national office. Mayhew himself concludes that, although "probably all the utility that can be wrung from the electoral realignments analogy has already been wrung," realignment theory still works in the case of 1860. However, a closer examination of the political campaigns in the state, particularly the words and actions of Governor Oliver P. Morton, reveals that Hoosiers interpreted national issues on the local level. The election in Indiana confirms Mayhew's critique and the alternative interpretations he put forward in his book. The election of 1860 in Indiana turned on local and state understanding of national issues and the context on the ground, because contingency, short-term strategy, and valence issues complicated what appeared to be purely national concerns when they were brought down to the level of Hoosier politicians and voters.[1]

In his critique, Mayhew provides an explanation of realignment theory that focuses on the major claims of the genre, which asserts that American politics are marked by electoral realignments that occur about every thirty years. Among those claims are contentions that demonstrate how the theory can be applied to the election of 1860. First, a few elections in American politics are realigning ones, although most are not. Certainly, 1860 fits well with this assertion, although most writers in the genre actually carry the Civil War shift in politics back through most of the 1850s. A second claim readily applied to 1860 involves what Mayhew calls the "second motor" of realignment, "a strengthening and weakening of party identification." Again, 1860 fits the classic pattern, with the collapse of the Second American Party system collapsed in the 1850s and the blurring and shifting of lines of party identification. A third assertion confirmed by 1860 is that realignment elections "are marked by turmoil in presidential nominating conventions." Obviously, the breakup of the Democratic Party convention and the following confusion, which resulted in sectional candidates running as Democrats, fits the bill. Still another, fourth, claim is that "good showings by third parties tend to . . . take place shortly before" realignments. Here, again, 1860 holds to the interpretation, because the Liberty Party, the Free Soil Party, and the American Party were only three of the third-party movements preceding the election that brought on the Civil War. A fifth claim also fits 1860, that "a new dominant voter cleavage over interests, ideological tendencies, or issues replaces an old one" in realignments. With the rise of the issue of slavery and its territorial expansion in the 1850s, sectional differences deepened and tore apart the existing party system. Related to that is a sixth claim, that "elections at realignment junctures are marked by insurgent-led ideological polarization." This assertion by Walter Dean Burnham fits well with 1860, when increased intensity over slavery within and between the parties gave rise to a style of politics much more polarized than before.²

Still more claims by the scholars of realignment can be applied to 1860, including a seventh that is at the heart of this examination of the election in Indiana, that "realigning elections hinge on national issues, nonrealigning elections on local ones." Again, this seems obvious for 1860, because the issue of slavery and the expansion of the institution dominated the campaign. The campaign of 1860 also fits well with an eighth assertion, that realignments "are associated with major changes in government policy." The growth of governmental power and the centralization of that power by the Republicans during the Civil War clearly mark a major shift in policy. Further, the end of slavery and the exponential expansion of industrial capitalism during and after the war are major landmarks that not only reflected a change in policy but also divided American history. A ninth claim, that realignment elections "bring on long spans of unified party control of government," also confirms the realignment interpretation for 1860. After all, the Republicans dominated national politics for decades after the Civil War. The election of 1860, then, seems to fit all of these contentions, and it seems to demonstrate the utility of the interpretative framework of realignment theory.³

Thus, David Mayhew's point-by-point refutation of the realignment genre leaves the interpretation standing in regard to 1860. Although he doubts that much more can be learned from applying the theory to that particular election, he admits that 1860, along with 1932, might justify "settling for a stripped-down version" of the theory that uses "the term *realignment* to characterize the two genuine outlier eras of American political history—the 1860s and the 1930s." Still not satisfied with such a suggestion, Mayhew argues that even those two electoral realignments do not hold because the differences between them are just too great. After all, 1860 brought not only the collapse of one party system and the rise of another but also a civil war that led to mass destruction. Nothing like it "occurred in the 1930s." Still, rather than leave 1860 standing alone as the sole example of a discredited realignment theory, Mayhew suggests that future analysis should be "cross-national," as scholars take up questions about how "civil wars intersect with elections" and whether or not "party identifications" are "hardened by civil wars." He points to Switzerland in the 1840s, Ireland and Finland after World War I, "Spain in the 1930s, and Greece after World War II," as case studies for comparative analysis.

Although those are certainly legitimate questions and interesting possibilities, Mayhew is too quick in conceding even as much as he does to the traditional application of realignment theory in explaining the election of 1860. Indeed, applying his critiques and alternative frameworks of analysis casts doubt on the strongest election claim of the realignment genre.[4]

Contingency, as Mayhew uses the term, means that outcomes are not certain, that the results are not predictable or inevitable. Various events and issues arise and influence decisions, making the outcome uncertain and likely to turn in any of a number of alternative ways. *Short-term strategy* refers to the tendency of candidates and parties to aim at electoral victories rather than issues dictated by realignment cycles. In other words, elections are much more likely to be about the immediate period than some long-term pattern. *Valence issues* are those on which parties claim to represent best what the voters want—arguing that they are better choice to do the same thing that the other party would do if elected. In Indiana, the 1860 campaign turned on local interpretations of national issues. The case of the Hoosier state confirms Mayhew's own suggestion that contingency, short-term strategy, and valence issues are more useful explanations than realignment theory when it comes to explaining elections in American history.[5]

The election in the Hoosier state attracted a lot of attention in 1860. Indiana, along with some other states such as Pennsylvania, still held separate October elections for state and congressional offices; voters cast ballots for the presidency in November. The October elections were a bellwether for the presidential campaign and were thus closely watched. Furthermore, in 1856, Indiana had supported the Democrat James Buchanan, and Republicans regarded the state as one of several that they had to carry if they hoped to win the presidency. Though not so important as Pennsylvania's 27 or New York's 35 electoral ballots, the Hoosier State's 13 electoral votes still could mean the difference between victory and defeat. Although Indiana voted for Buchanan in 1856, the opposition to him had been divided. The Know-Nothing candidate, Millard Fillmore of the American Party, garnered 9.5 percent of the vote in a race in which the Democratic victor won a slight majority of 50.4 percent. The Republican John C. Frémont took 40.09 percent. Percentages aside, when the actual totals are considered, Buchanan beat his combined opponents by fewer than two thousand votes. If no third-party candidate interfered and the Republicans could attract those votes most likely to go to such a candidate, they might very well carry the state. If they won Pennsylvania and Indiana, picking up only two of the five Northern states that they had lost in 1856, they would put their man in the White House.

Still further, the Republicans had been gaining strength in the state since the formation of their party in the wake of the 1854 Kansas-Nebraska Act. The numbers of seats held in the House of Representatives tell the story. In 1852, the Democrats held 10 of Indiana's congressional seats, whereas the Whigs had one. The unpopularity of the Kansas-Nebraska Act combined with the issue of temperance to sweep a Fusionist party to victory in the 1854 election, with the Democrats holding on to only two seats. But in 1856, the new Republican Party took five seats; the Democrats regained their majority with six. In 1858, the Republicans won control again, this time with seven of the eleven seats. This steady advance made the future seem bright for the new party, especially when other rivals, such as the Know-Nothings, faded and the issue of slavery and its territorial expansion continued to divide the dominant Democrats. The Republicans rightly hoped for victory in Indiana in 1860, both in the October elections, which would decide statewide offices, including the governor's seat as well as the congressional delegation, and in the November contest, which would decide the presidency.[6]

But the Republicans could not be sure. Stephen A. Douglas, the favorite to win the Democratic nomination, hailed from neighboring Illinois and was a popular figure in Indiana. Although he wrote the Kansas-Nebraska Act, and his brainchild had divided Northerners and his own party and been widely unpopular in much of Indiana, many Hoosiers still regarded him as the best man to defend the antislavery position. Most people in Indiana held an antislavery view, although for a variety of reasons. The antislavery view meant that they opposed the expansion of slavery and did not want the institution in their own state. Some opposed it on moral grounds, some on economic terms, still others for racist reasons, not wanting slavery in their own state because they did not like African Americans. Many Hoosiers joined other Northerners in seeing popular sovereignty (or squatter sovereignty), expressed in Douglas's Kansas-Nebraska Act, as a betrayal of the Missouri Compromise, which had limited slavery to territory south of the 36° 30′ line. Some saw Douglas's actions as an expansion of slavery and saw him as selling out to the Slave Power. But as the election of 1860 approached, some feared that the Republicans would support an abolitionist candidate. In the eyes of many Hoosiers, an abolitionist

Fig. 29. Hon. Oliver
P. Morton, Gover-
nor of Indiana in
1861. (Library of
Congress)

would be worse than a "Doughface" who sold out to the South. If the choice came down to Douglas or a radical abolitionist, Indiana would probably vote Democratic and help put the Little Giant in the White House. Realizing this, Indiana Republicans urged their party to nominate a conservative candidate rather than someone like William Seward, whose comments about slavery had won him a reputation as a radical. Indeed, Indiana's delegates to the Republican convention in Chicago supported Abraham Lincoln because he was a "safe" candidate who could possibly win their state.[7]

But Indiana Democrats worried about Douglas as well. Like the party as a whole, the Indiana Democracy divided over issues and personalities. This division created a contingency of the kind that Mayhew asserts should be considered an antidote to the grand scope of inevitability asserted by realignment theory. Some Democrats, including Oliver Morton, left the party in 1854 over the Kansas-Nebraska Act and ended up joining the Republicans. The Democrats divided still further when President Buchanan supported the proslavery Lecompton Constitution in Kansas, setting off a storm of controversy and causing some candidates to run under the label "Anti-Lecompton Democrat." In Indiana, the Democratic divisions broke along lines defined by the party's leader, Jesse D. Bright, elected to three terms in the Senate. In 1860, Bright held a seat in the United States Senate and was the most powerful Democrat in the Hoosier State. His grip on the party and on Indiana politics grew out of his service on committees, which enabled him to build a political machine based on the control of patronage and important funding for infrastructure projects in the state. In addition to dominating Indiana, Bright hoped to be the party power broker at the regional level. A native New Yorker, Bright owned land and slaves in Kentucky and was an unabashed supporter of slavery. His stand on slavery opened the door to his rivals within the Democratic state party. By the mid-1850s, Joseph A. Wright emerged as the most visible leader of the anti-Bright Democrats, who aligned themselves with Stephen Douglas. Bright hated Douglas because the Little Giant had frustrated the senator's ambitions throughout the 1850s, beginning with moves that thwarted his dreams of the vice presidency as the running mate of Franklin Pierce. Douglas then opposed Bright's reelection to the Senate in 1856, when voting irregularities led to a challenge by the People's Party, which soon became the Republican Party. Both Democratic senators from Indiana eventually took their seats, and the opposition candidates were rejected, but Bright was not one to forgive and forget. He longed for revenge on personal grounds.[8]

Beyond this, Douglas and Bright also divided on their views of James Buchanan. Bright staunchly supported the president and helped outmaneuver Douglas in 1856 to secure the party's nomination for the Pennsylvania moderate. This endeared him to the new president, who even offered Bright the most prestigious Cabinet post, that of secretary of state. Although he refused the job, Bright remained a powerful ally of the administration in the Senate. Douglas, meanwhile, openly broke with Buchanan on the issue of the Lecompton Constitution. When the president supported this proslavery document in 1857, Douglas opposed it, believing that the majority of voters in Kansas wanted a free state. This not only restored Douglas to credibility as a defender of the antislavery position but also allowed Wright and other Hoosier Democrats in Indiana to challenge the Bright machine. The senator's support for Buchanan and Lecompton made him vulnerable to charges of being proslavery, a tool of both the administration and the South, and a mere pawn of the Slave Power. Deriding their longtime enemy as a "Doughface," the anti-Bright forces rallied to support Douglas for the 1860 presidential nomination.[9]

Fig. 30. Jesse D. Bright, Senator from Indiana, 1859. (Library of Congress)

Bright fought back, hoping to keep control of his party and to defeat his archenemy, Douglas. Using all of his influence, including outright bribery, the senator tried to sway the state convention when the Democrats met in January 1860. But the Douglas faction won the day, and Indiana Democrats officially supported the Little Giant. When the national party convention in Charleston ended in chaos and the party then split along sectional lines, Bright saw an opportunity to strike back. Northern Democrats generally supported Douglas; John C. Breckinridge was the standard bearer for Southern Democrats. Bright vigorously supported Breckinridge. Not only did Breckenridge and Bright share ideological positions on slavery but Breckenridge's candidacy also offered Bright an opportunity to defeat Douglas and, perhaps, regain control of the Democratic Party in Indiana. Although he and his supporters managed to pull some votes away from the hated Douglas, almost all of them in southern Indiana, Bright's efforts failed, and he did not regain control of the party. Instead, many Hoosier Democrats blamed Bright for the electoral disaster. His enemies within the party continued looking for ways to curb his power and, if possible, rid themselves of him once and for all. Such an opportunity eventually presented itself. Bright's work for Breckinridge drove him further into the pro-Southern camp. This opened the door to charges of treason when he unwisely wrote a letter of recommendation to Jefferson Davis on the behalf of a friend. Bright addressed his old Senate colleague and ally in the Democratic Party as "His Excellency, Jefferson Davis, President of the Confederation of States." Despite his protestations that he had written the letter before hostilities had begun, at a time when many Northerners were in communication with Southern leaders, the letter and the charges of treason surrounding it led to his expulsion from the Senate in 1862. To add insult to injury, Governor Oliver Morton, a Republican, replaced Bright with his old enemy, Joseph A. Wright.[10]

On the surface, then, the national issues surrounding slavery and state's rights divided the Indiana Democrats just as they did other state parties across the land. But that division actually played out in a local, state context. In other words, many national issues mattered in the election in Indiana, but those issues influenced the contest in ways that reflected the particular situation in the state. As important as the issues were, the personalities involved mattered even more. In his refutation of realignment theory, David Mayhew suggests "alternative lines of thinking," including one that is "nominalistic, dissolvent, skeptical; it questions the very idea of constructing anything as grand as realignment theory." He argues that such a nominalist approach offers "three distinct ideas that can be seen as antidotes, so to speak, to the system-building ambition of the realignments genre." The first of his antidotes is "the idea of *contingency*." Mayhew contends that "electoral politics, as new events trigger new issues, is to an important degree just one thing after another." Indeed, "elections and their underlying causes are not usefully sortable into generation-long spans." Instead, a "scandal, a fancy, a blunder, a depression, or a world war may come along and swerve voters. A terrorist attack may do that. Any kind of contingency-free theorizing about real politics has serious limitations." The battle among Indiana Democrats between the Bright and Wright-Douglas forces presents just such a contingency when we examine the electoral situation in 1860.[11]

Another contingency that influenced the 1860 election in Indiana makes Mayhew's own list, which includes "a depression." The Panic of 1857 has too often been neglected by historians attempting to explain the coming of the Civil War. Brought on by the failure of the Ohio Life Insurance and Trust Company, the largest Ohio bank, the panic, like other depressions, had varied and complex causes. Many states had adopted so-called free banking systems in the wake of Andrew Jackson's Bank War and the decentralization of banking that followed. Far from being actual free banking, these banks were established under a system of regulation by state governments that allowed for suspension of specie payments whenever the banks overextended themselves. Although the new systems did allow for the creation of more banks, the "free banking" laws tied the expanded printing and circulation of bank notes and deposit to the amount of state government securities that the bank bought. This set up a pyramid scheme in which banks could overexpand through the purchase of government bonds. The Ohio Life Insurance and Trust Company collapsed when it was discovered that the manager of the New York branch had embezzled large amounts of money. Bank failures occurred throughout the decade, so this was nothing new. Indeed, the crisis might have been limited, but it spread as the failure coincided with other problems to bring on a widespread economic downturn. The withdrawal of British investment funds from U.S. banks coincided with the collapse of grain prices following the Crimean War. Peace brought the resumption of European trade, and a bumper U.S. crop meant still lower prices. With Europeans no longer buying Western commodities and prices dropping, the crisis spread to farmers. Further stress came when the bank failure led to a dramatic drop in railroad stock prices. Speculators began losing money, and more banks began to fail. Plans for railroad construction came to a halt, further endangering the farmers, because routes that promised easy access to markets were now uncertain. The Panic of 1857 and the crisis that followed caused the most damage in the North. Southern states largely escaped the depression, thanks to the strength of the cotton economy. This gave slaveholders confidence that their institutions, including slavery, were better than the free-labor system practiced by Northerners. The economic crisis bolstered a Southern sense of superiority. No wonder, then, that James Henry Hammond rose to his feet in the Senate in 1858 and declared, "Cotton is king."[12]

Across the North, the depression wreaked havoc on the economy and society. Leaders in some states, especially New England, declared bank holidays, hoping to prevent more failures, but their efforts fell short. President Buchanan and his secretary of the Treasury, Howell Cobb, "began a policy of retrenchment" to head off the crisis created by less revenue and larger government debt. But they did not cut expenditures enough, because revenues proved even smaller than predicted. By May of 1858, the administration warned Congress "of impending fiscal disaster." Cobb urged more spending cuts to balance the budget, requesting the government to borrow $15 million at 6 percent interest, with the bonds to be paid in ten years. This desperate move broke with the traditions of Jacksonian fiscal policy and set off a political storm over economic issues. Some called for using the tariff to ease the crisis; others insisted that laissez-faire policies must be maintained to ensure a shorter depression. The Republicans generally favored a protectionist tariff, whereas most Democrats were free traders, with some of them supporting a free-market approach across the board. Eventually, the government authorized $20 million in loans, but Cobb borrowed only half of that amount. The Democrats used the crisis as an opportunity to attack protectionism and passed the Tariff of 1857, which lowered rates to about 20 percent.[13]

As the depression spread, a religious revival swept across the North. Although some historians labeled the Revival of 1857–58 the "Businessman's Revival," the spiritual awakening (like others before and after it) had many roots and complex causes. The evangelical movement began in New York City in the fall of 1857 and spread from there—a different pattern from earlier revivals, which started in the countryside and small towns before spreading to urban areas. Another difference that marked this revival was that its leaders were not prominent revivalist preachers. Rather, it sprang from prayer meetings led by laypeople. Many evangelicals saw the financial panic and depression as a sign of God's judgment on the nation for its wicked ways. Political corruption, intemperance, and myriad other sins joined the long list of faults, which always included greed. American avarice caused evangelicals to repeat the biblical verse declaring that "the love of money is the root of all evil" (1 Timothy 6:10). In the North, slavery made the list of sins; Southern Christians included Northern fanaticism. The sectional rift in the evangelical churches, which had occurred the 1840s and had created separate Southern Baptist and Southern Methodist denominations, continued to deepen. As the depression intensified, many of those who found themselves bankrupt, out of business, or unemployed flocked to the religious services held by the evangelical churches. The revival lasted throughout 1858 and followed the typical pattern of revivalism in feeding a new round of growth for the evangelical churches. The Methodists, especially, enjoyed increased numbers in the 1858 revival, particularly in the North, where the Wesleyan doctrine of holiness appealed to those seeking to experience a life free of sin.[14]

The revival spread rapidly, visiting Indiana as well as other states. In the spring of 1858, Calvin Fletcher, a prominent Indianapolis lawyer and banker and a devout Methodist, reported his attendance at a series of prayer meetings and revival services associated with the broader awakening. He noted that the meetings were conducted with good order and remarked on how the financial crisis provided time for people to attend to their religious state: "I can see nothing in the revival more than a very general attention and from individuals who have been careless about the matter heretofore, but now find they have leisure to attend to what a good man, woman or child should do every day and have perhaps for years." Fletcher also praised the interdenominational nature of the revival: "So far very little sectarian feeling has been manifested—less than usual. It will be death to the movement if the different denominations shall fall out and contend for accessions." One Indianapolis newspaper reported on the same meetings that Fletcher attended by saying that "the religious revival is gaining strength and interest daily in this city. With very few exceptions all the churches in the city hold meetings twice a day, and a people's or business man's meeting, at the hour of noon, is largely attended, with good results." The depression made this possible, and "with a large class of citizens church going is the greatest business of the day, nothing being allowed to interfere with it."[15]

In Indiana, as elsewhere, the Revival of 1857–58 provided a renewed impulse for social reform. This reinvigorated the temperance and anti-slavery movements in the Northern states and brought calls for cleaning up the political corruption that had marked the Buchanan administration. On September 11, 1860, Calvin Fletcher accused the Democrats of voter fraud in his diary: "In politics the Republicans are greatly alarmed lest the Democracy will import so largely on them that will be beat again by the Frauds. The Catholic Irish & Germans indeed most of the Catholics in the U. States go for Douglas. They are Democrats not by choice but from arrangements . . . by the Catholic Bishops." The Hoosier banker thought that the Democrats had used immigrants in fraudulent ways before: "They use the Irish laborers to vote twice or ten times at a single election." By the end of the month, he worried that the Republicans were committing fraud as well, having learned of corrupt methods while on a business trip to Morgan County. In that rural area southwest of Indianapolis, "a large number of persons had been brought in from other states & from decidedly Republican districts of this state to vote & [were] quartered on the farmers. . . . I fear the Republicans have determined to act in a defensive & aggressive manner. But it is decidedly wrong & destructive of the purity of the Ballot box." By the following day, he was again concerned about the Democrats using Catholic immigrants to win the election and lamented, "I regret I have lived to see such corruptions."[16]

In addition to fears of corruption in the electoral process, moral issues sprouted new wings to take flight in the election of 1860. The Republicans rushed to claim the mantle of reform. Stephen Douglas and his supporters denounced the corruption of Buchanan, simultaneously attacking the Republicans as nativists and zealots bent on legislating morality and depriving law-abiding citizens of their liberty. Southern Democrats also chimed in, laying corruption at the feet of Northern Democrats while blasting away at Republican extremism. To Breckinridge supporters, the term "Black Republican" meant more than just abolitionism and a desire for racial equality. It meant socialism, free love, women's rights, and other new ideas that would tear at the very fabric of society. But it also meant corruption. All parties, then, cried out against graft and the abuse of power, insisting that they were the true reformers. In such a context, Abraham Lincoln's appellation "Honest Abe" took on new meaning. The Republicans moved quickly to claim the moral high ground and win evangelical Christian support. More complicated than a movement spawned by the depression, the Revival of 1857–58 spurred political action and was clearly intertwined with economics.[17]

The economic crisis following the Panic of 1857 also brought widespread social unrest. Jacksonian hatred of banks meant heated verbal onslaughts against the financial institutions; fears about the instability of the nation's financial system soon led to change. The long-standing Suffolk system of redemption, a free-market system of specie redemption created by New England bankers in 1818, came under attack. In the wake of the Panic of 1857, some state legislatures passed laws favoring Boston banks. Many leaders began calling for competition to curb the power and profits of the Suffolk system. This eventually led to the creation of Bank for Mutual Redemption in 1858 and the demise of the Suffolk bank, perhaps the most successful free-market banking system in history.

But other economic matters also caused protest. The depression brought unemployment for many Northern workers, causing, strikes, protests, and riots in many Northern cities. Many Southerners saw this turmoil as evidence of the superiority of slavery. Their criticisms of free labor and defense of bondage made them seem callous and eager to spread slavery to the North. Their talk of "wage slavery" and the supposedly superior Southern institution fed fears of the Slave Power conspiracy, which held that evil Southern planters hoped not only to spread slavery to the North but also to enslave poor whites. Worries that Southerners controlled the national government through their influence in the Democratic Party fueled the growth of the free-labor ideology espoused by Republicans. Although an economic recovery had begun by 1859, the crisis remained fresh in the minds of Americans for the next several years.[18]

Despite the fact that many historians have given the Panic of 1857 too little attention in their interpretations of the coming of the Civil War, James L. Huston has shown that the economic crisis played a critical role in the 1860 election, especially in Pennsylvania. The panic and depression it caused injected "specific economic policy questions into the controversy between North and South." Instead of sectional economic arguments being pro- or antislavery, the debate now shifted to "a controversy over the preservation of the free labor system." The Republicans "seized upon . . . the need to protect northern free labor society by appropriate federal enactments" and made it an effective political weapon against the South, arguing that "southerners not only cared little about northern free workers but also actively sought their degradation." This placed "the Panic of 1857 within the conceptual framework of the Slave Power conspiracy" and fanned the flames of fear "that southern political domination could destroy the viability of the North's free enterprise economy." Republicans, then, claimed to defend white liberty and free labor against the threat of the Slave Power. Democrats responded by arguing that the Panic of 1857 taught a valuable lesson in that it showed that "northern prosperity and social harmony depended upon a sure access to the southern market."[19]

Huston argues that, beyond political rhetoric, "the Panic of 1857 played a major role in shaping party campaign strategy" in 1860. Realizing that some critical states, "especially Pennsylvania," were unsure in the presidential election, politicians worked to create strategies that appealed to voters in those uncertain states. In Pennsylvania, this meant that Republicans would push for a high tariff. In doing so, they hoped, especially, to attract workers and capitalists in the iron industry who demanded higher tariff rates to protect them from foreign competition. Beyond the Keystone State, the Republicans hoped to gain support by advocating for a homestead bill. Favored by some Democrats as well, this legislation granted free land to actual settlers (instead of selling government lands in Western territories to speculators), a move that appealed to farmers ruined by the depression and hoping for a fresh start as well as out-of-work laborers in urban areas. When Republicans pushed for the protectionist Morrill Tariff and a homestead bill in 1859–60, the Democrats in Congress postponed the former, and President Buchanan killed the latter with a veto.[20]

This set the stage, then, for the political strategies in the election of 1860, as Republicans used economic issues to rally support in certain states and generally paint their opponents as enemies of free labor. Democrats responded by arguing that economic woes would follow a Republican victory, because that would mean the end of the Union. Douglas and his supporters tried to outmaneuver the Republicans by deflecting criticism on economic issues. They blamed Buchanan and the Southern Democrats for the party's failure to pass legislation favored by some Northern voters. In Pennsylvania, Douglas the free trader set aside his principles and argued that "a proper tariff" was in order. When Election Day came, the Republican strategy worked in Pennsylvania, with coal and iron districts abandoning the Democrats. As Huston puts it, "The Keystone State had become the foundation of Republican victory. By winning Pennsylvania, Lincoln had entered the White House." Lincoln's election, of course, led to Southern secession, which led to the Civil War. In Huston's words, "The immediate cause of the southerners' action was Lincoln's election; the immediate cause of Lincoln's election was the transformation of Pennsylvania from a Democratic to a Republican state. The Panic of 1857 played no small part in that transformation."[21]

Although Huston notes that Indiana also helped to elect Lincoln, he does not see the Panic of 1857 as playing a major role in the Hoosier State. He argued that Indiana did not experience the banking collapse like other Northern states. In fact, Indiana was one of four states that "maintained specie payment" during the panic and depression. In part, this was because the state's banking system had already weathered a crisis when "a regional panic in 1855 had already destroyed weaker banks and had placed the financial systems on a more prudent basis." Instead of economics, Huston points to the Bright-Douglas and Lecompton–anti-Lecompton split in the state party to explain the Democrats' defeat: "Indiana Democrats, however, still suffered the party division that had cost them" in earlier elections. At first blush, then, it seems that the Panic of 1857 did not play an important role in the Hoosier State in 1860. Historians of Indiana in the period remark that it must have played a role but do not explain how. Emma Lou Thornbrough put it this way: "Economic conditions, although they did not receive much attention in political speeches or in the press, were no doubt an ingredient in the political upheaval" of the 1850s. Kenneth M. Stampp concluded much the same: "While recent events, particularly the panic of 1857, made some men more ready to meet issues squarely and risk a crisis, the politicians continued to rival each other in affirming their devotion to conservatism." But Stampp reached a different conclusion about the importance of the crisis in Indiana: "The panic of 1857 severely checked the economic growth of Indiana, and even as late as 1860 recovery was far from complete." A second look reveals that the Panic of 1857 helped shape the 1860 campaign in Indiana, just as it did elsewhere. The economic crisis was a contingency on which the outcome of the electoral contest depended.[22]

Although economic issues did not dominate the campaigns in the Hoosier State, they certainly played a part in the election. The ways that the Panic of 1857 shaped the political strategies of Republicans elsewhere shaped them in Indiana as well. On March 18, 1860, early in the campaign, the Republican candidate for lieutenant governor, Oliver Morton, delivered a speech at Terre Haute that included economic issues. To be sure, he began with a lengthy discussion of Douglas's idea of popular sovereignty and an insistence that the Democrats were the true sectional party while Republicans were the party that hoped to save the Union. He denounced the Dred Scott decision and gave grudging support to the enforcement of the Fugitive Slave Act, which he thought "a fit subject for revision, amendment, and improvement." Morton denied that he was an abolitionist but argued, "I am opposed to the diffusion of slavery. I am in favor of preserving the Territories to freedom, of encouraging, elevating, and protecting free labor," but "with slavery in the several States we have nothing to do, and no right to interfere." In the wake of the Panic of 1857, the Hoosier Republican argued that his party defended free labor against the encroachment of the Slave Power. The Northern Democrats now served the interests of the South: "Power has passed from the democratic party in nearly all the Northern States. Its vitality and force are concentrated in the South."[23]

Having spent most of his speech on the issues surrounding slavery and its extension and the nature of the two parties, Morton came at last to the economy. He turned to "Protection to American Industry," arguing that "In collecting the revenues of the nation, the duties upon imports should be so adjusted that adequate protection be afforded to American industry." He tried to preempt Democratic charges of favoritism and the creation of monopolies by noting that "it is not the duty of the government to build up and maintain monopolies at the expense of the body of the nation." Still, it "is entirely within the power of the Congress, by a proper regulation of the tariff, to afford just encouragement and protection to the agricultural and manufacturing interests of our country." Although Morton did not mention the tariff until the end of his speech, it still played a part in his appeal to voters.[24]

He next turned to the "Homestead," an issue that attracted support from across the political spectrum in Indiana. Morton reminded his audience that many political leaders had long argued that "the public lands should not be treated as a source of revenue, but that they should be donated, in limited quantities, to actual settlers, who would improve them, and thus build up new communities and states." The Republican recalled that the previous policy of selling government lands had resulted in widespread speculation: "The greater portion of these lands have hitherto been purchased by non-residents and held for speculation." This hurt the "actual settler," who "has thus been compelled to purchase at second hand and at advanced rates, while the poor man has been debarred from a home and from a field for his industry." Morton extolled the virtues of "the hardy pioneers, braving the dangers and submitting to the hardships of the wilderness," and argued that the settlers themselves were the ones "who erect new States and enlarge the boundaries of our national wealth and power." Indeed, the settlers "are public benefactors and should not be required to pay tribute for their benefactions." Instead, "their homes should be given to them by the nation, upon conditions that they improve them, and thus add to the aggregate of our national prosperity." Anticipating Democratic arguments that the Republicans favored the rich at the expense of the poor, Morton closed his Terre Haute speech by saying, "It is not important that we have very rich men in this country, but it is important that all have homes and competence, and be made to feel that their country is a nursing mother, whose devotion to their interest, and protection of their rights can only be requited by a life of patriotism." Thus, the Republican ideology of free labor combined with economic policy in his call for a Homestead Act.[25]

Although these economic issues faded as the campaign wore on and Morton mentioned them less often, the Panic of 1857 still loomed large in the background. More important, the Republicans continued to cast themselves as the defenders of free labor in the North while accusing the Democrats of being the enemies of the working man. Time and time again, in speech after speech, Morton reminded his audience that the Republicans were the true friends of labor. He constantly and consistently unfurled the banner of free labor ideology as he attacked the Democrats and the forces of slavery. In a speech he made in Fort Wayne later in the campaign, the Republican candidate argued that the "mission of the republican party is to prevent the further extension of slavery, and to rescue the government from the corruption and abuses of the party in power." The antislavery position lay at the very heart of the party. But "embraced within it as its great central idea, its very existence, is the protection, dignity and elevation of free labor." Morton asked, "Who is so dull as not to see that labor is degraded and put beneath the dignity of free men, when it is performed by slaves?" Thus, even slavery had to be understood in the terms of a free-labor ideology, the doctrines of which were made real and concrete by the Panic of 1857. The crux of the matter was the struggle between slavery and free labor. "We believe that slavery is a moral, social, and political evil," Morton declared. Republicans thus opposed this evil on moral grounds. "But there are other considerations of a more personal and selfish character. If we do not exclude slavery from the Territories, it will exclude us. Free labor will not go to any considerable extent where slave labor exists, because it is degraded and dishonored by the association." Indeed, Morton argued, "Free labor and slave labor will not flourish in the same bed." He appealed to Hoosiers as working men, reminding them, "Where slave labor strikes its roots deep into the soil of a Territory, free labor will not grow but perish at the threshold." He urged them to realize that "we are all personally interested in this question—not indirectly and remotely as in a mere political abstraction—but directly, pecuniarily, and selfishly." Morton asked, "How can you, my democratic friends, labor for or even consent to the building up of an institution in the Territories which turns you and your children out? If you do not care for yourselves, at least care for your children."[26]

Even in this Fort Wayne address, which focused primarily on the slavery question, Morton did not merely interpret the issues in light of free labor but also found time to take up economic issues directly. Much of his speech attacked Stephen A. Douglas, now the Northern Democratic candidate and Lincoln's clear rival in Indiana. After blasting away at the Little Giant on matters surrounding the Democrat's positions on slavery, Morton now bombarded his "Impudence on a Large Scale" in economic matters. The Republican reminded his audience that "Mr. Douglas has been distinguished throughout his public life as an ultra free trade man. He has upon every occasion denounced protection in every form." But Douglas no longer held to his principles and flip-flopped on the tariff issue. Now, in a speech in Pennsylvania, "he came out boldly for a protective tariff, declaring that it was the duty of Congress to protect the coal and iron interests of Pennsylvania." Morton said that Douglas argued that "it was the improper intrusion of the slavery question into Congress which had prevented consideration and action upon the manufacturing and mining interests of Pennsylvania." Later in the same speech, the candidate for lieutenant governor defended the Republican Party against charges that they had used the Swamp Lands Committee to take good land by fraud. Corruption intertwined with economic matters, Morton hoped to convince Hoosier voters that the Republicans stood for honest government as well as new economic measures that would protect them from another panic and depression.[27]

Morton closed his campaign speech in Fort Wayne with praise for "Honest Old Abe." Evangelical voters motivated by moral issues liked the label "honest." And character mattered in other ways as well. Among the many attributes that recommended Lincoln to the voters of Indiana, Morton found the chief economic issue of the day: "His boyhood and early manhood were spent in honest toil in forest and in field, and he is thus preeminently qualified to be the candidate of the republican party at a time when free labor and slave labor are brought in conflict face to face." Lincoln "is in his own person the representation of free labor, and what it can do in ennobling and dignifying the human character. His hands, like yours, have been hardened with toil, and his brow has dripped with the perspiration of honest labor." If Indiana voters had, "by your honest industry and toil," managed to acquire "a home and a competence, Old Abe can sympathize with you. He knows just how you came by it." Morton's final words rang out: "[I]f . . . you believe that freedom is better than slavery—that the Territories should be preserved for free men and free labor—that freedom should be national and slavery sectional, then vote the republican ticket." If they did, he assured them, "you will vote your sentiments, and do your duty to your country and your God!" By embedding economic issues in the ideology of free labor, the Republicans not only promised that they would prevent another panic but also meant that Hoosiers must support Lincoln and his party if they hoped to protect their own self-interest, their own way of life, and the nation as a whole, and to please the Almighty. According to Morton, God clearly planned to vote Republican.[28]

Although contingency decided much in the Indiana election of 1860, another of David Mayhew's nominalist alternatives to the grand theory of realignment also came into play. He urges scholars to consider "*short-term strategy* as it is plied by candidates and parties, both of which tend to cater to the electorate as well as to emanate from it." In this view, analysis of elections assumes to some degree "that parties and candidates seek election victories above all else." This means that the parties "tend to converge at the voter median and bring on close elections." Thus, the parties employ strategies designed to guarantee victory rather than seeking to embrace or evade major issues that animate the electorate. In 1860, both parties tried to portray themselves to Hoosiers as the true defenders of freedom and the antislavery position because that was the view of the majority of voters in the state. This dictated the short-term strategy employed by the Republican Party in particular.[29]

In 1856, the Indiana Republicans nominated Oliver Morton as their candidate for governor. Morton, a native of Wayne County, earned a reputation as an attorney before turning to politics. A Democrat early in his career, Morton broke with that party on the Kansas-Nebraska Act. After wavering on what to do, he walked out of the state party convention and joined the People's Party, which eventually became the Republican Party. He campaigned against the Kansas-Nebraska Act and for the People's Party candidates in 1854 and in 1856 became the standard bearer for the Republicans. He held his own against Ashbel P. Willard, the popular orator who ran for the Democrats in the race for governor. Morton lost the election by fewer than six thousand votes, but his strong campaign made him the favorite for the gubernatorial nomination again in 1860. Now known around the state, with a growing reputation as a speaker and skillful debater, and respected for his leadership in the party since its inception, it seemed that he should readily get the nod for another run at the governor's chair.[30]

But Indiana Republicans developed a short-term strategy designed to win the election that put Morton into the lieutenant governor's slot instead of at the top of the ticket. Hoping to bring more voters into their party's fold, Republicans angled at attracting more former Whigs. By the late 1850s, the party consisted of a fusion of ex-Whigs, former Democrats opposed to the Kansas-Nebraska Act, Know-Nothings hoping to broaden their appeal, temperance advocates calling for a "Maine law" to prohibit alcohol in Indiana, and a variety of opponents of slavery, many of whom had belonged to the Free Soil Party. With their long-standing political organizations around the state, the Whigs moved easily into leadership positions, first in the People's Party, then in the Republican camp. They hoped to assert their nationalist economic and political agenda in the new party and believed that bringing in the rest of the former Whigs would solidify their position, both with the electorate and within the party. They distrusted former Democrats such as Morton and hoped to replace him with an ex-Whig. Furthermore, a well-known former Whig would reassure voters fearful that the Republicans were too radical in their opposition to slavery. Nominating an old Whig would dispel charges of abolitionism and portray the Republicans as conservative and mainstream.[31]

With this in mind, many in the Republican leadership sought to put Henry S. Lane in the governor's slot. A Kentucky native who had long opposed slavery, Lane had been a disciple of Henry Clay, the great leader of the Whigs. As such, Lane had worked tirelessly for his party, stumping for Clay in the presidential contest in 1844 and running for office himself. A Crawfordsville attorney and banker and a veteran of the Mexican-American War, Lane had all of the credentials necessary for winning high office. He had plenty of experience: over the years, he had served in the state senate, run unsuccessfully for Congress, and, arguably, had been elected to the U.S. Senate in the disputed election of 1856, which resulted in the Senate's refusal to seat the People's Party candidates in favor of the incumbent Democratic senators. His many campaigns had won him widespread name recognition. Furthermore, Lane had joined the Republican Party early and had been active in organizing it in the state. In addition to being loyal, he was popular and respected. Still further, he was a good speaker and a fine debater. When those who called for rotating candidates for office to avoid making the party seem like a tool for any particular individual added their voices to the chorus of those supporting Lane, he seemed like a fine choice.[32]

But Lane had other ideas. He coveted a seat in the U.S. Senate and thought he might be elected to the position if the Republicans won control of the state legislature. And Morton wanted to be governor, and his many friends and supporters backed him in seeking the office. Moreover, if he did not win the nomination for governor, Morton thought he should be given the nod for the Senate. For a while, it seemed that the Republicans in Indiana might follow the Democrats into division, with separate factions gathering around individual leaders ambitious for office. Instead, the party leadership worked out a compromise that implemented their short-term strategy. A deal was reached in which Lane would run for governor and Morton for lieutenant governor with the understanding that, if the Republicans controlled the legislature, Lane would become senator and Morton would fill the vacant governor's chair. Morton had to set aside his ambition to make the compromise work, a move he made with some difficulty. One Wayne County Republican, a Quaker, came to Morton and urged him to make the deal and run with Lane. In reply, Morton argued that he wanted to be governor and, if he could not have that, he should be the candidate for the senate instead of letting Lane have the advantage in both positions. The Quaker listened to Morton's arguments and replied, "Oliver, we can't let thee go to the Senate." When Morton asked why not, the man answered, "Because thee is a good man for either of these places, and Henry Lane would make a good Senator but would not make a good Governor. So he must go to the Senate and thee must stay and be governor." With such appeals to his vanity, Morton reluctantly made the deal, and the Republicans set their strategy into motion. In the October elections, the Lane-Morton ticket carried the day with a majority of about ten thousand votes. After two days in office, Lane was elected senator and Morton took over as governor. The Indiana Republican short-term strategy had worked.[33]

The Republican strategy of running Lane and Morton together in hopes of putting Lane in the Senate and Morton in the governor's mansion centered on the belief that the Republicans had to portray themselves as conservative if they hoped to win over more voters. Their thinking illustrated the importance of *valence* issues in 1860, the third nominalist antidote to realignment theory suggested by David Mayhew. First introduced in the 1960s by Donald J. Stokes and covered primarily in scholarship dedicated to "gauging the effects of ups and downs of the economy on elections," valence issues "hinge chiefly on perceived government management: my party can manage the economy or the war, for example, better than your party has been doing." This shifts the interpretation of elections away from "the staple kind of cleavage in the realignments genre," namely the ""position" issues, with one party favoring policy X and the other party favoring policy Y." Mayhew argues that the "more one examines American electoral history, the more it seems to tilt toward valence-issue as opposed to position-issue junctures." Indeed, valence issues "exemplify contingency and often bring into play opportunistic candidate or party strategies." In 1860 in Indiana, Republicans used valence issues to outmaneuver the Democrats on the question of slavery and win the election. Once again, the campaign speeches of Oliver P. Morton illustrate the point.[34]

Numerous historians have noted that the Republicans nationwide tried to portray themselves as more conservative than their Democratic opponents in the electoral cycles leading up to the Civil War. But what did that mean? In Indiana, at least, it meant that the Republicans used the valence issue of slavery to defeat their opponents. In essence, they argued that their party could better defend the antislavery position than the Democrats. The Republicans contended that if elected, they would do better than the corrupt, incompetent Democrats when it came to stopping the expansion of slavery into new territories. They claimed that the Northern Democrats could not be trusted on the issue, because they had changed their position time and again in opportunistic moves designed to win elections. Further, the Republicans charged their rivals with complicity in the peculiar institution. The Slave Power, they said, controlled the Democratic Party. Hoosier voters could not trust the Democrats to defend free labor and stop the extension of slavery. Whether caused by corruption or conspiracy or incompetence, the Democratic record made it clear that the party had failed to do the job on the most vital issue in the 1860 election.[35]

Although some Republican candidates in Indiana, including Lane, downplayed the slavery issue as a means of seeming more conservative and moderate by avoiding charges of abolitionism, Oliver Morton faced the issue head on. In his Terre Haute speech early in the campaign, he argued that the Democrats actually were the radical party, because they had been the ones to overturn the long-standing Missouri Compromise. Here, Morton's personal views clearly entered in. He had been an anti-Nebraska Democrat who left the party over the issue of Douglas's Kansas-Nebraska Act in 1854. He defined a "sectional party" as one "which, in its principles and purposes, seeks to consult and promote the interests of one section of the Republic, regardless of, or at the expense of the interest and prosperity of all other sections." He charged that the Democrats were the true sectional party, because Republicans were not even allowed to operate in the Southern states. Morton quickly made much of "The Conservatism of the Republican Party" in answer to the "common charge made against" Republicans that the party was "radical, revolutionary, and subversive in its character." He denied this, arguing that "this charge is manifestly unjust." In fact, he claimed that "the republican party is the historical and conservative party of the nation." To make his point, Morton defined a conservative as "one who aims to preserve from ruin, innovation, injury, or radical change; one who wishes to maintain an institution or form of government in its present form." By showing that the Republican "policy of opposition to the general diffusion of slavery, the preservation of the Territories to freedom, and the protection and elevation of free labor, is coeval with, or antecedent to the adoption of our Constitution," he argued that the party's "claim to conservatism is fully established." If the Republicans were the conservatives by this standard, then "the democratic party will be found to be radical, revolutionary and subversive, departing from its own creed, revolutionizing a long course of judicial decisions, and subverting the practice of the government from the time of its creation." Morton argued that the Democratic Party "has erected, into an article of faith, the new, dangerous, and portentous dogma, that the Constitution, by its own inherent power, establishes slavery in all the Territories, and that there is no power . . . that can exclude it therefrom." Here, he cast conservatism in terms of a valence issue, turning on its head the Democratic argument that the Republicans were radical and argued just the opposite.[36]

After denouncing the violence of John Brown, Morton blamed the "agitation of the slavery question" on the Democrats, noting that it could be "traced to the repeal of the Missouri Compromise." The Kansas-Nebraska Act "found the country at peace, and has left it stained with blood and torn by civil dissensions. It re-opened the slave question in a form most offensive and under circumstances most aggravating to the anti-slavery sentiment of the North." Far from defending Northern antislavery views, Stephen A. Douglas and the Democrats had caused the turmoil and strife that threatened to tear the country apart. Furthermore, Morton asked, "[W]hat is the cause of the hostility pervading the Southern mind toward the people of the North?" He answered his own question: "There are many causes, but the chief one is to be found in the policy of the democratic party." Morton argued that the Democrats had used the slavery issue to their political advantage and in so doing, had indoctrinated the two sections of the country to distrust and even hate one another. In tying the protection of slavery only to themselves, the Democrats made the South suspicious of any other party, because slaveholders feared that Northerners wanted to destroy their institutions. By demonizing the Republicans as abolitionists, the Democrats made it impossible for their rivals to circulate their newspapers or even speak in the South. The slavery question had "been invoked and fostered by the democratic party as a source and means of power." However, the Republican Party "has not produced this agitation, but has been produced by it. It is the creature rather than the creator. It sprang like a phoenix from the ashes of decayed parties, not as a sword, but as a shield" to protect freedom.[37]

Morton argued that "the policy of the democratic party is the extension of slavery, not only into all the Territories, but all the States." Democrats planned to accomplish this goal by using "the supreme court; an irresponsible tribunal, the members of which hold their offices for life, and who are not elected by nor amenable to the people." The Court "for many years, has been used as a place of retiracy for broken, spavined and asthmatic politicians." He claimed that far from fulfilling the vision of the founders, who hoped the Supreme Court would be a "court of appeals for the decision of questions of law and equity, legitimately arising in the lower federal courts," the Court had "been converted into an engine for the subversion of free institutions and the propagation of human slavery." The first step in extending slavery across the nation had been the repeal of the Missouri Compromise through the doctrine of popular sovereignty. The second step was the Dred Scott decision. Only the Republican Party stood in the breach against the growing Slave Power. Only it could protect Northern free labor from slavery. Only it could save the Union from the tide of revolutionary radicalism promoted by the Democratic Party. The true use of the word *republican* did not employ the term "in a narrow, sectarian, or party sense." Instead, Morton asserted that "by republican doctrine, I mean that sentiment which is opposed to the general diffusion of slavery; desires the preservation of the Territories to freedom, and seeks the elevation and protection of free labor." When Republicans such as Morton combined contingency issues such as the Bright/Douglas battle, the Panic of 1857, and the Revival of 1858 with valence issues such as which party would better protect the country against corruption and preserve the ideals of free labor, valence issues joined contingency in the minds of Hoosier voters. Not only would Republicans best protect them from economic crisis but would also defend freedom against the forces of slavery. The Democrats could no longer be trusted on the slavery question, because (as quoted above), "Power has passed from the democratic party in nearly all the Northern States. Its vitality and force are concentrated in the South." Democrats had actually created the problem and certainly could not be expected to fix it.[38]

Time and time again throughout the campaign, Morton returned to these themes, casting the decision facing Indiana voters in the language of a valence issue. Politicians of each party accused those of the other of being radical while portraying themselves as conservatives. In Morton's actions and speeches in 1860, contingency, strategy, and valence issues all came together, reflecting the way that those nominalist antidotes, suggested by

David Mayhew, "tend to infuse elections." In Indiana, the contingencies of the Democratic split and the Panic of 1857 shaped the election of 1860. Despite his own ideological preferences on the slavery issue, Jesse Bright's attempt to defeat Douglas and regain control of the state Democratic Party by supporting Breckinridge was a major blunder that only increased the Republican momentum. Indeed, David Turpie, the Democratic candidate for lieutenant governor, blamed Bright for the party's defeat in 1860: "In October we suffered a defeat not unexpected. . . . The majority against us in the state corresponded somewhat with the vote cast for Breckinridge in November. . . . Our discomfiture was principally due to the Breckinridge movement."[39]

The Panic of 1857 remained fresh in the minds of Indiana voters and further influenced the election of 1860. Republicans such as Morton used economic issues to appeal to Hoosiers still trying to recover from the depression and offered such remedies as the tariff and the Homestead Act. Here, too, valence issues mattered, with the Republicans railing against the Democratic failure to prevent the economic crisis and deriding the Buchanan administration's inadequate response. The Republicans could do better, they argued. But the economic crisis also made the Republican ideology of free labor real and concrete. No longer did Northerners view the conflict between free labor and slavery as an abstraction. The Panic of 1857 and the depression that followed put the terms of the debate into real-life situations that voters could understand. In Indiana, as well as in Pennsylvania, economics mattered. The Republicans designed a strategy to take advantage of the situation. Another valence issue involved corruption, especially in the wake of the Revival of 1857–58. Moral issues, especially political corruption, mattered. All candidates sought to blame someone else for the scandals of the past while claiming the mantle for reform. Short-term strategy also played a role in 1860, when Hoosier Republicans devised a plan that allowed them to appeal to a wider spectrum of voters by putting Henry Lane at the top of the state ticket. This was a risky move, requiring ambitious leaders to compromise for the good of the whole. Lane and Morton made their deal and implemented the Republican plan. When the plan was combined with their argument that they were the conservative party and the view of Abraham Lincoln as a moderate, this strategy paid off in victory. Lane and Morton and a majority of the Republican congressional candidates won election in October. Lincoln drew an even larger majority in Indiana's November vote for president.

Contingency and strategy came together in a valence issue in 1860, with the Republicans outflanking the Democrats in arguing that they could do a better job of protecting freedom than their rivals. Morton and his fellow Republicans took up the mantle of conservatism and painted the Democrats as radical revolutionaries. They blamed the Democrats for causing the sectional crisis and denounced Northern Democrats such as Douglas as corrupt opportunists. The Republicans wrapped themselves in the flag of patriotism and claimed the inheritance of the founding fathers. They denounced the Supreme Court as an undemocratic "tribunal" removed from the people, a tool in the hands of the Slave Power. The Democrats, controlled by the South, provided the means by which proslavery advocates held the reins of power. The Democratic Party, far from defending freedom in the North, actually extended slavery and threatened to destroy free labor. Only the Republicans could be counted on to promote antislavery policies and stop the expansion of slavery. Only they could prevent the Slave Power from invading the North and spreading the evil of slavery throughout the land.

The election of 1860 in Indiana, then, confirms both David Mayhew's critique of realignment theory and his nominalist antidotes to that grand theory. Far from being another part of a cyclical pattern of political realignments that occur about every thirty years, the most critical election in American history was actually much more complicated and complex, hinging on local or state interpretations of national issues that had little to do with realignment theory. Indeed, the case of Indiana supports Mayhew's contention that realignment should be set aside not only because "it does not come close to working" but also "because other stories can be told." He suggests three other narratives that might prove more insightful than the ones constructed using realignment theory. One "is about *bellicosity*," because war certainly shaped at least "the first third or so of American national history." Obviously, bellicosity played a role in 1860. A "second story is about *race*." Historians have already constructed stories about the role of race in American history, and it remains one of the most powerful forces in explaining the coming of the Civil War. The third narrative Mayhew suggests "is about *economic growth*." He argues that questions about how voters respond to the economy, rewarding or punishing parties and politicians for financial prosperity or downturns, might prove insightful. Surely, 1860 offers just such a story. The Panic of 1857 shaped the election, and Republican policies during the Civil War accelerated the rate of industrialization. Indeed, as Mayhew concludes, "the realignments way of thinking adds little or no illumination, but it does exact opportunity costs. Other lines of investigation might be more promising." The 1860 election in Indiana, at least, confirms Mayhew's refutation of realignment theory and underscores his contention that "it has come to be too much of a dead end." Other stories—not just general ones about war, race, and economic growth, but particular studies that emphasize contingency, strategy, and valence issues—need to be told.[40]

1. For several of the most important studies in the genre, see William Nisbet Chambers and Walter Dean Burnham, eds., *The American Party Systems* (New York: Oxford Univ. Press, 1967); Walter Dean Burnham, *Critical Elections and the Mainsprings of American Politics* (New York: Norton, 1970); and Paul Kleppner et al., *The Evolution of American Electoral Systems* (Westport, Conn.: Greenwood Press, 1981). A clear statement and defense of the ethnocultural historians' utilization of realignment theory can be found in Michael F. Holt, *Political Parties and American Development from the Age of Jackson to the Age of Lincoln* (Baton Rouge: Louisiana State Univ. Press, 1992), esp. 291–302. The claim that realignment elections are nationalized is made by David W. Brady, *Critical Elections and Congressional Policy Making* (Stanford: Stanford Univ. Press, 1988). For the critique and the interpretive framework behind the argument made in this essay, see David R. Mayhew, *Electoral Realignments: A Critique of an American Genre* (New Haven: Yale Univ. Press, 2002), esp. 24, 100–102, 147–53. For Mayhew's conclusion about 1860, see *Electoral Realignments*, 162–64. A number of political historians have criticized realignment theory and have cited to serious problems with it, including the difficulty in periodization political systems. For an example, see Joel H. Silbey, "Beyond Realignment and Realignment Theory: American Political Eras, 1789–1989," in *The End of Realignment?* ed. Byron E. Shafer (Madison: Univ. of Wisconsin Press, 1991), 3–23. Silbey offers a very different chronology that itself challenges realignment theory; see Joel H. Silbey, *The American Political Nation, 1838–1893* (Stanford: Stanford Univ. Press, 1991).

2. Mayhew, *Electoral Realignments,* 7–33. In this section of his book, Mayhew explains and challenges fifteen different claims within the realignment genre. Others not addressed in the text of this chapter but some of which may also be applied to 1860 include: "electoral realignments have appeared in a pattern of regularity—that is, periodicity"; "a dynamic of tension buildup has caused the oscillation in and out of the thirty-year-or-so realignment cycles"; "voter concern and turnout are unusually high in realigning elections"; realignments "are distinctively associated with "redistributive" policies; the "American voting public expresses itself effectively . . . during electoral realignments, but not otherwise"; and "there existed a 'System of 1896.'"

3. Mayhew, *Electoral Realignments,* 7–33.

4. Ibid., 162–64.

5. Ibid., 147–49. For the purposes of this essay, I am accepting Mayhew's assertion that contingency is a more valuable approach to history. Although contingency

is popular among historians today, determinism and inevitability remain significant to scholars of the Civil War era. I do not agree entirely with those who argue for contingency, but my own views are less important here than showing that the still widely held theory of realignment breaks down when we examine Indiana as a case study. Edward L. Ayers explores the divide between contingency and inevitability among scholars explaining the causes of the Civil War in *What Caused the Civil War: Reflections on the South and Southern History* (New York: Norton, 2005), esp. 131–44. On the question of inevitability, see also James Huston's piece on Stephen A. Douglas in chapter two of this volume.

6. For these election results, see Emma Lou Thornbrough, *Indiana in the Civil War Era* (Indianapolis: Indiana Historical Society, 1965), 52–54, 59–67, 71–77, 81–83; Kenneth M. Stampp, *Indiana Politics during the Civil War* (Indianapolis: Indiana Historical Bureau, 1949; repr., Bloomington: Indiana Univ. Press, 1978), 4–17; and Kenneth C. Martis, *The Historical Atlas of Political Parties in the United States Congress* (New York: Macmillan, 1989). For the breakdown of each congressional election, see the *House Journal* for the first forty-three sessions of Congress at the American Memory section of the Library of Congress Web site, available at http://memory.loc.gov/ammem/amlaw/lwhjlink.html, accessed March 9, 2012. For an older book that is still useful for any examination of the election of 1860, see Roy F. Nichols, *The Disruption of American Democracy* (New York: Macmillan, 1948). Nichols's conclusions reflect the Progressive Era during which he wrote, but his insights on the Northern Democrats remain valuable. For a fine historical study that emphasizes the Republicans, see William Gienapp, *The Origins of the Republican Party, 1852–1856* (New York: Oxford Univ. Press, 1987).

7. Stampp, *Indiana Politics during the Civil War,* 34–41; Thornbrough, *Indiana in the Civil War Era,* 87–88. As Joel Silbey has shown, other issues than slavery remained vital to the Democrats, even amid the sectionalism of the 1850s. For his analysis of the role of religion, culture, and local issues, see his *Partisan Imperative: The Dynamics of American Politics Before the Civil War* (New York: Oxford Univ. Press, 1985), 87–115.

8. Thornbrough, *Indiana in the Civil War Era,* 41–43; Nichols, *The Disruption of American Democracy,* 4–5, 13, 176. Wright continued to be a threat to Bright despite accepting the post of ambassador to Prussia in Berlin when Buchanan offered him the position to him in 1857 after several other men refused it. Wright would return to the ambassadorship after the Civil War.

9. Thornbrough, *Indiana in the Civil War Era,* 69–71, 78, 81; Nichols, *The Disruption of American Democracy,* 15.

10. Nichols, *The Disruption of American Democracy,* 294–309, 314–22; Stampp, *Indiana Politics during the Civil War,* 15–21, 97; Thornbrough, *Indiana in the Civil War Era,* 115; Richard F. Nation and Stephen E. Towne, *Indiana's War: The Civil War in Documents* (Athens: Ohio Univ. Press, 2009), 44, 53–55.

11. Mayhew, *Electoral Realignments,* 147–48.

12. James L. Huston, *The Panic of 1857 and the Coming of the Civil War* (Baton Rouge: Louisiana State Univ. Press, 1987), 14–28; Murray N. Rothbard, *A History of Money and Banking in the United States: The Colonial Era to World War II* (Auburn, Ala.: Ludwig von Mises Institute, 2005), 90–114. In addition to Huston, another historian who gives the Panic of 1857 more than a passing reference is Kenneth M. Stampp, *America in 1857: A Nation on the Brink* (New York: Oxford Univ.

Press, 1990), 221–38. Allan Nevins also gave a more thorough look at the panic and resulting depression in the third volume of his eight-volume classic study of the Civil War era, *The Ordeal of the Union;* see Nevins, *The Emergence of Lincoln: Douglas, Buchanan, and Party Chaos, 1857–1859* (New York: Charles Scribner's Sons, 1950), 176–97. A more typical example is Nevins's fellow Progressive historian Roy F. Nichols, who gives the crisis three pages out of more than five hundred in *The Disruption of American Democracy,* 132–34. The consensus scholar David M. Potter mentions the Panic of 1857 on only once in his nearly six hundred pages of *The Impending Crisis, 1848–1861* (New York: Harper & Row, 1976. Sean Wilentz manages about five pages out of some 150 dedicated to the 1850–61 period in *The Rise of American Democracy: Jefferson to Lincoln* (New York: Norton, 2005), 719–25.

13. Huston, *The Panic of 1857,* 130, 131–38.

14. On the Revival of 1858, see, especially, Timothy L. Smith, *Revivalism and Social Reform in Mid-19th-Century America* (New York: Abingdon Press, 1957), esp. 63–79; Richard J. Carwardine, *Evangelicals and Politics in Antebellum America* (New Haven: Yale Univ. Press, 1993), 292–96; Stampp, *America in 1857,* 236–38.

15. Calvin Fletcher, diary, Saturday, March 27, 1858, quoted in Gayle Thornbrough, Dorothy L. Riker, and Paula Corpuz, eds., *The Diary of Calvin Fletcher,* vol. 6, *1857–1860, Including Letters to and from Calvin Fletcher* (Indianapolis: Indiana Historical Society, 1978), 208–9. The *Indianapolis Locomotive,* March 27, 1858.

16. Calvin Fletcher, diary, September 11, 1860, in Thornbrough et al., *Diary of Calvin Fletcher,* vol. 6, 596; Fletcher, diary, Friday, September 28, 1860, in Thornbrough et al., *Diary of Calvin Fletcher,* 602–3; Fletcher, diary, Saturday, September 29, 1860, in Thornbrough et al., *Diary of Calvin Fletcher,* 603.

17. For the revival's role in the election of 1860, see Carwardine, *Evangelicals and Politics,* 296–307. For the true meaning of "Black Republican," see, for example, J. G. Randall, *Lincoln the President: Springfield to Gettysburg* (New York: Dodd, Mead, 1945), 1:182. Corruption also mattered in the context of republicanism, the ideology that underlay much of antebellum politics. For more extensive discussions of republican ideology, see my essays in chaps. 3 and 4 in this book and the insightful piece by Thomas E. Rodgers in chap. 6.

18. Rothbard, *History of Money and Banking,* 115–22; Huston, *The Panic of 1857,* 210. For more on the Panic of 1857, the Republicans and free labor ideology, see Eric Foner, *Free Soil, Free Labor, Free Men: The Ideology of the Republican Party before the Civil War* (New York: Oxford Univ. Press, 1970), 24–29.

19. Huston, *The Panic of 1857,* 231.

20. Huston, *The Panic of 1857,* 231–32, 246–48.

21. Huston, *The Panic of 1857,* 251, 260. Huston clearly takes a deterministic view in his analysis, making my use of his work in support of contingency somewhat ironic. However, at some point, something determines an outcome. At what point does a contingency make the result inevitable? In this case, I see the election as hinging on the contingency of the economic situation, among other factors. Huston would argue that the economic context determined the election. So in a sense, we are saying the same thing about this particular instance in history. For more on Huston's view of contingency and determinism, see his excellent essay on Stephen A. Douglas in chap. 3 of this book.

22. Huston, *Panic of 1857,* 23; Thornbrough, *Indiana in the Civil War Era,* 84; Stampp, *Indiana Politics during the Civil War,* 43, 10.

23. Oliver P. Morton, "Speech delivered at Terre Haute, March 18th, 1860," in William M. French, ed., *Life, Speeches, State Papers and Public Services of Gov. Oliver P. Morton* (Cincinnati: Moore, Wilstach, & Baldwin Printers, 1866), 31–53.

24. Morton, "Speech delivered at Terre Haute," 54–55.

25. Morton, "Speech delivered at Terre Haute," March 18, 1860, 55.

26. Oliver P. Morton, "Campaign of 1860, Speech at Fort Wayne," in French, *Life, Speeches of Morton*, 81–102.

27. Morton, "Campaign of 1860, Speech at Fort Wayne," 103–15.

28. Morton, "Campaign of 1860, Speech at Fort Wayne," 117–18.

29. Mayhew, *Electoral Realignments*, 148.

30. Thornbrough, *Indiana in the Civil War Era*, 72–73, 76; Stampp, *Indiana Politics during the Civil War*, 27.

31. Stampp, *Indiana Politics during the Civil War*, 22, 27.

32. Ibid., 27. For more on Lane, see James E. St. Clair, "Henry S. Lane, January 14–16, 1861," in Linda C. Gugin and James E. St. Clair, *The Governors of Indiana* (Indianapolis: Indiana Historical Society Press, 2006), 136–39.

33. William Dudley Foulke, *Life of Oliver P. Morton, Including His Important Speeches* (2 vols. Indianapolis: Bowen-Merrill, 1899), 1:66–67; Stampp, *Indiana Politics during the Civil War*, 27–28. For the deal between Lane and Morton, as well as a similar arrangement on the Democratic side, see David Turpie, *Sketches of My Own Times* (Indianapolis: Bobbs-Merrill, 1903), 183–84.

34. Mayhew, *Electoral Realignments*, 149–52.

35. For historians outlining the Republican claim to conservatism in Indiana, see Stampp, *Indiana Politics during the Civil War*, 43; and Thornbrough, *Indiana in the Civil War Era*, 90–92.

36. Morton, "Speech delivered at Terre Haute," 31–38.

37. Morton, "Speech delivered at Terre Haute," 38–47. In the political turmoil of the 1850s, Kansas came to be a symbol of white liberty, making Morton's use of it as a valence issue all the more significant. See Nicole Etcheson, *Bleeding Kansas: Contested Liberty in the Civil War Era* (Lawrence: Univ. Press of Kansas, 2004).

38. Morton, "Speech delivered at Terre Haute," 47–54.

39. For more of Morton's 1860 campaign speeches, see French, *Life, Speeches of Morton*, 31–135; and Foulke, *Life of Morton*, 67–84. Mayhew, *Electoral Realignments*, 152; Turpie, *Sketches of My Own Times*, 188.

40. Turpie, *Sketches of My Own Times*, 156–65.

8

The View from Abroad

Europeans Look at the Election of 1860

Lawrence Sondhaus

In sharp contrast to the depth of European interest in the bloody war that resulted from it, the U.S. presidential election of 1860 attracted relatively little attention across the Atlantic. Few European commentators foresaw the outcome of the election campaign or appreciated its significance after the results were known. Fewer still accurately predicted what would happen next, after an entire region of the American republic refused to accept the overall verdict of the electorate. From the party conventions of May 1860 to the shelling of Fort Sumter eleven months later, the quantity and quality of information about the looming American crisis depended first and foremost on the traditional diplomatic channels, with European diplomats in the United States, along with their American counterparts in European capitals, shaping European opinion about the crisis by the way they interpreted it. Second, and no less significant, were the impressions of prominent American visitors to Europe and European visitors to the United States. The former included the Republican leader William H. Seward, in Europe from May to December 1859; the latter, Albert Edward, Prince of Wales (the future King Edward VII), visiting the United States in September and October 1860. Decades before the onset of international news services, essentially the same articles would appear in the press of both continents; London newspapers copied New York newspapers and vice versa. Diplomats, foreign travelers, and the press alike suffered from the problem that their dispatches, letters, and newspapers took time to cross the Atlantic. The transatlantic telegraph cable, operational as of July 1858, failed that September and would not be replaced by

Fig. 31. His Royal Highness, Albert Edward, Prince of Wales. (*Harper's Weekly,* October 6, 1860)

a second, permanent cable until July 1866. Until then—and thus through-out the Civil War—the United States once again was separated from Eu-rope by roughly two weeks, a fast steamer's average passage time from New York or Boston to British ports.

Whereas European intellectuals viewed the United States as a laboratory for the political ideals of the Enlightenment (liberals generally sympathizing with the republican experiment, conservatives viewing it with skepticism), European interest in American affairs naturally centered on the economic importance of Southern cotton production and the slave labor that made it possible. In the average year during the decade of the 1850s, the Ameri-can South accounted for 72 percent of the raw cotton imported by Britain; in 1860, "a bumper crop in Dixie" drove it to 85 percent. France's much smaller textile industry was even more dependent on the South, which produced 93 percent of French raw cotton imports during the 1850s. In some years, cotton textiles accounted for as much as 55 percent of all British exports, and at least 4 million British workers depended on the textile industry for their livelihood. Such statistics fed the "King Cotton" arguments of slave-state politicians, who entered the crisis of 1860–61 increasingly confident that an independent union of Southern states would be both economically viable and supported by powerful allies abroad.[1] Because Britain had abolished the slave trade in 1807 and slavery in 1833, with France following suit in 1848, the slave labor essential to American cotton production posed a moral dilemma for the leading European states. Well before mid-century, a majority of Britons from across the political spectrum condemned slavery on humanitarian or religious grounds. This should have predisposed most of them to sympathize with the free states of the North, but patience had its limits. British abolitionists and other idealists considered the Compromise of 1850 morally bankrupt; afterward, some had difficulty identifying with a North whose leading politicians could be so pragmatic when it came to the greatest moral issue of the age.

Their despair soon gave way to fresh hope with the publication of Harriet Beecher Stowe's *Uncle Tom's Cabin*. The first London edition of the novel appeared in May 1852, and by the end of that year, it had sold over a million copies in Britain, at least triple the number it sold in the United States. Stowe toured Britain in 1853, then again in 1856 and 1859, reigniting interest in the issue of American slavery and the politics surrounding it.[2] Before the decade ended, *Uncle Tom's Cabin* had been translated into at least sixteen other languages, including Serbian, Slovenian, Welsh, and Armenian. Eleven different French editions appeared in 1852 alone. After Napoleon III established the Second Empire later that year, French liberals barred by the censor from discussing most domestic affairs found their catharsis in the drama unfolding across the Atlantic, where the future premier Émile Ollivier credited Stowe with sparking "a moral revolution."[3] In 1859, as France went to war with Austria on behalf of Sardinia-Piedmont, setting in motion the unification of Italy, the country's liberals kept an eye on events in the United States. John Brown's raid had an electrifying effect on them. Victor Hugo, then in exile for his opposition to Napoleon III, lionized Brown and, more than most European observers, fully appreciated the significance of his execution: "Brown's gallows stands between North and South. Solidarity is no longer possible."[4]

Fig. 32. William H. Seward, Senator from New York, 1859. (Library of Congress)

Prominent Americans who heard the news of John Brown's raid while in Europe included the Republican leaders William H. Seward and Charles Sumner. Seward, confident that he would be his party's nominee for the presidency the following year, spent seven months abroad in 1859. After embarking from New York in May (to the tune of a band playing "Hail to the Chief"), Seward spent the summer in Britain, where he had a private audience with Queen Victoria. He was a guest in the homes of the prime minister, Lord Palmerston, and the foreign secretary, Lord John Russell, before touring France, where he was visiting at the time of Brown's raid, then Italy. In Rome, he had an audience with Pope Pius IX, who expressed sympathy with his quest for "higher advancement." Seward went on to visit Egypt and Palestine before returning home in December.[5] Sumner likewise was vacationing in France when news arrived of Brown's raid, but had spent much more time across the Channel, where he had become "almost an idol to antislavery Britons" in the wake of his caning on the Senate floor at the hands of South Carolina's Preston Brooks. Brooks had attacked him in May 1856 following a venomous speech Sumner had delivered against slavery and the South. Sumner did not resume his Senate seat until June 1860, in the meantime spending much of his convalescence in Britain.

Fig. 33. Hon. Charles Sumner of Massachusetts, between 1855 and 1865. (Library of Congress)

A frequent visitor to Europe since the late 1830s, Sumner spoke several languages and had a large network of admirers; one historian credits him with being a transmitter of "humanitarian, reformist ideas in a movement which embraced both continents, and one who helped associate the New England cultural elite with the British intelligentsia."[6]

Sumner may have been the most admired American politician in Britain, but even his friends there doubted that such a polarizing figure could ever become president. Seward, in contrast, had few British admirers; indeed, his reception in the highest circles in 1859 instead reflected the general assumption that he would likely be elected president in 1860, an assumption Seward himself did nothing to dispel. The New York senator figured prominently among the leading American politicians whom British diplomats stationed in the United States during the 1850s had labeled "anti-British." Their list included figures in both parties, among them the Democrats Stephen A. Douglas and Jefferson Davis, but they considered Seward particularly untrustworthy and, because of his dependence upon New York's Irish vote, likely to engage in irresponsible demagoguery targeting Britain. As early as 1856 British diplomats reported loose talk among a wide variety of American politicians about using a war against

Britain to rally the country and overcome sectional divisions. In this regard, Lord Lyons, appointed the ambassador to Washington in December 1858, worried about Seward in particular.[7]

Throughout the U.S. election campaign of 1860, European attention focused on dramatic developments closer to home. In an unintended consequence of France's defeat of Austria in Italy the previous year, the liberal revolutionary Giuseppe Garibaldi invaded Sicily on May 11—a week after the adjournment of the deadlocked Democratic convention in Charleston and a week before Abraham Lincoln's nomination by the Republican convention in Chicago. Over the summer, Garibaldi proceeded to conquer not just the island of Sicily but also all of the Kingdom of Naples. Meanwhile, the army of Sardinia-Piedmont advanced southward, overthrowing several smaller and weaker northern Italian states in its path. For the sake of Italian unity, Garibaldi subsequently turned over his conquests to the Sardinian king, Victor Emmanuel II, who would be recognized as king of Italy early the following year. On November 7—the day after Lincoln's election—Garibaldi and Victor Emmanuel rode side by side into Naples. Reflecting on Europe's view of the dramatic events of 1860, Britain's conservative *Saturday Review* likely did not exaggerate when it claimed that Garibaldi "was the subject of more discussion in a day than all the parties and all the orators in America in a year."[8]

Prominent Europeans visiting the United States during the election campaign naturally took an interest in it, which was reflected in their diaries and letters home. Baron Salomon de Rothschild, the heir to one of Europe's greatest nonroyal fortunes, arrived in New York from Paris in 1859 at the age of twenty-three, to live and work for two years in the service of his family's international banking house. His travels included a visit to Washington in the spring of 1860, before the party conventions but with speculation about their outcome well underway. After meeting the leading men of American politics, Rothschild repeated the conventional wisdom that Seward would win the Republican nomination. Sensing the deep divisions among Democrats, he concluded that "the Democrats will lose the game and Seward will win out." Among the contenders, however, he had the highest regard for the Democrat John C. Breckinridge of Kentucky. "Breckinridge . . . has all my sympathies. He is a young man, charming, full of fire, intelligent, and, what is rare, a perfect gentleman." Breckinridge, in his capacity as James Buchanan's vice president, personally guided Rothschild on his tour of Capitol Hill. The banker intended to travel to Charleston in late April for the Democratic convention, where he hoped to see Breckinridge nominated, but after becoming aware of rumors that Rothschild money would be used "to buy a President," he canceled his plans.[9] The Austrian ambassador, Ritter von Hülsemann, had a similarly positive view of Breckinridge. Reflecting a conservative diplomat's preference for continuity, Hülsemann noted that the vice president came with the added advantage of having "the same principles as Mr. Buchanan, and in case he should enter the White House it would only be a change of persons," not policies.[10]

By 1860, Hülsemann had been in United States longer than any other foreign envoy, having been posted to Washington in 1838, and functioned as acting ambassador for several years before receiving the appointment formally in 1855. He understood the United States better than most foreign diplomats, as evidenced by his years of insightful and remarkably accurate reports on American society and politics.[11] But neither he nor Rothschild fully appreciated the ominous consequences of the combination of the Democrats' failure to nominate a candidate in Charleston and Lincoln's nomination by the Republicans in Chicago two weeks later. Whereas the Democrats, adjourned in disarray on May 3, after ten days and fifty-seven ballots, with Douglas clearly leading but also well short of the two-thirds majority required for the party's nomination, on May 18, the Republicans nominated the dark horse Lincoln on the third ballot, rejecting the favorite, Seward. Rothschild remarked that the nomination of "Lincoln of Illinois, an extremist," had added interest to an otherwise "insignificant and monotonous week politically" and assumed a candidate with such narrow appeal could not possibly win the election: "to a great degree this assures the presidential chances of Douglas."[12] Hülsemann, reflecting on the Republican convention months later, considered Lincoln's selection somewhat of a fluke, because "his only claim to the nomination was his local popularity in Illinois as a rival of Douglas who, at the moment of the nomination of Mr. Lincoln, was regarded as the inevitable candidate of the Democratic Party." Otherwise, Lincoln had nothing to offer the electorate. "He has passed his life in a village in the West" and "has no experience in great affairs."[13]

At this stage, European observers assumed a continuation of the pattern that had held since 1840—that the American presidency would be decided in a two-man race between the candidates of the leading parties, with any other competitors being of little significance. They logically assumed that

Douglas, backed by a united Democratic Party, would win easily against Lincoln, a weaker candidate than Seward whose support would be limited to the Northern states. Their assumptions were invalidated when the Democrats failed to rally behind Douglas after they reconvened in Baltimore on June 18. The ensuing split, which resulted in the nominations of Breckinridge by Southern Democrats and of Douglas by Northern Democrats, left both men less likely to win than Lincoln, but few European observers could yet imagine the Republican from Illinois taking the White House. By early July, Hülsemann pinned his hopes on the election's fourth candidate, John Bell of Tennessee, nominated by the new Constitutional Union party two months earlier but considered a hopeless underdog prior to the Democratic schism. The Austrian ambassador lauded Bell's simple Unionist platform ("the Union, the Constitution, and the enforcement of the laws") and concluded that "his views are very wise, and he would be an excellent president." He conceded that Bell "is not popular," because "the masses have been too agitated by the demagogues that control the two great parties," yet concluded that "his election would be a triumph for the wise men" of America, because Bell had "the distinctive character of an anti-demagogue."[14] Rothschild likewise speculated that Bell and his distinguished running mate, Edward Everett of Massachusetts, as "candidates of the moderate party of the Union," could be an attractive alternative to the sectional candidates Lincoln and Breckenridge and the now hopelessly weakened Douglas.[15]

The last weeks of the election campaign coincided with a visit to the United States by Queen Victoria's eldest son, the eighteen-year-old Albert Edward, Prince of Wales, whose presence on American soil preempted election news in the headlines of most major U.S. newspapers. Following an eight-week tour of Canada, the future King Edward VII crossed from Windsor, Ontario, to Detroit on September 20 to begin a one-month visit to the United States. Because his American tour was not an official state visit, the prince traveled under the name "Lord Renfrew," one of the least in his long list of titles, but from the start the private, unofficial nature of his visit was a farce: thirty thousand people turned out to welcome him in Detroit. The prince traveled 2,600 miles in thirty days, venturing as far west as St. Louis before embarking for home at Portland, Maine, on October 20. Everywhere his entourage was mobbed by enthusiastic, curious crowds, the largest for his arrival in New York, where at least 200,000 people (some estimated 500,000) lined the parade route up Broadway.[16] During his tour the prince met a host of prominent Americans, including the literary figures Henry Wadsworth Longfellow and Ralph Waldo Emerson, as well as the senior officer in the U.S. Army, General Winfield Scott. But aside from President Buchanan, who hosted him for three days at the White House, he met few American politicians above the rank of mayor and none of the four presidential candidates.

Because of his position, the Prince of Wales refrained from commenting directly on the presidential election even in his letters home. But by visiting the United States on the eve of the most divisive election in its history, he had stepped into a political firestorm and could hardly avoid being swept up in it. In designing his itinerary, British officials made their prewar sympathies known: aside from St. Louis, in slaveholding Missouri, there would be no stops in slave states. They cited the South's "unhealthy climate" as the formal reason for the snub, but Southern leaders refused to accept it.[17] As soon as Albert Edward began his visit and his itinerary became known, Lord Lyons received a petition signed by "a number of Southern gentlemen from different States" appealing for a city in the South to be added to the tour on the grounds that "the cotton fields of that fertile and extensive region supply the material from which much of the wealth and power of the British Empire is derived, and . . . that, nowhere in this Republic does there exist a higher appreciation of that great nation than in the plantation States." The petition closed with the hope that such a visit would allow the prince to develop "an increased respect for our institutions" and thus "overthrow the barriers" created by the "misguided philanthropy" of the abolitionist movement.[18]

The British relented, and added a visit to Richmond the weekend of October 6–7, following the prince's stop in Washington. After attending Sunday services at St. Paul's Episcopal Church, he and his companions journeyed a few miles into the Virginia countryside to tour the Haxhall plantation (but "without getting out of the carriage," as the *New York Times* noted with some satisfaction). Later on Sunday, a rumor that the prince would attend evening services at Richmond's First African Church caused thousands to congregate in lower Broad Street. Maintained by the white families of the nearby First Baptist Church for the benefit of their slaves, the church had a unique interracial congregation, with some whites attending its services to make it compliant with a Virginia law prohibiting all-black assemblies even for religious observances. The prince's appearance there would have made a strong political statement, which the British ultimately decided not to make, though three members of entourage did attend the service.[19] In the prince's remaining tour stops (Baltimore, Philadelphia, New York, and Boston) he faced larger crowds but an atmosphere far less politically charged. On a side trip from New York to the U. S. Military Academy at West Point, he made the acquaintance of an artillery instructor whom fate would place in a most difficult position the following spring. Captain Robert Anderson, one of the faculty members assigned to conduct the prince around the grounds, in mid-November was assigned to Fort Sumter in Charleston harbor. There, as Major Anderson, he would be the commanding officer when the Civil War's first shots were fired.[20]

A month after the Prince of Wales visited Richmond, Lincoln's Republican ticket triumphed over his rivals Douglas, Breckinridge, and Bell, even though Lincoln received no votes in the deep South and very few ballots were cast for him in the slave states as a whole. The steamer *Asia,* the fastest of many leaving American ports for Europe on Wednesday, November 7, the day after Lincoln's election, had the distinction of being the first to reach Europe with the news. The *Asia* made port at Queenstown (today Cobh), Ireland, on November 18 and docked at Liverpool the following day, with mail including the New York newspapers of the 7th. The next edition of the *Times* of London, appearing on November 20, offered no analysis of its own, instead excerpting verbatim the accounts of the New York press. Though careful to balance the views of three different papers, the *Times* no doubt raised false hopes for the future of the Union in quoting the *New York Herald*'s conclusion that those "who still believe in the strength of the Union will be comforted with the assurance of an anti-Republican majority in both Houses of Congress. The success of Bell . . . in several of the Southern States is also considered as affording a powerful guarantee for the maintenance of the Union in the South." Such optimism appeared to be supported by an estimate of the vote of the Electoral College accompanying the article, which overestimated Bell's showing while making the Republican victory appear slightly less overwhelming and less polarizing than it actually was. Lincoln's 180 electoral votes were underestimated at 169. The estimate gave California and Oregon to Douglas and assumed that New Jersey's seven votes, ultimately split between Lincoln and Douglas, would go to Bell. The count also assumed that Bell, not Breckinridge, would carry Maryland and Delaware, adding two more slave states to the three Bell actually won, and giving him 57 electoral votes instead of 39 while leaving Breckinridge barely ahead of him with 61, instead of the 72 he actually carried. Even Douglas appeared to have suffered slightly less of a debacle with the placement of Lincoln's West Coast states in his column along with Missouri (but minus the split vote of New Jersey), leaving him with 16 rather than 12. Of course even the inaccurate figures first reported in Europe still gave the Republican candidate a clear and decisive victory, with more electoral votes than his three rivals combined. "The presidential result may be summed up in three words—Lincoln is elected."[21]

In the weeks that followed, through their ambassadors in Washington, the European governments received (with the usual two- to three-week delay) the latest rumors regarding the secession of Southern states or the resignation of Southerners from federal service. In his first postelection dispatch to London, dated November 12, Lord Lyons reflected the conventional wisdom in characterizing Lincoln as a moderate Republican; like many foreign diplomats, he expressed hope, if not confidence, that the Union would weather the storm.[22] In a dispatch to Vienna four days later, Hülsemann continued to indulge his fascination with Bell as a unifying figure, speculating that Lincoln would make the Southern Unionist his secretary of state in a coalition Cabinet.[23] Rothschild, reflecting the sensibilities of Seward and other Republican rivals of the president-elect, observed that "Lincoln . . . is not up to his position and the Republicans themselves regret nominating him." [24] Under the circumstances, Lincoln had to unify the Republican Party before reaching across party lines; that winter he shrewdly built a Cabinet including Seward and his leading rivals within the party and would wait until 1864 to offer a high-profile position to a Southern Unionist—Andrew Johnson, his second-term vice president, who in an irony had been a Breckinridge Democrat in 1860. Lincoln's failure to make a bold, nonpartisan gesture disappointed Hülsemann; as early as December 7, two weeks before South Carolina's secession, he lamented that "the North and the South . . . are like two enemy camps."[25] Other long-serving diplomats in Washington soon shared his pessimism. Russia's Eduard de Stoeckl, posted to the United States since 1850, likewise considered the Union "permanently destroyed."[26]

Nevertheless, the European press continued to report the aftermath of the election as if it were "of no immediate danger to the Union," as one historian has noted, because "the slavery controversy" had assumed the character of "a constant quarrel between North and South."[27] Slavery had caused crises before, and they had been resolved peacefully, most notably in 1820 and 1850. Distant observers could see no reason why this crisis, too, would not end in compromise. Following the straightforward initial reports in the *Times* and other daily newspapers, the first extensive British analysis of the election result came on Saturday, November 24, when the weekly *Economist, Saturday Review,* and *Spectator* all included articles on Lincoln. The liberal *Economist* lauded Lincoln as a moderate and emphasized his position, often repeated during the campaign, that he sought only to stop slavery from spreading to the western territories, not to abolish it in states where it already existed. Only the conservative *Saturday Review* sounded a cautionary note, observing that although Britain had experienced its share of difficulties with previous Democratic administrations, the Democrats were a known quantity, but the Republicans were not. At least the Republican victory had not made Seward president; two months would pass before the European powers learned he had accepted Lincoln's offer to become secretary of state.[28]

The *Times* soon echoed the generally positive appraisals of Lincoln. On November 27, Britain's leading daily reproduced a piece from the *New York Tribune* suggesting that the president-elect's personal story would have a unifying effect at least for ordinary Americans. The brief biography hailed Lincoln as "a noble specimen of true moral courage and manhood," a product of "the fostering influences of American institutions and society" and concluded that "every labouring man in the country toiling under the weight of poverty with a view to better days, and every student struggling for knowledge and advancement under whatever difficulties, has stock in Old Abe."[29] A host of European intellectuals, with convictions ranging from liberal to revolutionary, not surprisingly saw the election through this lens, because the rise of a self-made man of such humble origins confirmed their view of the limitless possibilities a free society offered its citizens. They had long idealized the United States as a beacon of hope for the ultimate triumph of republican (or at least parliamentary) democracy, and in their eyes, America never shone brighter than in the afterglow of Lincoln's victory. In far-off Russia, Nikolai Chernyshevskii—whose novel *What Is to Be Done?* inspired Lenin to write the 1902 revolutionary pamphlet of the same title—was numbered among the intelligentsia's most interested observers of the events in the United States over the winter of 1860–61; he had no equal in his passion for Lincoln and the cause of preserving the Union.[30]

The news of South Carolina's ordinance of secession (December 20, 1860) ended this general optimism about the immediate future of the United States. On January 10, 1861, over two weeks before the British foreign secretary, Lord John Russell, received word of other states seceding from the Union, he wrote to Lyons that he did "not see how the United States can be cobbled together again by any compromise." He hoped that "the right to secede should be acknowledged" and that "no force will be used."[31] Such pessimism appeared vindicated when European leaders learned of the secession of another six states within a span of twenty-four days, culminating with Texas on February 1, and the establishment of the Confederate States of America by these seven states the following week.

During the first weeks of the new year, the British press for the most part condemned the seceding states for placing their highest priority on "the preservation of an evil institution," but this solidarity of opinion gradually crumbled. On January 19, the conservative *Saturday Review* characterized the South's secession from the Union as a principled quest for liberty and compared it with the rebellion of the thirteen colonies against Britain. But Britons who accepted the dissolution of the Union were not necessarily pro-Confederate. Indeed, the most liberal voices argued for a good-riddance mentality on the part of the loyal states of the North, which, no longer encumbered by the need to compromise with the slave states, could in the future be more true to their democratic and egalitarian ideals. Among the leading organs of the British press, the *Economist* made this assertion as early as January 12. Regardless of whether they mourned the North-South split or considered it beneficial for one or both regions, European commentators now were almost unanimous in their conclusion that it was permanent.[32]

Anticipating Lincoln's victory against an opposition divided among Douglas, Breckinridge, and Bell, some Southern leaders had begun to sound out European support for an independent union of slave states long before Election Day. In August 1860, South Carolina and Mississippi sent commissioners to France to meet with Napoleon III, giving rise to rumors that the Southern envoys had offered to make him or one of his Bonaparte relatives their monarch. In November 1860, shortly after Lincoln's election, the future Confederate secretary of state, Robert Toombs, further fueled Northern suspicions of Southern monarchism when he "expressed preference for the British over the United States constitution" in a speech in the Georgia legislature. In January 1861, news of a second meeting between Napoleon III and the Southern commissioners caused such a furor in the North that the French government subsequently denied it had encouraged or promised assistance to the Confederacy.[33] The denial did not specifically refute the charge that a Confederate throne had been discussed, most likely because it had, indeed, been discussed. A coinciding case in Paris involving the claims of the American descendants of Jerome Bonaparte, Napoleon I's rebellious younger brother, fueled speculation. Jerome had married an American, Elizabeth Patterson, then acceded to his brother's wishes and divorced Elizabeth. He married a German princess prior to becoming king of Westphalia (1807–13). When the ex-king Jerome died in June 1860, his long-estranged first wife, now seventy-five years old, hastened to France and filed suit to have the American Bonapartes recognized as legitimate members of the imperial family. The case, ultimately successful, went to trial in January 1861, just as the six remaining states of the Deep South were preparing to follow South Carolina in secession.[34] Attention soon focused on Patterson's grandson, Jerome Napoleon Bonaparte, born in 1830, a first cousin once removed of Napoleon III. Jerome Napoleon had graduated from West Point in 1852 but soon after resigned his American commission to serve in the French army, where he would remain until Napoleon III's defeat in the Franco-Prussian War (1870–71) made France a republic once again. Despite the speculation swirling around him in 1860–61, he never showed interest in becoming king of the Confederacy. In any event, an attempt to establish a monarchy in the South would have been doubly disastrous for the rebel cause. Its leaders and citizens did not want a strong central government, and the presence of a crowned head on American soil would have only energized the North further.[35]

The lame-duck Buchanan administration did nothing to respond to rumors of European interference in the secession crisis, or of efforts to exploit American weakness. But even before Lincoln's inauguration, Seward let it be known that the Republicans would not tolerate foreign meddling in U.S. domestic politics or foreign challenges to the Monroe Doctrine. In early February, the future secretary of state threatened Lord Lyons with a war to unite America against foreign interventionists.[36]

Seward's bombast only further alienated the European powers at a time when, in their eyes, the new administration's stock was already falling. Indeed, British reaction to Lincoln's first inaugural address, on March 4, reflected the degree to which his stature had diminished in the four months since his election, even though he had yet to serve a day as president. Although some British commentators praised the "statesman-like" and conciliatory address, more saw it as a weak speech. From the perspective of the Foreign Office, Russell considered the Confederacy to be in an "impregnable" position, with a slave revolt being the only thing that could possibly undermine it.[37] As winter gave way to spring, European condemnation of the secessionists on moral grounds gave way to rationalizations of Confederate independence. On March 12, the *Times* of London published its first pro-Southern editorial, speculating that, within the future family of nations, a slaveholding Confederacy could be just as respectable as the empire of Brazil. Despite its slavery, Brazil had distinguished itself by "good faith and good conduct" that contrasted sharply with the behavior of many of the republics of Spanish Latin America, which had no slavery.[38] But British observers in the South found "King Cotton" Confederates to be just as insufferable as Seward. The *Times* of London's military correspondent, William H. Russell, sent to Charleston to cover the crisis over the resupply of the federal garrison at Fort Sumter, witnessed firsthand the "cocky buoyancy" of the universal (and wrongheaded) assumption that the South controlled Britain because of cotton.[39]

By March 1861, North-South tensions focused on Fort Sumter because it was the most significant remaining vestige of federal authority in any of the South's major seaports. By then, however, the European powers had for months wrestled with the problem of how to acknowledge the de facto control that the seceded states exercised over the ports of the South. The Buchanan administration advised foreign shippers to pay the local authorities whatever fees or duties they demanded, but to do so "under protest." After Lincoln's inauguration on March 4, Seward quickly signaled that the new administration would no longer accept this accommodation. At the British embassy in Washington on March 25, Seward shocked his host, Lord Lyons, and a dinner-party crowd of foreign diplomats with the threat "to confiscate without compensation" any foreign ships leaving Southern harbors "without papers required by United States law"—papers which, of course, none of them now had. In this tense atmosphere, both Britain and France came as close as they had yet to recognizing the Confederate government. Five days before Seward's outburst, Lyons had issued his own threat to the secretary of state that Britain would recognize the Confederacy "if a considerable rise were to take place in the price of cotton, and British ships were to be at the same time excluded from the southern ports." Within days of attending the British embassy dinner, the French ambassador in Washington, Henri Mercier, echoed these arguments in advising Napoleon III to extend recognition to the Confederate States.[40]

The deepening North-South breach made Seward's threats of a unifying war against Britain and/or France appear increasingly hollow.

Meanwhile, Spain became the first European power to exploit the crisis. During 1860, a pro-Spanish faction of Dominicans led by Pedro Santana had seized power in the Dominican Republic; Santana subsequently negotiated a Dominican reunion with Spain, announced formally on March 18, 1861. Spanish troops from Cuba landed in Santo Domingo later that month. Prior to leaving office, Buchanan had been aware of Santana's machinations but made no attempt to stop him; indeed, his own minister in Madrid, the secessionist William Preston of Kentucky, likely encouraged the Spanish to believe they could act without fear of consequences from the United States.[41] Spain's reacquisition of the Dominican Republic was, of course, temporary, lasting only until 1865, but it set the precedent for a Spanish attempt to restore colonial rule in Peru and, more ominously for the United States, Napoleon III's quest to establish a puppet empire in Mexico. Preston likewise played a role in the latter case, placing his diplomatic skills and knowledge of Spanish at the service of the Confederacy as its ambassador to Emperor Maximilian. In the short term, Spain's annexation of the Dominican Republic led to the last iteration of Seward's foreign-war-to-rally-the-nation scheme, which would have exploited the affair by having the United States go to war with Spain and conquer Cuba (long coveted by Southern filibusterers) along with Puerto Rico. This far-fetched plan seemed plausible enough at the time to prompt Lord Russell to lecture the Spanish ambassador in London about "foolishly risking an eventual American takeover in Cuba and Puerto Rico." Russell's fears proved unfounded, because Lincoln did not accept the logic that the road to reconciliation in the United States passed through Santo Domingo. On April 1, the president rejected Seward's plan.[42]

Writing to Lyons on Friday, April 12, 1861, Russell passed along news of the Palmerston cabinet's latest deliberations regarding the United States and the new Confederacy, informing the ambassador that the British government was "in no hurry to recognize the separation as complete and final."[43] When Lyons received the letter two weeks later, he could not have failed to appreciate the irony that it had been written a matter of hours before the Confederates had begun shelling Fort Sumter. Neither Britain nor France ever formally recognized the Confederate States of America, but by declaring neutrality before the first major battle was fought (Britain on May 13, France on June 13), they gave the Confederacy de facto recognition as a belligerent on an equal footing with the Union. Their ships, and those of other foreign countries, soon faced a Union naval blockade of

Southern ports. But their economic interests suffered still more when the Confederacy embargoed its own cotton exports, causing the international market price of raw cotton to soar, then used the warehoused cotton as collateral for bonds floated on European money markets. However, this strategy failed to force the leading powers to recognize the Confederacy, and its bonds sold well only until the following year, stabilized prices by importing more raw cotton from Egypt and India. Meanwhile, Britain and France did a brisk business with the Confederacy despite their purported neutrality, selling the rebels everything from small arms to commerce-raiding warships, and even building ironclads for them (none of which saw action in the Civil War). The resulting bad blood between the United States and the leading European powers did not diminish until the fol-lowing decade, when the French Third Republic replaced the regime of Napoleon III (1870) and Britain signed the Treaty of Washington (1871), the preamble of which included a near apology for its material support of the Confederacy.[44] The treaty resolved longstanding issues, including a Pacific-coast border dispute (involving islands in the bay between Van-couver and Victoria), and led to arbitration resulting in the payment to the United States in 1872 of reparations totaling $15.5 million. These were the so-called *Alabama* claims, named after the most famous British-built Confederate commerce raider.

From the onset of the presidential election campaign in May 1860 to the shelling of Fort Sumter in April 1861, European reports and reviews of political developments in the United States reflected the prejudices of the sources and interpreters of information on both sides of the Atlantic, as well as the delay in the transatlantic communication of all news owing to the state of technology at the time. What historian Ephraim Adams has concluded in regard to Britain holds just as true for France and, with far less emphasis on the economic factor, for other European powers as well: within the context of 1860–61, Europeans faced a dilemma in reconcil-ing their "commercial interests" with the "sentiments of humanity" that caused most of them to oppose slavery, all within the context of their "cer-tainty that a new state was being born."[45] They felt this certainty because, up to that time, "[h]istory failed to record any revolution on so large a scale that had not succeeded."[46] Indeed, after the original seven seceding states were joined by the slave states of the Upper South, the new Con-federacy grew to include 770,000 square miles (2 million square kilome-ters) of territory, home to 5.5 million whites and 3.5 million black slaves.

The failure of a rebellion of such sweeping scope was unprecedented. If we consider that its failure was rooted in the foundation established in 1860–61, it appears more understandable that even the most knowledgeable European observers of the election failed to foresee the outcome of the campaign, did not fully appreciate its consequences, and lacked the vision to forecast the ultimate result.

1. D. P. Crook, *The North, the South, and the Powers, 1861–1865* (New York: Wiley, 1974), 16, 20.

2. Crook, *The North, the South, and the Powers*, 37; Ephraim Douglass Adams, *Great Britain and the American Civil War*, 2 vols. (New York: Russell & Russell, 1924), 1:32–33.

3. Serge Gavronsky, "American Slavery and the French Liberals: An Interpretation of the Role of Slavery in French Politics during the Second Empire," *Journal of Negro History* 51 (1966): 36–37; Ollivier quoted, 37.

4. Quoted in Gavronsky, 40.

5. John M. Taylor, *William Henry Seward: Lincoln's Right Hand* (New York: HarperCollins, 1991), 113.

6. Crook, *The North, the South, and the Powers*, 43. See also Adams, *Great Britain*, 1:33; John Bigelow, *Retrospections of an Active Life*, vol. 1, *1817–1863* (New York: Baker & Taylor, 1909), 124.

7. Crook, *The North, the South, and the Powers*, 35.

8. Quoted in Crook, *The North, the South, and the Powers*, 38. See also Donaldson Jordan and Edwin J. Pratt, *Europe and the American Civil War* (Boston: Houghton Mifflin, 1931), 4.

9. Salomon de Rothschild, *A Casual View of America: The Home Letters of Salomon de Rothschild, 1859–1861,* ed. and trans. Sigmund Diamond (Stanford: Stanford Univ. Press, 1961), 33.

10. Ritter von Hülsemann, report of July 2, 1860, in *Wien-Washington: Ein Journal diplomatischer Beziehungen, 1838–1917,* ed. Erwin Matsch (Vienna: Böhlau, 1990), 189.

11. Hülsemann, report of July 2, 1860, in Matsch, *Wien-Washington*, 7–217; includes his dispatches from the years 1838–63.

12. Rothschild, *A Casual View of America*, 43.

13. Hülsemann, report of March 8, 1861, in Matsch, *Wien-Washington*, 198.

14. Hülsemann, report of July 2, 1860, in Matsch, *Wien-Washington*, 190.

15. Rothschild, *A Casual View of America*, 83.

16. Ian Radforth, *Royal Spectacle: The 1860 Visit of the Prince of Wales to Canada and the United States* (Toronto: Univ. of Toronto Press, 2004), 313–14, 336–37. The prince's own letter home to his father, Prince Albert, estimated the New York crowd at 300,000. See Radforth, 346.

17. Radforth, *Royal Spectacle*, 314.

18. "Slavery Agitation: Invitation for the Prince of Wales to Visit the South," *New York Times*, September 21, 1860.

19. "The Prince at Richmond," *New York Times,* October 8, 1860. See also Radforth, *Royal Spectacle,* 321–23. On the First African Church, see "An Old Landmark [The First African Church, Richmond]," *Harper's Weekly,* June 27, 1874, 545.

20. Bigelow, *Retrospections,* 297.

21. "America," *The Times* (London), November 20, 1860.

22. Adams, *Great Britain,* 51.

23. Hülsemann, report of November 16, 1860, in Matsch, *Wien-Washington,* 192.

24. Rothschild, *A Casual View of America,* 90.

25. Hülsemann, report of December 7, 1860, in Matsch, *Wien-Washington,* 192.

26. Adams, *Great Britain,* 53n.

27. Adams, *Great Britain,* 37; see also Jordan and Pratt, *Europe and the American Civil War,* 4.

28. Adams, *Great Britain,* 38–39. Lyons wrote to Russell on January 7, 1861, with the news that Seward would be heading the U.S. State Department. See Adams, *Great Britain,* 59.

29. "The President Elect of the United States," *The Times* (London), November 27, 1860.

30. Hans Rogger, "Russia and the Civil War," in *Heard Round the World: The Impact Abroad of the Civil War,* ed. Harold Hyman (New York: Alfred A. Knopf, 1969), 200.

31. Adams, *Great Britain,* 52–53.

32. Adams, *Great Britain,* 45, 47, 54.

33. A. R. Tyrner-Tyrnauer, *Lincoln and the Emperors* (New York: Harcourt, Brace & World, 1962), 18–19.

34. "Paris Gossip . . . the American Bonaparte Case," *New York Times,* February 4, 1861.

35. Tyrner-Tyrnauer, *Lincoln and the Emperors,* 22, erroneously attributes Jerome Bonaparte's lack of interest in a Confederate crown to his marriage to the daughter of a Massachusetts millionaire, which caused him to fear "the confiscation of his family's American property if he should identify himself with the cabal against Washington." Jerome did not marry Caroline Edgar of Massachusetts until 1871, after he returned to the United States from France.

36. Crook, *The North, the South, and the Powers,* 47–48.

37. Crook, *The North, the South, and the Powers,* 36, 40.

38. Adams, *Great Britain,* 56.

39. Crook, *The North, the South, and the Powers,* 21.

40. Lyons to Russell, March 26, 1861, quoted in Crook, *The North, the South, and the Powers,* 48; see also ibid., 51. Philip E. Myers, *Caution and Cooperation: The American Civil War in British-American Relations* (Kent, Ohio: Kent State Univ. Press, 2008), 36–37, presents a much different account of the Lyons-Seward exchange of March 20, in which the ambassador made no threat to Seward, and a conciliatory secretary of state assured Lyons of his opposition to any blockade of Southern ports that "compromised British trade."

41. See Crook, *The North, the South, and the Powers,* 54–55 (where Santana is misidentified as "Sanchez"), and Jordan and Pratt, *Europe and the American Civil War,* 247.

42. Crook, *The North, the South, and the Powers,* 54, 61. On the Dominican question, Myers, *Caution and Cooperation,* 37–38, once again portrays a more conciliatory

Seward, arguing that "the secretary of state's peaceful gestures negated his 'foreign war panacea' bluster," which in any event "Seward was half-hearted about."

43. Russell to Lyons, April 12, 1861, quoted in Adams, *Great Britain,* 74.

44. Myers, *Caution and Cooperation,* 248.

45. Adams, *Great Britain,* 59.

9

"An Inscrutable Election?"

The Historiography of the Election of 1860

Douglas G. Gardner

"Altogether, it was a very curious, a very mixed, and except for its grand central result, a very inscrutable election." So Allan Nevins in 1947 judged the presidential contest of 1860, back in an era when political history, and especially the political history of elections, was incontestably at the center of the historical profession's interests.[1]

Outside of the immediate context of the argument Nevins was making about how the popular and Electoral College votes in 1860 had not lined up with each other (a common enough result in American presidential elections), it is difficult to see how anyone can regard the election of 1860 as really having been inscrutable. Defined by the *Oxford English Dictionary* as "that [which] cannot be searched into or found out by searching; impenetrable or unfathomable to investigation; quite unintelligible, entirely mysterious," the term *inscrutable* does not seem to fit the circumstances of the canvass that made Lincoln president. Odd, bizarre, unexpected, comic, tragic—all of these adjectives and more aptly apply to the election of 1860 and its short- and long-term consequences, but not "inscrutable." Nevins himself wrote over a hundred fact-filled, lucid, coherent, narrative-driven pages on what happened at the national political level during the campaign of 1860.

For over a century, the major historical analyses of the election of 1860 have concentrated on a few key issues, creating a historiographical tradition whose confines may be ready to be shattered at this sesquicentennial moment. The primary focus of the tradition has been on Abraham Lincoln and his candidacy's impact on the shape of the election and on the attitudes of the body politic. A narrative counterpoint to the success of the Republican candidate has been the concomitant failure of Stephen A. Douglas to achieve victory in the fall elections in the wake of the split of the Democratic Party. This combined concentration on Lincoln (and also his supporters and advisors) and Douglas (and the ripping apart of his party) has varied only occasionally over the past century as historiographical generations have succeeded one another. It continues even into the current crop of book-length reconsiderations of the election.

As an adjunct to this traditional focus on the candidates and their candidacies, an overwhelming sense of "inevitability" about some part of Lincoln's emergence, or his nomination, or his election, of the dissolution of the Union in the wake of his inauguration has been expressed in many of these accounts. It is true that some accounts have allowed for more contingency from the actors and circumstances, but most writers take a deterministic view of the presidential contest. *Inevitability* is a word that sends shivers through Civil War scholars as they contemplate how to explain best the road to war, and there is no need to re-cover that familiar ground at any length. Instead, the purpose of this essay is to focus on how a few specific narratives about the election do or do not encapsulate the concept. Of course, "contingent" is not precisely the antonym of "inevitable," but it has become an historical buzzword over the past two or three decades, as academic historians have sought to explicate the role that chance, accident, and fortuity played in—to use more buzzwords—the "social construction" of past worlds. Further complicating the inevitability-contingency divide is the fact that the exact terms of the inevitability that various authors have identified over the decades have been so imprecise that at times the concept is prone to rhetorical drift even within the same sentence or paragraph. The pall of the historiographical division over the possibility of inevitability in the literature is so strong that it calls to mind what Edward L. Ayers has recently categorized as the fundamentalist position on the entire problem of Civil War causation, which in his words "emphasizes the intrinsic, inevitable conflict between slavery and free labor."[2] For such fundamentalists, the differences over slavery (and anything else, but mostly slavery) between the sections were so intertwined with such deeply felt and basic notions of sectional identity and security that war at some point became inevitable.

This historiographical tradition about the election of 1860—focused on Lincoln and Douglas, and usually, but not always, stressing inevitability—

was encapsulated in a number of accounts throughout the twentieth century that still deserve to be read and considered by scholars of the sectional conflict and its political ramifications. During the ongoing 150th anniversary of the Civil War years, four authors have published important and solid book-length accounts of the election, in which they extend this familiar formula in ways congenial to the sensibilities of the current generation. This current crop of narratives on the election mostly rejects the notion of inevitability by emphasizing the importance of political interplay and conflict. The opportunities for future scholarship on the election, its players, and its contexts are immense as historians move through and beyond the sesquicentennial.

The analysis that follows is generally chronological in organization. It seems most convenient to proceed from the first to the last, to begin with writings from the end of the nineteenth century and conclude with those being produced at the start of the twenty-first. Although I have attempted to be wide ranging in including authors and works, no promise of comprehensiveness is implied or should be inferred. Instead, this chapter provides a brief survey of how, over time, historians—mostly historians based in universities—have viewed the conduct and consequences of the presidential election of 1860. Although the focus is on authors of major works, a few scholars who wrote minor works or offered important observations while engaged in larger projects receive consideration when convenient. The survey begins with James Ford Rhodes, the romantic amateur who wrote at the dawn of the professionalization of history in American universities, and who argued that the war had been fought over the fundamental moral issue of slavery. It then proceeds to the writing about Lincoln's election during the founding generation of the American historical profession by the Progressive historians and their contemporaries, focusing especially on the monographic treatment by Emerson David Fite. Like Rhodes, the Progressive generation emphasized fundamental and inevitable conflict in the shaping of the American past; unlike Rhodes, the Progressives saw conflict as crucial in shaping their own time as well. Much of Fite's analysis centered on Lincoln's opponents and their failure to unite behind some sort of anti-Lincoln compromise candidate or otherwise to manipulate the political system to prevent the election of a Republican with Free Soil values.

The chapter then moves on to the later Progressives in the middle decades of the twentieth century, when historians such as Reinhard H.

Luthin, Ollinger Crenshaw, and Roy Franklin Nichols modified the earlier emphasis on fundamental conflict by allowing for more contingency in events as the nation moved toward toward what Nichols memorably characterized as disruption. This emphasis on contingency and the flow of events sometimes led these historians away from a Lincoln-Douglas focus. Crenshaw wrote of the uncertainties and activities of Southerners white and black, and Nichols considered a bewildering array of Democratic actors. During the same mid-century period, scholars such as those anthologized in a volume by Norman A. Graebner repackaged inevitability while allowing for a more complex and interactive political scene than had historians of the Progressive generation. A decade and a half later, the Consensus historian David M. Potter, in his masterful synthesis on the antebellum years, followed suit. This essay concludes by considering the historical writing on the election in the last few decades, and especially in the last few years, during an emerging general revival of Civil War political history. In fitting this collection of essays into the literature, the chapter also offers suggestions for future work that might move beyond what has become a stale formula that limits the imagination of historians as they seek to understand and reconstruct past worlds.

James Ford Rhodes, a Republican industrialist who retired from the economic strife of the Gilded Age to pursue the writing of historical narrative, regarded the sectional presence of slavery—an institution "out of tune with the nineteenth century"[3]—as an irreconcilable difference that undermined national unity and led to war. When in his *History of the United States from the Compromise of 1850* (the first edition appeared in 1893), Rhodes came to the gory details of the canvass of 1860, some readers might have wondered who the Republican candidate was. Rhodes claimed that "the personality of Lincoln counted for little in the campaign. It was everywhere conceded that he was thoroughly honest, but his opponents sneered at his reputed capacity," finding him at best a potential leader of "respectable mediocrity."[4] For Rhodes, the efforts of William H. Seward, the New York senator who in 1858 had posited famously that there was "an irrepressible conflict" between the slavery and antislavery forces, and who had been the presumptive Republican nominee in 1860 before being outmaneuvered by Lincoln's supporters at the Wigwam, dominated the Republican campaign at the national level. Seward stumped the North with a series of serious, reflective, and morally centered speeches appropriate to the vexed issues surrounding slavery. Rhodes also found it possible to offer grudging praise for the perseverance of Stephen A. Douglas, fighting the good fight in a lost cause as he took the unprecedented step of publicly campaigning on his own behalf. In the end, the white South would find itself sufficiently united to the expansion of slavery by fear of Lincoln and his party to come together and to hold together during the secession winter. The two other major candidates, John C. Breckinridge and John Bell, are peripheral players in Rhodes's story. It all seems to have been so terribly foreordained and inevitable, with Northerners such as Seward and Stephen A. Douglas on the side of history and national unity, and white Southerners . . . not. Rhodes believed that, fortunately, the inevitable conflict that had shaped the events of 1860—to which Lincoln seems almost to have been a bystander—had been resolved. The result was the national, social, and economic unity of the Gilded Age during which Rhodes had prospered and was writing.

If Rhodes was an intermediate voice on the way to academic professionalization, the Progressive Era produced the first full generation of academic historians trained in the new-style graduate programs. The Progressives rejected the romantic aspects of Rhodes's nationalism. They found conflict not just during the antebellum period but also after the war and in their present of the early twentieth century. Indeed, for the Progressive historians who spoke most famously and influentially of the Civil War and related events, the war had heightened conflict in postbellum American society. Charles A. Beard and Mary Ritter Beard glossed their concept of the "Second American Revolution" in this way: "At bottom the so-called Civil War was a social war, ending in the unquestioned establishment of a new power in the government, making vast changes in the course of industrial development, and in the Constitution inherited from the Fathers."[5]

In *The Presidential Campaign of 1860* (1911), Emerson David Fite provided a monograph-length Progressive exploration of the election. For Fite, the election year was full of political machinations and disputes, some of them barely remembered in his time or ours, but in the end the events of 1860 mattered little as the nation hurtled toward the sectional split. Fite began his book by claiming that "never has a campaign been waged in which the people of the whole nation have taken a more calm, serious, and intelligent interest." Although the campaign was conducted in the aftermath of the John Brown raid and the speakership crisis of 1859–60 was linked to Hinton Rowan Helper's *Impending Crisis of the*

South, "physical violence and offensive personalities, as a rule, were conspicuously absent." Somewhat contradictorily, Fite also emphasized how the heightened emotions of the day ("John Brown must, therefore, bear the immediate responsibility for the extremes of the presidential campaign of 1860") led all parties and all leaders alternatively to stake out extreme positions and engage in rhetorical evasion as the nation hurtled toward destruction. Events occurred largely beyond the control of either individuals or political groups. "It was a situation that political conventions and platforms might recognize but could not control. The people were in command, and they themselves were being hurried along by unseen and irresistible forces, now by this seemingly small event and now by that." The daily rush of political debate throughout the year—in and around Congress before and after the speakership crisis, continuing through the political conventions and on to the campaign trail—masked the inevitable sectional fissure. The lead-up to the various election days was anticlimactic. "How the vote would go never once seemed in doubt," especially because Lincoln's opponents were unable to find ways to fuse themselves into a potentially successful opposition. Even more consequential than the vote was the growing inflexibility of Southern political leaders of many stripes as they signaled that they would be unable to accept a Republican president. This warning led Douglas to switch from barnstorming for his own election to barnstorming, particularly in the South, for the future of the Union. Like Rhodes, Fite seemed to imagine a past where it would have been more efficient to proceed from Harpers Ferry to Fort Sumter, because everything in 1860 was a playing out of forces already in motion as that year began.[6]

In 1944, a third of a century after Fite's work, Reinhard H. Luthin published a book entitled *The First Lincoln Campaign.*[7] Luthin was much less certain than Fite or Rhodes about the inevitability of sectional rupture, and he was not afraid to find political conflict everywhere he looked, not just in one section or surrounding one group of actors. Luthin was a student of Allan Nevins and Harry J. Carman at Columbia University, where he, too, taught for much of his career. Luthin wrote during World War II and in the historiographical shadow of a generation of scholars—many of whom rejected the fundamentalist position on Civil War causation—who mixed their own despairing, antiwar impulses of the interbellum period of the twentieth century with a harsh critique of the politics and politicians of the antebellum era. This critique was applied usually and especially to the politics of the North and of Northern, antislavery, anti-Southern politicians. Charles W. Ramsdell had ridiculed the sincerity of Republican free soilism as early as 1929 in an article entitled "The Natural Limits of Slavery Expansionism." In 1940, James G. Randall, a noted Lincoln biographer, had reduced the war's main causes to the missteps and misleadings of a "Blundering Generation" of politicians in an article which was a substantial critique of the Beardian orthodoxy. Randall's student and another future Lincoln biographer, David Herbert Donald, would blame "An Excess of Democracy" for causing the war. And Avery Craven would so condemn antislavery "extremists" that it takes almost an act of will today to remember that he was a Northern Quaker.[8]

Luthin provided an even deeper, thicker description of politics and politicians than had Fite, an account much more driven by contingency than by foreordination. Luthin's account started with 1856 and the emergence of a sectional Republican Party ultimately united more by opposition to the prevailing Democrats than by anything else. Lincoln was able to win the 1860 nomination because of his "availability," because he was the least objectionable to the most delegates. (For example, the small number of German delegates found Lincoln's lack of nativist ties appealing.) Lincoln's managers focused their postconvention attention on doubtful Northern states, especially Indiana and Pennsylvania (both swing states with October statewide elections that had been carried by the Democrat James Buchanan in 1856) and also New York. Focusing on questions of importance in those states—the tariff in particular—and exploiting existing Democratic divisions proved to be a powerful strategy for the Lincoln organization. Luthin moved beyond a fundamentalist emphasis on the looming inevitability of conflict. The political strategists and operatives he described were not mere pawns in some higher-level contest between slavery and antislavery, North and South, agrarianism or industrialism, but independent actors engaged in the practice of politics. He showed Democratic and Southern political leaders at work, not just the Northern Republicans at the center of the story told by Rhodes and Fite. These latter kept the leaders of Dixie largely off stage where they could only bellow faintly heard threats of disunion as Lincoln neared and achieved election.[9]

In 1945, the historian Ollinger Crenshaw extended this inclusion of actors besides Lincoln and Douglas and their key supporters and opponents in his *The Slave States in the Presidential Election of 1860*. Crenshaw argued that politics in the South were far more complicated than previous historians had shown—or, rather, assumed. Southern political leaders were not a unified "slavocracy" who manipulated events to achieve their own nefarious ends. Rather, disorganized and divided, Southern politicians devolved into "confusion and drift" as the campaign progressed.[10] And Crenshaw understood that even the South's and the nation's disenfranchised found ways to influence events as they lived through the period before the secession winter: he explored in a 1942 article the suggestion that slave insurrection panics in Texas and elsewhere during the spring and summer of 1860 helped set the stage for the white Southern reaction to Lincoln's election, an idea recently revived in the work of Donald E. Reynolds.[11]

It is difficult to summarize easily Roy Franklin Nichols's *Disruption of American Democracy* (1947), "Democracy" being used primarily in the sense of the Democratic Party, and only secondarily in the sense of the national political system.[12] The Democratic Party that Nichols described was a political coalition of local, state, regional, and personality-based groups that had endured and mutated over four decades but found itself unable to weather the storms of the years after 1856 in a united fashion. The level of detail in which Nichols indulged—his book wallows in the day-by-day, minute-by-minute recounting of politics and politicians—parallels that in the 1860 work of the journalist Murat Halstead, conveniently collected in *Three Against Lincoln* (1960), edited by William B. Hesseltine.[13] Like Luthin, Nichols allowed for the play of events, personalities, and issues big and little in a complex society, as he told the story of the dissolution of the Democratic Party, a truly national organization in a country that by the late 1850s had few such national institutions. (Nichols had evidently read Tocqueville.) The disruption of the Democracy by those varied pressures and agendas were a necessary precondition to the disruption of the Union, an idea that links Nichols's work to that in more recent years of Michael F. Holt. Nichols—and Holt after him—takes political infighting and its results seriously. Both historians view these events as substance rather than shadow, as what needs to be explored and explicated and explained rather than merely dismissed as markers on the road to a foreordained end. Nichols's joy in what some might call the minutiae of 1850s politics can be infectious even for those with only a moderate interest in such things. It is a shame that the Nichols book is out of print, because it provides an exemplar of the best of a previous historiographical generation.

Reinhard Luthin may have undertaken his project as a preliminary study to benefit Allan Nevins's account of the election of 1860 in his 1947 book *The Emergence of Lincoln,* the second of what would become eight

volumes on the Civil War era. Nevins covered the period from the opening
of the initial Democratic convention at Charleston to the election of his
titular hero in four chapters covering 112 brisk pages. Nevins mixed the
concentration on political leaders, alliances, campaigning, and rhetoric offered by Luthin and Nichols with something of a return to earlier notions
that the election of 1860, for all its clashes and pageantry, mattered for
little. The important outcome of the election of 1860—disunion and war—
was decided by the time of the conclusion of the speakership crisis . If one
of the advances Nevins made over the accounts of Rhodes or Fite or Luthin
was to devote a thorough chapter to the Democratic split into Douglas and
Southern wings, Nevins also wrote as if these political leaders and strivers
were playing parts in a drama that ultimately they could not control. Nevins believed that these two wings of the party had become irreconcilably
split from each other even before they gathered for a doomed attempt to
get a two-thirds agreement on a candidate, and that this division guaranteed the election of a Republican and, hence, war. Like Nevins, Nichols
believed that the failure of the Democracy meant a rift in the democracy,
although Nevins was much more certain than Nichols was about the un-
likelihood of partisan and sectional reconciliation. Nevins was aware that
he had little to add to the familiar story of Lincoln's supporters at the Republican convention in Chicago, offering some excuse for his standard account with the observation, "For decades to come, participants were to re-
tell the story of the convention until it became a part of the legendary lore
of the republic." Nevins gave the eventual Southern Democratic candidate,
Breckinridge, the backhanded compliment, "Not even Breckinridge could
give much grace or dignity to the thrust of the Southern Democracy" at destroying the national Democratic Party and, hence, the nation as a whole.

"By later summer," Nevins opined, "the question was no longer of Lincoln's election but of the results of his impending victory." With "the radicals of the South fervently whipping secessionist sentiment" there was "one
candidate alone, Douglas, dealing courageously with the issue." Nevins
showed how Douglas took to the hustings to campaign for union during
the summer and fall of 1860 and how attempts at fusion by Lincoln's opponents amounted to little. Nevins observed, "A full history of these movements would be tiresomely complex." Republicans throughout the North
conducted parades and sang songs while emphasizing their party's presumed moderation. Lincoln's party made local use of the tariff issue in the
more industrial states and the homestead issue in the more rural states.

Nevins was more enthusiastic than his predecessors in analyzing the distribution of final votes. As we have seen, he was also particularly ironic in his observations of the disjuncture between popular and Electoral College votes. "The nation had taken a mighty decision," Nevins concluded, a decision to limit slavery expansion at the cost of war. Nevins deserves full credit for being the first historian to cover adequately all four of the major candidates (even John Bell) and their campaigns and to present a fully synthesized view of a national canvas that varied wildly from place to place and state to state. And he wrote with a flair that reminds us that he was initially a journalist and biographer before being conscripted into the academy.[14]

The 1961 volume of articles by Don E. Fehrenbacher, Norman Graebner (who also was the volume's editor), Robert W. Johannsen, William S. Barringer, and Avery Craven was the result of a conference linked to the Civil War centennial. In various ways, each and all of the authors reasserted the fundamentalist position that by the time of the campaign of 1860, it was too late. A violent resolution to the contest over slavery was inevitable, or close to it, because of the accumulated intersectional fears and misunderstandings of the 1850s and earlier decades. Graebner's essay argued that the moralizing rhetoric of Northern antislavery workers led defensive white Southern apologists and leaders to overestimate the danger posed to their peculiar institution. Johannsen's essay recounted how those Southern leaders rejected Douglas as a candidate in 1860, destroying Nichols's Democracy and guaranteeing the election of the Republican candidate. Fehrenbacher claimed that these "Southern apprehensions, although fed by hysteria, were to some extent rooted in reality." Craven repackaged the 1920s Fugitive-Agrarian condemnation of industrial society in describing a conflict between a modern (modernizing?) North and a premodern (nonmodern?) South. He implied that the contest continued in his own time as the South and the nation experienced the changes of the post-1945 world, especially those wrought by the civil rights movement.[15] The emphasis by Graebner and his colleagues on the long-term divergence of the North and the South continued in David M. Potter's superb 1976 synthesis, *The Impending Crisis, 1848–1861*. Potter argued that in 1860 the splits had become so extreme that the nation had essentially two elections, one in the North and another in the South.[16]

In the period after the publication of the Graebner anthology and during the time in which Potter wrote his book, the social history revolution took hold and shook the historical profession. The writing of mere political history became largely unfashionable within the academy. Indeed, scholarly consideration of the war itself waned for two decades. Not until the late 1980s and after were the social and cultural historical approaches applied in substantial ways to the war's causes, conduct, and consequences.[17] One important marker in the revival of scholarly interest in the Civil War was James McPherson's 1988 *Battle Cry of Freedom.* McPherson sought to break little new ground in regard to the political events of 1860 as he synthesized the antebellum years with his fundamentalist, slavery-centered account of the war's coming. For this Pulitzer Prize winner, as for the scholars in the centennial celebration volume edited by Graebner, processes of modernization played an important role. The North modernized faster than the South, leading to irreconcilable differences and an inevitable conflict.[18] During these years and beyond, a few academic historians—Joel H. Silbey, Michael F. Holt, and Mark E. Neely most prominently—kept Civil War political history alive through a long interregnum of relative academic indifference.[19] Harold Holzer—with a background not in academe but in politics and public relations—wrote several useful accounts centered on Lincoln, including a study of the Cooper Union speech and a consideration of Lincoln's time as president-elect. Holzer's book opens with a brief, serviceable, and sufficiently complex overview of the election.[20] The popularity of Doris Kearns Goodwin's *Team of Rivals: The Political Genius of Abraham Lincoln,* published in 2005, should remind us that for those interested in the nineteenth century but not housed in the academy, political history never became irrelevant and that academics cede the subject to others at some risk.[21]

There has been a recent flurry of historiographical activity regarding the election of 1860 and its place in American history, a flurry that remains something of a moving target for those trying to keep track. Four important books focusing on the election of Lincoln have appeared in the last few years, written by Gary Ecelbarger, Bruce Chadwick, Michael S. Green, and Douglas R. Egerton.[22] Although these writers hold academic degrees and positions, three of them published their books with nonscholarly presses, and all of the volumes seem aimed as much at the ever-elusive general reader as at those in the academy. All four authors build on and seek to complicate and extend the long-running historical tradition of producing narrative histories of the election of 1860. They focus on major candidacies, doing so in ways cognizant of the last quarter century of work in Lincoln scholarship and the Civil War years. All the members of this

quartet offer accounts that show contingency and that allow for events being shaped by politicians committing politics and by the publics to which
those politicians appealed. For these current writers, Lincoln and his contemporaries were not caught in some teleological web as they contended
for preference in the democratic republic. Three of these recent books focus mostly on Lincoln while generally paying adequate attention to his
rivals. Egerton's account is more about the machinations of Douglas and
the Southerners within the Democratic Party opposed to him than about
the election's victor.

Gary Ecelbarger's narrative focus on the successful candidate is evident
in the title of his *The Great Comeback: How Abraham Lincoln Beat the
Odds to Win the 1860 Republican Nomination* (2008). His account is the
product of an era when political junkies and cable TV talking heads recognize that there is no downtime in campaigning for president. Ecelbarger's
antebellum political scene is like today's in that months and years before
nominating conventions, aspirants and their supporters are jockeying for
the big prize, even while those potential candidates are often denying or
otherwise rhetorically deflecting the possibility. For Ecelbarger, Lincoln's
road to the nomination was deeply contingent, the result of events driven
by humans making human decisions as they contended for political power.
He begins with Lincoln's formal defeat by Stephen A. Douglas for the Senate seat from Illinois in early 1859. Despite a bout of understandable psychological depression in the wake of the defeat, Lincoln resolved to take
advantage of the possibilities offered by his ongoing emergence as a national figure. Lincoln and his advisers used political speaking and writing
opportunities, and even the new medium of photography (a point Holzer
made at length in his Cooper Union book), to introduce him to ever more
parts of the Northern public, most especially potential Republican voters.
Ecelbarger's account of how Lincoln's Illinois supporters managed events
at the Chicago convention that nominated Lincoln, positioning him as "a
principled pragmatist," recalls and expands on what Nevins called "the
legendary lore of the republic." Ecelbarger tells his Lincoln-focused story
lucidly and takes account of the current scholarship and sensibilities in
Lincoln and Civil War studies. This book should appeal both to academic
historians and to those with an avocational interest in the life and times of
the sixteenth president.[23]

Bruce Chadwick's *Lincoln for President: An Unlikely Candidate, An
Audacious Strategy, and the Victory No One Saw Coming* appeared

in 2009 and bears a title that implies the considerable overlap between his book and Ecelbarger's. Chadwick begins by disputing the traditional notion—that of Rhodes and so many of his successors—that Lincoln achieved the presidency "through little effort of his own" by backing into office as others committed political suicide. Chadwick's Lincoln may be even more of a political player and striver than Ecelbarger's, as he makes much of Lincoln's political abilities and instincts in his retelling of the story. Chadwick writes well of the contingency of politics and political actors. Although he does not offer the passionate exploration of extravagant detail that Nichols did, his chapter-length excursions, which weave in important accounts of the candidacies of Douglas and Breckinridge and even of John Bell, hark back to Nevins's efforts at narrative inclusivity. These considerations of all four candidates are particularly welcome additions to a tradition that too often marginalizes candidates beyond the big two. This book about the election of 1860 places the winner in a broad and rich historical context and is likely to be friendly to all sorts of readers.[24]

Lincoln the political manipulator is evident in Michael S. Green's *Lincoln and the Election of 1860,* which expands on the themes of his essay in this volume. Green focuses as much attention on the political instincts of Lincoln as on those of his managers. "No one did more than Abraham Lincoln to make sure that he would be the candidate and victor, and the ability that he demonstrated in the process prepared him to lead the North to victory in the Civil War." His characterization of Lincoln as "Everybody's [in the Republican Party] Second Choice" is a pithy summary of larger truths. Green's most important contribution is his particularly clear and level-headed discussion of the possibilities of fusion ("Con-fusion") efforts by Lincoln's opponents, which might have thrown the election to the House of Representatives. This topic deserves much more exploration. Green's book is short, perhaps with the assigned-undergraduate-reading audience in mind, which may explain his opening excursion on the politics of slavery since the founding of the republic.[25]

Douglas R. Egerton's *Year of Meteors: Stephen Douglas, Abraham Lincoln, and the Election that Brought on the Civil War,* published in 2010, is a very long and dense book that in at least two ways is reminiscent of the classic account by Roy F. Nichols. Both authors offer an incredible amount of detail about the intricacies of political infighting in the period before the secession winter. This may ultimately limit the audience for Egerton to the most devoted of specialists while discouraging too many general readers or others without a deep professional interest. Also, like Nichols before him, Egerton shifts his central focus away from Lincoln and the victorious Republicans. Although the book is long enough that he can include a complete account of Lincoln's campaign and those of the other candidates as secondary supplements to his main narrative, he writes mainly about the Democrats and their internal struggles.

Most specifically, Egerton's attention is on Stephen A. Douglas and those Southerners within his own party so opposed to the Little Giant's candidacy that they were willing to destroy the party of Jackson before accepting Douglas. Egerton revives and reformulates the old conspiracy charge that Southern disunionsts—William Lowndes Yancey and Robert Barnwell Rhett are particular bogies—sought to split the Charleston Democratic convention along sectional lines. This view stands in stark contrast to Ollinger Crenshaw's vision of a Southern political class so divided as to be adrift and ineffectual. Egerton's Southerners designed a purposeful destruction of the Democracy in hopes of finding a way to throw the election to the House of Representatives. When they carried out their plan and none of Lincoln's other opponents succeeded, they guaranteed the election of a Republican president who would alarm Southern whites sufficiently to bring about the fire-eaters' ultimate goal of secession. Those readers who like watching televised political pundits doing Electoral College math will particularly enjoy the appendix, where Egerton tries to find a way for a non-Republican candidate (probably Douglas) to achieve a clear majority. The short answer is Douglas would have had to won *all* the states won by candidates other than Lincoln, to which he would have needed to add California, Oregon, the rest of New Jersey, and either Pennsylvania or both Indiana and Illinois. Beyond such mathematical ruminations, this is a book for those who love the interplay and conflict of politics among fallible, ambitious men only partially certain, and sometimes wrong, about where their decisions will lead the larger polity. Those who wish to avoid conspiracy theories as historical explanations should not be put off by what they fear they will find in this book. Egerton's hand is too deft and his research too deep to offer a simplistic or crude narrative of the events surrounding the election of 1860, though many will remain unconvinced. For those wanting one book on the election of 1860, this is probably it, though some will find the Lincoln-centered accounts of Ecelbarger or Chadwick more reader friendly.[26]

All four of these recent works are welcome and deserve a wide and appreciative audience among both scholars and general readers. Those who have not read Luthin, Nichols, and the rest will find any of the latest books worthy introductions to the electoral contest of 1860. But all four authors provide accounts that ultimately offer little interpretative novelty. They all end by replicating the historiographical tradition that has surrounded the election of 1860 since the time of Rhodes and Fite. It has been almost three score and ten years since Allan Nevins found himself apologizing for repeating "the legendary lore of the Republic," and it may be time for those creating the next generation of historiography to expand their horizons.

The essays in this volume offer a first step toward overturning the historiographical tradition, even as they also provide an in-depth exploration of the literature and engage many of the important and traditional issues surrounding the election. Of course, Lincoln and Douglas will always have to be accounted for when the political events of 1860 are considered. And these essays continue, in sophisticated ways, to ponder the philosophical divide among historians about whether events are predetermined or not. Today's scholars interested in the politics of the last antebellum election need to be wary of becoming overly ensnared in abstruse metaphysical discussions about inevitability or contingency as they seek out and ask questions of conventional and innovative sources in order to create a richer reconstruction of the past. It is not that these questions do not matter or cannot be decisive in shaping what historians write, but neither should historians of the Civil War era try to settle questions that resemble the enumeration of dancing angels on pinheads. The contrast between two of the essays in this volume show that it is possible to avoid the trap of offering metaphysics at the expense of history. James Huston's reconsideration here of Stephen A. Douglas's candidacy and doomed efforts to save the Union is an unyielding and spirited restatement of the inevitability position; A. James Fuller offers an informative and theoretically inflected account of politics in Oliver Morton's Indiana steeped in contingency.

Much work remains. Even as the essays in this volume contribute to the understanding of the election, they also suggest new avenues for research. One obvious path is in the potential exploration of the failed efforts by Lincoln's opponents to achieve some sort of consequential fusion. Contemplating the potential dynamics of fusion efforts reminds us that, as Tip O'Neill once said, all politics is local. Local and state and regional politics of parties and leaders and followers in 1860 need doing. This is particularly the case for actors and events in the South, as suggested by the questions raised and still unanswered in reading the works of Ollinger

Crenshaw, Avery Craven in his essay in the Graebner volume, and Douglas R. Egerton's recent book. How cohesive were Southerners and their political leaders as events unfolded? State-level and local studies need to deal with such issues and to test, generally, how well the traditional accounts actually fit what happened south of Mason and Dixon's line. Fuller's contribution to this volume on John Breckinridge's candidacy is particularly attractive, with its effort to marry the much-studied concept of "honor" to the motivations of a man not the immediately obvious candidate of the southern wing of the Democratic Party.

Although the existing literature marginalizes events in the South, yawning lacunae also exist in the understanding of what happened in 1860 in the North at state and local levels. Fuller's consideration of Indiana in 1860 needs duplication for other states and other Northern politicians. In his essay on John Bell and the Whig-dominated Constitutional Union Party, Fuller offers an analysis that points to the need for more studies of others in all parties who wished to work for further intersectional compromise. And, as with the South, state and local studies based in Northern sources should reveal new complexities about the election of Lincoln.

One of the virtues of Thomas R. Rodgers's effort in this volume to quantify and account for the high voter turnout in 1860 is his realization that the aggregate turnout and vote totals were the results of millions of individual decisions. Voters cast their ballots for all kind of reasons, ranging from party identification to the salience of passing issues to Election Day weather and distance from polling places. Where sources permit, we need microlevel studies of urban wards and rural townships and Southern electoral beats to help us better understand voter behavior in 1860. And the experiences—including experiences in the corporeal and sensory and material sense—of voters themselves need consideration and evaluation. Politics in the years before the Civil War had its physical aspects. The election of 1860 involved marching, nighttime illuminations and political banners, cartoons and sleazy journalism, singing, and drinking. The Republican Wide Awakes and their opposing counterparts intimidated opponents on behalf of their tickets even as they passionately promoted their own candidates' virtues.[27]

Not all in the democracy had a vote, and the ways in which the attitudes, activities, and impacts of white women, of slaves and free blacks, impinged by design or otherwise on political calculations deserve much further attention from a generation raised on social and cultural history.[28] Fuller notes

Fig. 34. Grand procession of Wide-Awakes at New York on the evening of October 3, 1860. Republican Wide Awakes in N.Y.—Lincoln-Hamlin Campaign. (Library of Congress) The famous Republican "marching club" and rival organizations that supported the other candidates helped bring out the vote in 1860.

the role of women in his chapters on Bell and Breckinridge and hints that the actions of candidates' wives deserve further study. John R. McKivigan's account of Frederick Douglass's conflicted and mostly negative attitudes about Lincoln in 1860 reminds us that not all blacks were disenfranchised in the decade of the Dred Scott decision, and that not all opponents of slavery united behind Lincoln. Douglass was an international figure in an abolitionist movement that crossed national boundaries, and Lincoln famously asserted that the Union was "the last best hope of earth." Lawrence Sondhaus's analysis of the European perspective on the election is as a starting point for placing such events, which seem so American, within the context of the transatlantic world. Thus, the essays in this collection engage and challenge the traditional historiography and ask new questions that prove that the election of 1860 is still in need of scrutiny.

1. Allan Nevins, *The Emergence of Lincoln,* vol. 2, *Prologue to Civil War, 1859–1861* (New York: Charles Scribner's Sons, 1950), 313. Subsequent references to this work are embedded in the text.

2. Edward L. Ayers, *What Caused the Civil War: Reflections on the South and Southern History* (New York: Norton, 2005), 132.

3. This same quote appears multiple times in the published works of James Ford Rhodes, most relevantly in *Lectures on the American Civil War* (New York: Macmillan, 1918), 10.

4. James Ford Rhodes, *History of the United States from the Compromise of 1850 to the End of the Roosevelt Administration,* new ed. (New York: Macmillan, 1928), 2: 493. Rhodes first wrote these words for an 1893 edition.

5. Charles A. Beard and Mary R. Beard, *The Rise of American Civilization* (New York: Macmillan, 1927), 53; see also Marc Egnal, "The Beards Were Right: Parties in the North, 1840–1860," *Civil War History* 47, no. 1 (2001): 30–56.

6. Emerson David Fite, *The Presidential Election of 1860* (New York: Macmillan, 1911), ix, vi, 32, 90–91, 232.

7. Reinhard H. Luthin, *The First Lincoln Campaign* (Cambridge, Mass.: Harvard Univ. Press, 1944).

8. Charles W. Ramsdell, "The Natural Limits of Slavery Expansion," *Mississippi Valley Historical Review* 16, no. 2 (1929), 151–71; James G. Randall, "The Blundering Generation," *Mississippi Valley Historical Review* 27, no. 1 (1940): 3–28; David Herbert Donald, "An Excess of Democracy," in *Lincoln Reconsidered: Essays on the Civil War Era* (New York: Knopf, 1956); James G. Randall. *Lincoln the President,* 4 vols. (New York: Dodd, Mead), 1945–55; David Herbert Donald, *Lincoln* (New York: Simon and Schuster, 1995); Avery Craven, *The Coming of the Civil War* (Chicago: Univ. of Chicago Press, 1943). Michael F. Holt attractively repackaged and reworked the "blundering generation" thesis to explain *The Political Crisis of the 1850s;* see Holt, *The Political Crisis of the 1850s* (New York: Norton, 1978).

9. Luthin noted, conventionally, that German immigrants and their children were one of the mansions, and a smallish one at that, within the house of 1850s Republicanism. For over a century, various German-American publicists and organizations have linked the election of Lincoln to German votes, and some historians have given the idea a hearing. (There seems little doubt that one of Lincoln's secondary strengths at the Chicago convention was his nonidentification with his party's nativist elements.) Frederick C. Luebke gathered together the strands of the controversies about German-American voting in a 1971 anthology, his short answer being "no." A longer one was that ethnocultural influence on voting for Lincoln or against slavery or for or against anything else was highly complex for German-Americans. In fact, ethnocultural influence required analysis so detailed and localized that the broader national question quickly becomes moot. See Frederick C. Luebke, ed., *Ethnic Voters and the Election of Lincoln* (Lincoln: Univ. of Nebraska Press, 1971). See also the level-headed discussion

by Joel H. Silbey, "The Civil War Synthesis in American Political History," reprinted in *The Partisan Imperative: The Dynamics of American Politics Before the Civil War* (New York: Oxford Univ. Press, 1985), esp. 7–9. For an example of a German-American publicist who retells the chestnut about the Germans (in this case) nominating Lincoln, see Annette R. Hofmann, *The American Turner Movement: A History from Its Beginnings to 2000* (Indianapolis: Max Kade German-American Center at Indiana Univ.–Purdue Univ. Indianapolis and Indiana German Heritage Society, 2001), 91–94.

10. Ollinger Crenshaw, *The Slave States in the Presidential Election of 1860* (Baltimore: Johns Hopkins Univ. Press, 1945), 73.

11. Ollinger Crenshaw, "The Psychological Background of the Election of 1860 in the South," *North Carolina Historical Review* 19 (July 1942): 260–79; and Donald E. Reynolds, *Texas Terror: The Slave Insurrection Panic of 1860 and the Secession of the Lower South* (Baton Rouge: Louisiana State Univ. Press, 2007).

12. Roy Franklin Nichols, *The Disruption of American Democracy* (New York: Macmillan, 1948).

13. William B. Hesseltine, ed., *Three Against Lincoln: Murat Halstead Reports the Caucuses of 1860* (Baton Rouge: Louisiana State Univ. Press, 1960).

14. Nevins, *The Emergence of Lincoln*, 251, 286, 297, 315. Though praising Stephen A. Douglas for his attempts to preserve the Union, Nevins elsewhere in the volume doubted that Douglas ever entertained much moral outrage at the institution of slavery. Graham A. Peck has recently pondered the question "Was Stephen A. Douglas Antislavery?" His answer is "no," in the face of a substantial historiographical and biographical tradition that argues Douglas was in some way "privately" opposed to the peculiar institution. See? Peck, "Was Stephen A. Douglas Antislavery?" *Journal of the Abraham Lincoln Association* 26, no. 2 (2005): 1–21.

15. Norman A. Graebner, ed., *Politics and the Crisis of 1860* (Urbana: Univ. of Illinois Press, 1961). The Fehrenbacher quote is from page 60.

16. David M. Potter, *The Impending Crisis, 1848–1861* (New York: Harper & Row, 1976).

17. I am thinking of works such as Joseph T. Glatthaar, *The March to the Sea and Beyond: Sherman's Troops in the Savannah and Carolinas Campaign* (New York: New York Univ. Press, 1985); Gerald F. Linderman, *Embattled Courage: The Experience of Combat in the American Civil War* (New York: Free Press, 1987); Reid Mitchell, *Civil War Soldiers* (New York: Simon and Schuster, 1987); and Maris A. Vinovskis, "Have Social Historians Lost the Civil War? Some Preliminary Demographic Speculations," *Journal of American History* 76, no. 1 (1989), 34–58.

18. James McPherson, *Battle Cry of Freedom: The Civil War Era* (New York: Oxford Univ. Press, 1988).

19. Mark E. Neely's works include *The Union Divided: Party Conflict in the Civil War North* (Cambridge, Mass.: Harvard Univ. Press, 2002) and *The Boundaries of American Political Culture in the Civil War Era* (Chapel Hill: Univ. of North Carolina Press, 2005).

20. Harold Holzer, *Lincoln at Cooper Union: The Speech That Made Abraham Lincoln President* (New York: Simon and Schuster, 2004); and Holzer, *Lincoln President-Elect: Abraham Lincoln and the Great Secession Winter* (New York: Simon and Schuster, 2008), esp. 11–14.

21. Doris Kearns Goodwin, *Team of Rivals: The Political Genius of Abraham Lincoln* (New York: Simon and Schuster, 2005).

22. Gary Ecelbarger, *The Great Comeback: How Abraham Lincoln Beat the Odds to Win the 1860 Republican Nomination* (New York: St. Martin's Press, 2008); Bruce Chadwick, *Lincoln for President: An Unlikely Candidate, An Audacious Strategy, and the Victory No One Saw Coming* (Napierville, Ill.: Sourcebooks, 2009); Michael S. Green, *Lincoln and the Election of 1860* (Carbondale: Southern Illinois Univ. Press, 2011); and Douglas R. Egerton, *Year of Meteors: Stephen Douglas, Abraham Lincoln, and the Election that Brought on the Civil War* (New York: Bloomsbury Press, 2009).

23. Ecelbarger, *The Great Comeback(* 230.

24. Chadwick, *Lincoln for President*, ix.

25. Green, *Lincoln and The Election of 1860*, 112, 43.

26. Egerton, *Year of Meteors*, passim.

27. For possible inspirations, see Mark M. Smith, *Tasting and Touching in History* (Berkeley and Los Angeles: Univ. of California Press, 2008); Santanu Das, *Touch and Intimacy in First World War Literature* (New York: Cambridge Univ. Press, 2008); T. H. Breen, *The Marketplace of Revolution: How Consumer Politics Shaped American Independence* (New York: Oxford Univ. Press, 2004); David Jaffee, *A New Nation of Goods: The Material Culture of Early America* (Philadelphia: Univ. of Pennsylvania Press, 2010); and Joan E. Cashin, "Trophies of War: Material Culture in the Civil War Era," *Journal of the Civil War Era* 1, no. 3 (2011): 339–67.

28. See Erika Rozinek, "Trembling for the Nation: Illinois Women and the Election of 1860," *Journal of Illinois History* 5, no. 4 (2002): 309–24. Rozinek argues that Illinois women—another disenfranchised group—used their female identities to influence the political contest at local and state levels in 1860.

Contributors

A. James Fuller is an associate professor of history at the University of Indianapolis. He has published five books, including *Chaplain to the Confederacy: Basil Manly and Baptist Life in the Old South* and *America, War and Power: Defining the State, 1775–2005*.

Michael S. Green is a professor of history at the College of Southern Nevada. He is the author, coauthor, or editor of seven books, including *Freedom, Union, and Power: Lincoln and His Party during the Civil War* and *Lincoln and the Election of 1860*.

Douglas G. Gardner is a lecturer in history at Indiana University–Purdue University, Columbus. His research interests center on the cultural history of the Civil War, especially the place of prison camps and race in memory.

James L. Huston is Regents Professor of History at Oklahoma State University. He is the author of numerous books, including *The Panic of 1857 and the Coming of the Civil War, The Lincoln-Douglas Debates of 1858,* and *Stephen A. Douglas and the Dilemmas of Democratic Equality*.

John R. McKivigan is Mary O'Brien Gibson Professor of United States History at Indiana University–Purdue University, Indianapolis. He is the editor of the Frederick Douglass Papers and is the author of several books, including *The War against Proslavery Religion: Abolitionism and the Northern Churches, 1830–1865*.

Thomas E. Rodgers is an instructor in history at the University of Southern Indiana. He is the author of a number of articles on mid-nineteenth-century American history, including "Billy Yank and G.I. Joe: An Exploratory Essay on the Sociopolitical Dimensions of Soldier Motivation," *Journal of Military History;* and "Liberty, Will, and Violence: Democratic Political Ideology in West-Central Indiana during the Civil War," *Indiana Magazine of History.*

Lawrence Sondhaus is professor of history at the University of Indianapolis. He is the author of many books, including *Strategic Culture and Ways of War, Navies in Modern World History,* and *World War I: The Global Revolution, 1914–1919.*

Index